IN QUEST OF
NATIONAL SECURITY

———————■———————

IN QUEST OF
NATIONAL SECURITY

ZBIGNIEW BRZEZINSKI

edited and annotated by Marin Strmecki

———————— ■ ————————

WESTVIEW PRESS
Boulder & London

Copyright © 1988 by Zbigniew Brzezinski

Published in 1988 in the United States of America by Westview Press, Inc., 5500 Central Avenue, Boulder, Colorado 80301

Library of Congress Cataloging-in-Publication Data
Brzezinski, Zbigniew K., 1928–
  In quest of national security.
  1. United States—Foreign relations—1977–1981.
2. United States—Foreign relations—1981–   .
3. United States—National security.   I. Strmecki, Marin.   II. Title.
E838.5.B79. 1988   327.73   88-10723
ISBN 0-8133-0575-6

Printed and bound in the United States of America

The paper used in this publication meets the requirements of the American National Standard for Permanence of Paper for Printed Library Materials Z39.48-1984.

10   9   8   7   6   5   4   3   2   1

Contents

Preface

THE ARTICLES AND SPEECHES appearing in this anthology, which span the years of the Carter and Reagan administrations, have been reproduced essentially as they were originally written or delivered. In order to preserve their authenticity in their specific context, no alterations of substance were made in these entries. Changes were limited to some minor stylistic copyediting and some short deletions from the older entries of highly dated material which illuminated only marginally the more timeless points under discussion. In this way, it is hoped that the reader will be able to trace both the threads of continuity in Dr. Brzezinski's views and the evolution of his thinking on the key issues related to U.S. national security.

I would like to thank several interns in Dr. Brzezinski's office whose assistance in word processing and proofreading were indispensable in producing this volume. They are Sabrina Spencer of Michigan State University, Creigh Yarbrough of Smith College, David Rea of Wesleyan University, Jean-Paul Paddack of Georgetown University, Cecilia Pulido of the University of California, Los Angeles, and Cindy Arends of Oregon State University.

Marin Strmecki

Introduction

THIS BOOK BRINGS TOGETHER essays and speeches I have written and delivered, both in academia and in government, on the perennial question of national security. I do not use the term *national security* in the narrow sense of military security. While military power is one important dimension of the historical rivalry between the United States and the Soviet Union, it is unlikely to determine which rival prevails unless the contest leads to an apocalyptic military clash. Instead, I believe that national security involves wider considerations, including political statecraft, economic strength, technological innovation, ideological vitality, and others. An attempt to achieve national security without addressing these aspects of the problem will be only partially relevant and will likely fail.

The point of departure for the quest for national security must be a correct diagnosis of the nature of change in our time. In my view, the contemporary world is being altered by four interrelated revolutions: a political revolution, a social revolution, an economic revolution, and a military revolution. Their cumulative impact has already profoundly affected the distribution of global power, the competitive relationship between the two principal global rivals, and the stability of the U.S.-Soviet military balance. And these four revolutions will have an ever-greater effect in the years ahead.

The central substance of the political revolution is the attraction of democratic ideals. Today, the idea of human rights, the concept of self-government, the notion of a truly pluralistic political order are concepts which reflect the universal aspirations of mankind. These are evident around the world, and it is no exaggeration to state that we are living in an age in which human rights and individual liberty have become the historical inevitability of our time.

In Western Europe, Spain and Portugal evolved from dictatorships into liberal democracies in the 1970s. These democratic transformations showed that even over decades of uninterrupted rule, one-party fascist

1

regimes could not muster the capacity to perpetuate themselves. The demise of these regimes stemmed from the fact that in their attempt to achieve total power they did not liquidate every island of autonomy in the social order. They did not eliminate every independent social and political organization, and as a result, these persisting islands of autonomy provided a jumping-off point for a gradual evolution away from the totalitarian model.

In the developing world, a spread of democracy has also taken place. In Latin America, nondemocratic countries are now a minority phenomenon, with such important states as Brazil and Argentina moving away from military dictatorships in recent years. The only significant exceptions to this trend are Chile, Cuba, and Nicaragua. In the Far East, democratic rule has returned to the Philippines and to South Korea. This phenomenon is clearly related to the spread of literacy, which has created more politically self-conscious and more self-confident publics, and to the process of urbanization, which has brought people closer together and fostered a more dynamic political interaction. It is also connected with the rise throughout the developing world of a professional and highly educated middle class.

Even in the Communist world, the manifestations of the global political revolution are clearly present. In China, the student demonstrations in late 1986 were an effort to expand the state's reform program into the political sphere. In Poland, the continuing strength of the underground Solidarity movement has led to a kind of self-emancipated society, complete with its own extensive daily press and publishing network. Moreover, in both, the state has sought to increase participation in the system—economic decentralization in China, and halting attempts at a limited political dialogue in Poland—not only on the basis of political initiatives from above but also as a consequence of social pressures from below. The outcomes are yet to be determined, but the phenomena are clearly present.

Not even the Soviet Union has escaped the impact of this worldwide trend. Mikhail Gorbachev has made it clear that he cannot undertake the reformation of the Soviet system without the active participation of the Soviet people. He has sought to animate the populace as an antidote to the stagnation of the system. In a recent address to the Soviet trade unions, he said, "The more democracy we have the faster we will progress along the path of restructuring, socialist renovation, and the more order and discipline there will be. So the question is this: Either we have democratization or we have social inertness and conservatism. There is no third way here." Also, in an extraordinarily suggestive public exchange during Gorbachev's recent visit to Prague, Gennadi Gerasimov, the Soviet spokesman, was asked what the difference was between Gorbachev and

Alexander Dubcek, the leader of Czechoslovak Spring in 1968. Gerasimov answered with just two words: "Nineteen years."

It was the answer of a supporter, but could also have been the answer of a critic. That is important to note because the limited steps Gorbachev has taken toward greater openness have clearly encountered strong institutional impediments and political opposition. These obstacles are deeply rooted in Russian and Soviet history, and they reflect powerful vested interests in maintaining the system unchanged. Where this will lead is uncertain, but the appearance of this phenomenon—even in this still ambiguous form—is a symptom of the wider, global political revolution.

The central thrust of this revolution is toward greater societal pluralism, greater freedom of expression, and gradual adoption and implementation of the standards enshrined in various international conventions, such as the UN Charter and the Helsinki Agreement. This trend is not geographically confined but global in nature. It is moving beyond the nineteenth-century concept of liberal freedom and beyond the early twentieth-century concept of equality. It is a reflection of a wider recognition that a modern society has to combine—in a variety of ways—pluralism, social autonomy, and self-government. The practical definition of this can differ from region to region, indeed from country to country. This process does not imply emerging uniformity in political systems, but a convergence around the principles of putting restraints on those who hold power, of promoting freedom of expression, and of opening up wider public access to information.

This final point ties into the global social revolution. It is based on a single revolutionary technological creation, the integrated circuit. Telecommunications, satellite, and computer technologies have literally changed the way the world works, not only altering the way people interact in a modern society, but also unleashing an explosion of innovation in almost all fields of human endeavor. And this process is bound to accelerate in the more advanced countries as newer and better technologies are brought on line with each passing year.

These developments do pose the question of whether society will become more or less subject to social control by the political center. Data bases store immense amounts of information; computers can exchange and cross-check information with each other in fractions of a second; telephone networks have become extraordinarily extensive; mobile communications are widespread. This all could contribute to strengthening central control, but on balance the opposite is likely to be the case. Such new technologies tend to break down the governmental monopoly on information, to make prohibitions on horizontal communications within a society an impediment to social progress, and to render insti-

tutionalized and state-enforced dogma irrelevant. Thus, the new information technologies create a thrust toward greater individual independence.

The social revolution will also probably have the effect of increasing
the gap between those countries that accept and adapt to the new reality
and harness these new capabilities and those that do not. The world is
already becoming increasingly stratified. It is no longer divided between
developing and industrialized countries. Instead, there are now countries
that are essentially undeveloped, others that are rapidly developing, still
others that have been industrialized, and a few that have leapt into the
postindustrial technetronic age.

Making that great leap forward requires full exploitation of modern
computer technology. From the creation of the first basic computer in
the late 1940s to 1977, an estimated half million such machines were
installed in the United States. From 1977 to 1985, more than 20 million
more were built. Today, there are 100,000 large-scale computers in the
United States, 24,000 in the European Community, 17,000 in Japan,
and 3,000 in the Soviet Union. Hand-in-hand with computerization
comes the introduction of quasi-intelligent industrial robots. There are
about 45,000 in the United States, 52,000 in the European Community,
68,000 in Japan, and 3,000 in the Soviet Union. These advances have
pushed productivity to levels scarcely thought possible even a few years
ago. Now, further advances are following up so rapidly that a computer
bought in today's market will be leapfrogged by technology within six
to nine months.

Steam-driven engines enabled people to accomplish physical tasks that
were, at one time, considered to be literally superhuman. In the same
way, the computer allows people to perform mathematical calculations
that are literally superhuman. Computer-assisted innovation—particularly
in designing complex products and industrial processes—has fostered a
surge in the creative power of society. Computer intelligence does not
yet approach human intelligence, but it is estimated that within ten or
twenty years there will be computers as complex as the human mind.
This process will profoundly change the way society functions, the way
it harnesses and adapts ultrascience and high-tech to its own use, and
even the way it evolves and transforms itself.

The pluralism of the political revolution and the massive innovation
of the social revolution have stimulated a revolution in the nature of the
world economic order. At the core of the economic revolution is the
globalization of economic activity. National autarchy is becoming a thing
of the past; it is simply not efficient. A country that seeks to develop
solely within itself, insulated from world prices and inhibited from

exploiting the benefits of productive comparative advantage, is likely to become increasingly a country that falls behind in economic development.

Those countries that have had the highest growth rates in the last ten years have been the ones that have deliberately capitalized on the globalization of the economic order. Indeed, the growth of eight of the world's ten fastest growing economies over the last five years was driven by exports. The great national economic success stories over the last decade—Japan, South Korea, Hong Kong, Singapore—all were based on capitalizing on the growth of world trade. While the population of these countries accounted for only 4.3 percent of the world's total population, their imports and exports accounted for more than 13.4 percent of world trade.

We can expect that the countries that will take the lead economically in the years ahead will be those that have political and social systems that maximize individual and collective innovation and that have the capacity to adapt rapidly to changing economic circumstances. This demands constitutional pluralism, freedom of social interaction, and economic flexibility. In the coming decades, the countries that will emerge on top in the global economic competition will be those with governments, not only capable of anticipating change and of planning for it, but also willing to tolerate and encourage a creative, pluralist environment.

The fourth revolution is taking place in the military realm. In the dialectic between offense and defense, the offense has been in ascendance since approximately 1917. But it appears that now modern technology may be giving rise to a new era of defensive ascendancy.

In the last stages of World War I, the military application of the tank and the airplane created the possibility for tactics of maneuver, for strategically decisive surprise offensives, even for the concept of preemptive victory. After the war, offensive doctrines were advanced and developed by such great inter-war military thinkers as Tukhachevski in the Soviet Union, Guderian in Germany, Douhet in Italy, and Mitchell in the United States. All developed a common notion that the combination of concentrated aircraft and tank operations gave a supreme advantage to a strategy based on offensive military operations.

After World War II, the atomic revolution affirmed offensive ascendancy, not only with the tremendous destructive power of thermonuclear weapons, but particularly with the introduction of intercontinental ballistic missiles. It seemed impossible even to contemplate defending against these strategic weapons. With the refinement of the ICBM guidance systems over the next thirty years, increasing missile accuracy created the possibility of achieving the ultimate offensive capability: a surgical first-strike preemptive attack that would leave the victim unable to fire in retaliation and that would render his whole society prostrate before the enemy. Offense truly seemed to have become supreme.

But today science and technology are creating new opportunities for defense. It is quite possible that in the foreseeable future, susceptibility of strategic forces to military preemption and national vulnerability to societal destruction will again be separated. While a perfect strategic defense to shield civilian populations—as envisioned by President Reagan—cannot be built in the foreseeable future, it will soon be technologically feasible to build a limited strategic defense of one's strategic forces, command and control systems, and national command authority. It will be possible to attrite an ICBM barrage so that a military planner will be unable to design a preemptive attack with a high degree of confidence in its success. Since failure in the nuclear age leads to societal suicide, no leader is likely to put all his chips on a long shot.

Thus, each side's cities will remain vulnerable to nuclear attack, but defensive weapons will be able to ensure the survival of its retaliatory forces. As a result, a condition of offensive supremacy through first-strike weapons may give way to deterrence through limited strategic defense.

In addition, on the conventional level, we may be moving into a phase of the offense-defense dialectic in which the defense becomes ascendant. Advanced countries will soon introduce into their armories a vast array of intelligent weapons, capable, for example, of recognizing and attacking a target, such as a tank, from great distances on their own. These weapons can detect the full spectrum of sound, heat, and electronic signals on a battlefield, analyze them in tiny on-board computers using complex formulas to differentiate the target from the background clutter, and then maneuver themselves along a chosen attack trajectory. Given these developments, an offensive thrust by a mass tank formation would be suicidal and advancing concentrations of infantry would become exercises in mass suicide. Even over an extended front, conventional forces will be localized as soon as they move forward and will be promptly destroyed without inflicting massive collateral damage.

In the coming decades, these four revolutions will have a profound affect on our national security. It is evident that the countries that most fully exploit the political, social, and economic revolutions will be in the best position to exploit the military revolution—and that should give the West a basis for some optimism.

First, it is clear that centralized bureaucratic rigidity will be the greatest danger to a country's development. A bureaucratic order seldom adapts quickly to change—and I state this on the basis of an intimate familiarity with the U.S. bureaucracy—and the capacity to adapt will be the key to success. Bureaucratic centralism stifles innovation, and without innovation no country will be able to respond to the four global revolutions.

If combined with ideological orthodoxy—as it is in the Communist world—such centralism represents the greatest possible hindrance to a society's development and the worst possible fetter on its productive forces. Institutional pluralism and open-mindedness are the preconditions for innovation in our age.

Second, it is likely that a highly variegated and sharply demarcated global stratification will emerge. Scores of countries lagging behind today will be left further behind, and only a select few will accelerate their development and improve their global position.

At the forefront is likely to be a kind of combination of the United States and Japan, both of which have entered the technetronic era and each of which will almost inevitably become engaged in a closer economic and political relationship with the other. Current protectionist sparring does not presage a fundamental breach between the two but rather represents the birth pains of a closer and increasingly complementary association. In a broad sense, the tensions are analogous to the difficulties among European countries at the start of the Common Market, when transcending specific problems was a general recognition that prosperity was possible only through cooperation.

Western European countries will occupy the second tier of states. Most will lag behind the United States and Japan because of Western Europe's internal social weaknesses. These are a result in part of the historical fatigue of the two world wars and in part of the cultural hedonism to which Europe has been prone in the postwar period. It is also largely caused by the continuing absence of the larger economic and political unity that would enable West Europeans to harness their full potential for rapid development and technological innovation.

The Soviet Union and Eastern Europe will lag further behind. They will continue to be plagued by systemic difficulties and will attempt, with varying degrees of success, to adapt overly centralized, bureaucratic economies to the requirements of the new age. This process of adjustment will doubtless move forward in some cases, increasing the scope of popular political and social participation despite major bureaucratic opposition, and will potentially lead to serious reversals in others. A few rapidly developing countries, capitalizing on their lower wage levels, on strong popular work ethics, and on growing world trade, will form another tier, perhaps in time surpassing the countries in the Soviet bloc.

Even further behind will be other countries that are unable to respond to the four global revolutions. These countries face the potential for a steady economic decline—despite their already low standards of living— and perhaps even for social collapse and disintegration. That sad prognosis could become the likely prospect in some of the poorer parts of the world.

Third, it will be increasingly possible to create greater international stability, particularly in the relationship between the superpowers. Given the potential for developing strategic and conventional force postures based on defensive technologies, the world may reduce the nuclear nightmare by diminishing the temptations of strategic military preemption and may move away from a situation in which the threat of mass societal destruction is a necessary corollary of welfare. It will be possible to develop forces capable of repulsing aggression on its own terms, with far less collateral damage in the theater of combat. This growing efficacy of defensive weapons systems is likely to create a more stable world militarily by denying the strategic advantage to the side that might attack.

That will not end the rivalry between the United States and the Soviet Union. A vigorous geostrategic competition between the two powers will continue. Stability in the military balance will not be automatic but rather will require continuous energetic efforts. If the United States checkmates Soviet military power, it will heighten the importance of the economic and political dimensions of the contest, where U.S. strengths match up well against Soviet weaknesses.

U.S. strategy in the U.S.-Soviet rivalry must show an understanding of the long-term importance of the four contemporary global revolutions. As John Maynard Keynes once wrote, "The great events of history are often due to secular changes in the growth of population and other fundamental economic causes which, escaping by their gradual character the notice of contemporary observers, are attributed to the follies of statesmen or the fanaticism of atheists." He was right to point out the importance of the broad secular trends—such as the four revolutions in our time—that influence the position and prospects of states in a competitive world. But we should also be aware that conscious national decisions determine not only how a country exploits these trends to enhance its potential power, but also whether it capitalizes on its potential power to achieve geostrategic results. It is to these sets of questions that we must devote attention in the quest for national security.

PART ONE

■

U.S. Strategy

Global power, strategic insight, and national will are three requirements for great power status. In these speeches and essays, Dr. Brzezinski examines the U.S. record in the postwar period in light of these fundamental elements.

After World War II, Dr. Brzezinski wrote in the first entry, the United States was the preeminent power. With its economy unscathed in a world devastated by war and with its monopoly on nuclear weapons, its position relative to other powers was unprecedented. It was able to shape the nature of the international system and to establish a framework to ensure the security of Western Europe and the Far East. In those years, the United States had the power and the will to follow through on its global strategy.

But beginning in the 1960s the United States suffered from an erosion of national will and a loss of strategic focus. U.S. actions in Vietnam and Cuba—both of which involved a failure to use U.S. power decisively to achieve national objectives—represented a loss of nerve. At the same time, as the rest of the world recovered from the war, the power of the United States became relatively less dominant. As a result, to achieve its international goals—to ensure its national security—the United States needed to compensate with a keener sense of global strategy. While some administrations were more successful in this respect than others, Dr. Brzezinski wrote in the second entry that in the Reagan years, U.S. actions appeared to be guided not by strategy but by reactive impulses to world events.

In his book Game Plan: How to Conduct the U.S.-Soviet Contest *(1986), Dr. Brzezinski charted a geostrategy for the United States, which he sketched out in the testimony before the Senate Armed Services Committee and in an article in* Foreign Affairs *that appear here. Geostrategy as such requires an understanding of the thrust of Soviet policy, a clear sense of U.S. geographic priorities in the U.S.-Soviet contest, and an appreciation of the strategic requirements for deterring Soviet aggression. The third and fourth entries represent his prescription for avoiding a loss of control over critical events, as Soviet actions and the world's inherent turbulence combine to endanger the vital interests in the West.*

CHAPTER ONE

— ■ —

From Loss of Nerve
to Loss of Control

FORECASTING THE THRUST OF international change in the 1980s, of course, is a dangerous intellectual sport. But to cope with the danger one must be bold. It is certainly easy and tempting to be guided by the maxim "plus ça change, plus c'est la même chose." But in periods of great change, timidity may be the greatest enemy of insight.

Certainly, on the surface, many of the concerns preoccupying us today are highly similar to those that dominated the headlines a quarter-century ago. A survey of newspaper headlines exactly twenty-five years ago demonstrates the parallels:

- The *London Times* reported that Prime Minister Macmillan, while reflecting on the division between the free world and the Communist world, affirmed that the free nations "can no longer afford to think parochially." He went on to say, "In the long run the free world will defend itself and will win adherence to itself because our way of life gives a better way of living, a fuller life to the individual, security and hope."

- *The New York Times* reported that Adlai Stevenson urged "the leaders of free nations to rally to achieve a functioning, expanding free trade system," adding that the United States must be willing to assume the role of world creditor. He also warned that "even the testing of nuclear weapons, let alone their use, is incompatible with human welfare."

- News dispatches also reported that Secretary of State John Foster Dulles had observed that the Soviets had decided that "brute force

---

Keynote address at the twenty-fifth anniversary conference of the Center for International Affairs at Harvard University, on June 9, 1983.

11

no longer brings results" and that they had therefore switched to policies "not obviously designed to be predatory." The media in general was convinced that an East-West summit conference would take place to discuss nuclear arms-control issues.
- *The New York Times* reported on continuing fighting in Lebanon between government and rebel forces.

In all, not very different from today's headlines! Yet the fact is that, despite this superficial similarity, discontinuity is the central reality of our times. An anecdote cited by General Sir John Hackett in his provocative work *The Third World War* illustrates the point:

> There is a nice story of a political prophet in Munich in 1928, who was asked to prophesy what would be happening to the burghers of his city in five, fifteen, twenty and forty years' time. He began: "I prophesy that in five years' time, in 1933, Munich will be part of a Germany that has just suffered 5 million unemployed and that is ruled by a dictator with a certifiable mental illness who will proceed to murder 6 million Jews."
>
> His audience said: "Ah, then you must think that in fifteen years' time we will be in a sad plight."
>
> "No," replied the prophet, "I prophesy that in 1943 Munich will be part of a greater Germany whose flag will fly from the Volga to Bordeaux, from northern Norway to the Sahara."
>
> "Ah, then you must think that in twenty years' time, we will be mighty indeed."
>
> "No, my guess is that in 1948 Munich will be part of a Germany that stretches only from the Elbe to the Rhine, and whose ruined cities will recently have seen production down to only 10 percent of the 1928 level."
>
> "So you think we will face black ruin in forty years' time?"
>
> "No, by 1968 I prophesy that real income per head in Munich will be four times greater than now, and that in the year after that 90 percent of German adults will sit looking at a box in a corner of their drawing rooms, which will show live pictures of a man walking upon the moon."
>
> They locked him up as a madman, of course.

*   *   *

In this spirit, I will first glance at what transpired in the 1960s, identifying the significance of its milestones, and then speculate on the historical meaning of the decade as a whole. I will, however, be much less specific than the Munich seer and will speak of larger trends and dangers.

In the 1960s, U.S. power reached its apex. Yet in those years the posture of the United States changed dramatically. At the outset, U.S.

policies shaped the world; at the close, the world shaped U.S. policies. It was a decade in which U.S. designs for a grand alliance with a united Europe faded and a decade in which the United States as a nation lost its nerve as the leading world power.

In the Bay of Pigs operation and the Vietnam War, the United States failed to act like a world power. In 1961, after calling the island of Cuba a mortal threat, the United States chose to respond to the threat by dispatching some 3,000 brave Cuban exiles to overthrow Cuba's new dictator—and promptly abandoned them when the expedition faltered. Without U.S. air support, the Bay of Pigs operation turned into a massive failure.

In the early 1960s, when faced with a geopolitical challenge in distant Vietnam, the United States chose to wage a limited but escalating war. It did not use its military power in a way to achieve a decisive outcome, but rather let itself become bogged down in a war that became increasingly unpopular. In addition, out of a fear that the Congress could not choose between guns and butter, the United States decided to conduct the war through inflationary deficit financing, thereby weakening both its own economy and the international economic system. In Vietnam, we chose the wrong war strategy because the selection of the right one would have required a clear-cut choice between war and peace. It was more comfortable to opt for a piecemeal engagement and to finance the war by weakening the dollar than to ask ourselves whether we wanted to make the requisite sacrifices necessary to achieve our objectives.

Even in the one instance in which the United States acted like a great power—the Cuban missile crisis in 1962—it failed to harvest the fruits of its effort. The United States did not exploit the success either to press the Soviet Union to withdraw from the Caribbean through an arrangement for the full neutralization of Cuba or to structure a more stable and more cooperative relationship with the Soviet Union in the area of strategic arms competition. Instead, we deluded ourselves with the comfortable belief—expressed explicitly in official statements in the mid-1960s—that the Soviet Union had accommodated itself indefinitely to strategic inferiority. In fact, the Soviet Union was already two years into what became a massive strategic buildup designed to erase the U.S. strategic advantage—the very advantage that had given our policymakers in the Cuban missile crisis the confidence to apply conventional pressure on Soviet forces.

During the 1960s, the United States failed to use its power to assert its global imperial status or to adjust consciously to a new reality and accept a lesser role. That failure was not attributable to individual policymakers but to the United States as a nation in the deepest historical sense. Unlike our performance in the years immediately after World War

II, we lacked a sense of historical direction and became increasingly uncertain about our role in the world. U.S. imperial purposes still defined our objectives, but we pursued them increasingly by half-hearted means shaped by a desire to evade difficult choices. We emerged from the decade chastened—aware that we could neither dominate the world nor withdraw from it.

We also emerged from the 1960s as a divided nation. The U.S. consensus about the world had collapsed, and public opinion in the United States became polarized. With that polarization, the center of gravity within each political party shifted toward its ideological extreme. As a result, instead of acting as it traditionally had to minimize our national disagreements, the political process magnified them.

In the 1970s, the United States essentially went into a holding operation. The decade was dominated by the disengagement from Vietnam. It also involved a new accommodation to the realities of Soviet power, though with Moscow exploiting its Cuban connection to expand its own strategic footholds in the Third World. But the United States did not resolve the fundamental dilemma of its role in the world: It remained torn by the conflicting imperatives of power and principle.

*   *   *

If the 1960s was in retrospect a decade involving a loss of nerve, do we have any clues to the significance of the 1980s? In 1983, some trends have already become visible.

Geopolitically, the cold war has become global in scope, while at the same time narrowing into a primarily U.S.-Soviet affair as Western Europe has gradually opted out of the East-West competition. It is unlikely that the countries of Eastern Europe will become significantly more emancipated, and Poland—given its catastrophic economic condition and mounting social and political ferment—is more likely to be crushed than to become more stable and democratic. The Soviet Union may be beset by massive domestic crises by the late 1980s, but these problems will probably still be contained by the highly regimented and bureaucratically assertive Soviet political system. For the United States, the principal constructive focus of world affairs will increasingly become the Pacific Basin. It will replace Western Europe as our most important partner in the world—and not only in the economic sphere. A new strategic triangle— the United States, Japan, and China—could become more significant than NATO.

In addition, two regions and three specific issues will probably become critically important. The first region is the Middle East. U.S. policymakers have persistently failed to use the massive leverage available to them to push both parties into genuine negotiations. This failure has prompted well-founded concerns that the continuing stalemate could gradually undermine the more moderate Arab elites and facilitate a large-scale reentry into the region by the Soviet Union as a political force.

We have to ask ourselves some critical questions. In the absence of peace—and given the likely de facto incorporation of the West Bank and the Gaza Strip into Israel—what are the prospects for the long-term survival of Mubarak's rule in Egypt, of Hussein's reign in Jordan, and even of the ruling dynasty in Saudi Arabia? Will the Gulf states—the vitally important Hanseatic League of our times—also be threatened by such regional instability, with radicalism and fundamentalism chipping away from opposite sides at their fragile internal political systems? Without a broader peace settlement, are not the chances now becoming overwhelming that Israel itself will be transformed into a binational garrison state almost permanently isolated from its neighbors? Will not these developments lead to a wider parting of U.S. and European perspectives on the Middle East issue and thereby to a more dangerous split in the transatlantic partnership?

The second critical region is Central America. Are we not likely to see the turbulence now confined to the relatively small states of the isthmus spread to Mexico itself? The danger stems not from a domino theory. Rather, it exists for internal Mexican reasons. There are some ominous parallels between Mexico and Iran. Social modernization has imposed growing strains on the political system, though the Mexican system has involved a more flexible and participatory pattern. Large-scale migration to urban centers by displaced rural populations has created a mass of people susceptible to demagogic mobilization. The objective reality of inequality of wealth—which has been widening—has been accompanied by a growing subjective rejection of that reality as profoundly unjust. Unlike Iran, Mexico also has the burden of external indebtedness, which imposes truly painful choices on policymakers. Like the Iranians, Mexicans focus on the United States as an external source of their internal problems and tensions, thereby making extremist appeals both more attractive and more explosive.

If Mexico were to become the next Iran, previous U.S. dilemmas regarding Cuba and Central America, which have focused so heavily on Cuba's connection to the Soviet Union, would be dwarfed in historical significance by the national security, political, and economic challenges posed by an indigenous Mexican crisis.

There is also a special dimension to the Mexican problem: the large Mexican population within the United States. Mexican-Americans differ from all other groups of immigrants because they enjoy a de facto linguistic autonomy. This inhibits or slows their cultural and political assimilation, and that fact becomes politically relevant since their country of origin has a living historical memory of a genuine territorial grievance against the United States. No other immigrants to the United States have been in that position. This carries serious implications in the event of a major internal upheaval in Mexico, which could also generate a simultaneous crisis in U.S.-Mexican relations.

In addition to these regional dangers, concern is justified over our ability to handle three issues. The first is national defense. The United States has increasingly slipped into a pattern of unilateral disarmament by dithering. Congress has now asserted a role as co-shaper of U.S. defense policies, both at the tactical and the strategic levels. More and more senators and representatives consider themselves to be putative secretaries of defense, each articulating his or her own defense strategy, each developing his or her own arms-control scheme, and each focusing funding on his or her preferred weapons systems (which usually turn out to be those that need large-scale appropriations only in the 1990s or that are manufactured in the home state or district). Given the absence of bipartisanship, it is difficult to imagine the United States making critical defense and arms-control decisions in a fashion consistent with a comprehensive long-term strategy.

While the overall U.S.-Soviet strategic balance is unlikely to change dramatically, given the scale of existing arsenals and additional deployments, internal indecision will make it more difficult for the United States to build a more stable security and arms-control relationship with the Soviet Union. This, in turn, will fuel widespread uncertainty about the credibility of U.S. deterrence for purposes beyond the most narrowly confined scenario of a central attack on the United States itself.

The second issue is nuclear proliferation. Nuclear peace will become more precarious as nuclear weapons proliferate to tertiary powers. The result will be a rise in the probability that these weapons will be used in anger in a local or regional conflict. It is idle speculation to try to pick a target or to imagine a scenario. But it is not idle speculation to note that by the end of this decade, crises in several parts of the world may be susceptible to the use of nuclear weapons by states that will have recently acquired them. A highly congested and vulnerable country, such as Israel, is bound to offer an attractive focal point for extremist and radical elements with access to nuclear weapons technology.

The third issue is the shift in the international division of labor in the world economy. It has already proved to be disruptive to U.S. industries. It is likely to produce even more domestic tension in the future. More ominous, it will be increasingly probable that some major financial collapses will take place among the heavily indebted countries, thereby endangering the stability of the international financial system as a whole. In the last year, the system withstood the first test. But it is like a dike straining to contain a flood. Seepage and overflow are the twin dangers. They pose the threat not only of an economic upheaval but also of political turbulence. Austerity and democracy do not easily go hand in hand. Events in Mexico, Brazil, Poland, and Nigeria—countries with very different political systems—represent only the first wave of a larger financial crisis that will spread more widely in this decade.

Our current economic recovery from the recession that began in 1981 may mitigate in the short run the danger of a global financial collapse. But the international financial system remains very vulnerable to the next shock. So do the economies of some key countries. Margins of safety have narrowed, and if the next U.S. recession occurs within several years, the world financial system may find itself unable to withstand the strains.

In the 1980s, we are likely to experience a collective loss of control over global change. I emphasize the word *collective* because global change is clearly no longer susceptible to unilateral control by the United States, though the United States remains the most important participant in any collective effort to manage change in ways to avert catastrophes.

A progressive loss of collective control does not presage a Pax Sovietica. Moscow simply lacks the capacity to exercise effective political and economic world leadership. Instead, it foreshadows increasing global anarchy. This is abetted by a loss of national purpose and national discipline in the United States, of which the absence of bipartisan consensus on world affairs is an important symptom. In the 1980s, the danger is that U.S. foreign policy will become increasingly paralyzed in an increasingly turbulent world.

*   *   *

We therefore need to reflect seriously on these prospects and consider which actions can be taken to avert the most dire consequences. In this context, the purpose of prophesy is not self-fulfillment but self-denial. We need to identify the key dangers in order to avoid them. I will not end these remarks with an immodest prescription for averting a decade out of control. Instead, I will try to sketch out some ideas that can serve as a point of departure for addressing our problems.

First, we cannot chart an effective course without a deliberate revival of a bipartisan foreign policy. Only such a policy can provide the necessary impulse for a wider international alliance, for a global effort to shape international arrangements capable of absorbing the inevitable tensions. Only such a policy can ensure that the United States will have a sense of direction that others can understand and will be prepared to follow. Only such a policy will generate consistency in our international actions and will be able to compensate for the frequent changes in our presidents.

Only under a bipartisan foreign policy will the United States steer a moderate course avoiding swings from right to left and vice versa.

Invoking the need for a bipartisan foreign policy does not amount to uttering an empty cliché. It means the deliberate choice of presidential candidates who are capable of surrounding themselves with advisers from the middle of the political spectrum, who are able to work with the leaders of the opposite party, who can articulate and implement policies derived from a national consensus. Public opinion polls show that the potential for such a political consensus exists. We must work to make our political process develop that consensus, rather than fracture it, as has happened in recent years.

Second, to avert catastrophes in the critical regions of the Middle East and Central America, we must begin by realizing that their problems are not susceptible to resolution by U.S. fiat or U.S. passivity. In the Middle East, we cannot dictate a solution. But the alternative should not be the adoption of a posture that checks radical Arab unilateralism but renders a unilateral Israeli solution the only probable outcome. We must become more actively engaged in promoting an equitable outcome. That means using U.S. leverage to set in motion genuine negotiations designed to give Israel the security to which it is entitled and the Palestinians the political dignity for which they yearn. In brief, Ben Gurion's old formula of "peace for land" needs to be pressed forward energetically before it is too late. We can achieve meaningful results more easily if we associate ourselves with the views of our democratic friends in Western Europe and the Far East, all of whom also have an enormous stake in avoiding a regional disaster.

In Central America, we need to be especially responsive to Mexico's internal dilemmas. We should adopt a compassionate and far-sighted policy on immigration, trade, and financial cooperation. We cannot premise a policy to avert an internal Mexican catastrophe on the condition that Mexico accommodates itself to our view on the Central American issue. On the contrary, in coping with the current turbulence in Central America, we must strive above all to work closely with other concerned Latin American countries, especially Mexico, Venezuela, Colombia, and Panama. That means we must show a greater willingness to accept their perspective on the problem. This includes the need for recognition by the United States of the indigenous socioeconomic character of the sources of these revolutionary conflicts—even though they are clearly abetted and exploited by the Soviets and the Cubans.

In many respects, this is less a matter of what we actually do and more a matter of how we interpret historically what is happening. The worst outcome would be for us to allow these conflicts to become so Americanized that the rest of the hemisphere comes to view the conflict as an anti-Yankee crusade. That would not only help the Soviets and the Cubans in Central America, but would also poison the political climate for any constructive U.S. response to the Mexican dilemma.

Third, we need to remind ourselves that the issue for the remainder of the decade is not so much the decline of the U.S. capacity to act purposefully but the waning of U.S. will to act as a great power.

The objective dimensions of our power still make us the preeminent force in the world. In 1983, U.S. share of the world economy was approximately 25 percent—more than double the share of the next largest country. In terms of availability of energy, vulnerability to external economic pressures, and access to markets, the United States remains in a better position than any other industrial power. It also has a better chance of preventing the erosion of its share of the world economy in the near term. In the event of major disruptions in the supply of resources and even critical raw materials, the United States remains in a better position than most of our friends and rivals, except for the Soviet Union. Moreover, given the fact that worldwide food shortages are likely to grow, U.S. economic leverage is likely to increase because of the extraordinary productivity of our agricultural sector.

Finally, U.S. technological advantage and economic potential is tremendous. With the application of microelectronics to weapons technology, the United States will alter qualitatively the U.S.-Soviet military balance. With major U.S. research and development expenditures from both government and private sources, U.S. leadership in the area of high technology is unlikely to fade.

U.S. loss of nerve and the collective loss of control are not products of objective circumstances but rather a matter of subjective indecision. Given our national tradition, Americans do not wish to become an imperial nation, exercising its power in the manner of a hegemonic power. But given the scale of our power and given the dependence of our basic interests and values on global stability, it is absolutely essential that we remain committed to an internationalist, outward, and activist posture regarding world problems. Turning inward, emphasizing protectionism, engaging in endless bickering over foreign policy and security decisions, subjecting ourselves to continual lamentations about our inability to influence events in regions as centrally important as the Middle East and Central America are a prescription for a decade out of control, which, in turn, will have disastrous consequences for us at home.

While shaping a political climate congenial to renewed bipartisanship, we can and should pursue an activist and assertive foreign policy designed to promote the emergence of a new, post-European, and truly global international system. Indeed, the only alternative to a decade out of control is a U.S. policy of constructive globalism.

CHAPTER TWO

■

Reagan's Ominous Legacy
in Foreign Policy

AS THE POST-REAGAN ERA APPROACHES, a startling paradox is beginning to haunt people who take national-security issues seriously: A strong-minded president who has presided over an apparently successful foreign policy is likely to bequeath to his successor an ominous global agenda.

Reagan's political skills help to obscure these difficulties. But it seems likely that this century's most popular (and seemingly successful) president may leave office with a dangerously deteriorating state of affairs in four broad areas of our national security: the geostrategic, the regional, the economic and the political. And since the next president is almost certainly going to be less popular and less powerful than the incumbent, effective leadership will be more difficult to assert.

This bleak prognosis is not likely to change because of next week's summit in Reykjavik, Iceland. Indeed, that hastily prepared summit illustrates the most serious failing of Reagan administration foreign policy: its improvised and reactive character. Despite President Reagan's earlier and categorical assurances that he wouldn't meet with a Soviet leader next time outside the United States, he's now rushing off to Reykjavik to hold a summit with a Soviet leader who two weeks ago branded him, in effect, a liar. There is thus the real likelihood that any agreement in Iceland will be either cosmetic or concessionary.

By conventional standards, the president and his team have many reasons to be proud. Only a carping partisan critic would begrudge the president's claims that he has restored American self-confidence; increased markedly our defense spending; called the Soviet bluff in the INF talks;

This chapter appeared in *The Washington Post, Outlook* section, October 5, 1986. Reprinted by permission.

put the Soviets on the defensive with his bold Strategic Defense Initiative; increased thereby the chances of inducing genuine Soviet concessions in the arms-control negotiations; demonstrated, despite unfair Democratic criticism, the capacity to use force decisively, as in Grenada, with positive regional results; improved personal relations with our top allied leaders; maintained the new U.S.-Chinese connection (despite some initial fumbling); and projected once again an image of America as the future's innovative social laboratory.

That is an impressive list. Whether much of it is the product of luck—as critics would allege—or of personal leadership—as devoted Reaganauts would claim—is irrelevant. A true leader is a lucky leader. He generates his own "fortuna," to use Machiavelli's formula for the secret of the Prince's success. Reagan did benefit from the drop in the price of oil and from Brezhnev's senility. But he also inspired a sense of confidence and projected personal strength, and true leadership requires both.

Another criticism is more germane. A closer scrutiny of Reagan's successes reveals a perplexing reality. Almost all of these accomplishments are reactive in nature. They are responses to problems or challenges that imposed themselves on the president and his advisers. Except for the emphasis on defense, they are not part of a larger grand design either to shape a significantly new geostrategic relationship with the Soviets or to cope with major regional dilemmas.

This condition is due in part to the president's own style of leadership and in part to the continuing dilution of effective executive control over foreign policy in the American system as a whole. The president has not imposed a systematic top-down decision-making system either on the executive branch as a whole or on his associates. Since World War II American presidents typically either shaped national security policy by relying on clearly dominant secretaries of state, or did so themselves by elevating their national security advisers into the preponderant players exerting control from the White House. Alexander Haig apparently thought that Reagan would follow the first model, and shortly thereafter Haig was decapitated by the White House staff.

Paradoxically, the president then did not opt for the second variant, and the frequent changes in the leadership of the NSC have contributed to the progressive attrition of its central role. Today, the decision-making process at the very top is institutionally more fragmented than at any point since World War II. This is so even though the philosophical differences among the top players are probably less acute than they were under President Carter's centralized NSC system.

This condition is made worse by the continuing and expanding intrusion of Congress into the tactics of foreign policy, not to speak of congressional battles over broad foreign policy directions. Almost every congressman sees himself as a putative secretary of state, surrounded by personal staffers who make it their business to make the life of the secretary of state as miserable as possible. Some legislators have even gone as far as to designate some of their assistants with the pretentious title of national security adviser. Much of the press, too, views foreign policy not as a matter to be approached with a shared concept of national interest but rather as an opportunity to embarrass the administration in office, to leak its secrets, and even to expose its truly sensitive plans or activities.

The Reagan legacy of unsolved problems—geostrategic, regional, economic, and political—begins with the U.S.-Soviet relationship. Some limited progress on arms control is to be expected, though probably not much more than in SALT II. Reagan is to be credited for whatever progress occurs because he improved the U.S. bargaining position by not permitting arms control to become the fetish of his administration. That, in turn, convinced Moscow that it had to make genuine concessions. Especially important for the future of the SDI has been Reagan's recent decision, urged upon him by this writer among others, to gradually inject into the arms-control negotiations the question of revising and perhaps eventually scrapping the ABM Treaty.

Nonetheless, the fact remains that the long-term strategic decisions for the 1990s, and for the century beyond, have not yet been made by this administration. Our strategic doctrine and our weapons technology are out of kilter, and there is no obvious connection between our strategic requirements and our arms-control policies. The MX deployment was needlessly derailed; the strategic rationale for a new land-based mobile ICBM remains debatable; the emphasis on deep cuts in Soviet first-strike strategic forces has been abandoned; and the SDI has been elevated into a grand but distant vision that has probably accelerated covert Soviet strategic defense efforts without giving the United States a more limited, essentially counter-first strike SDI deployment that would provide by the next decade a prudent mix of strategically offensive and limited defensive forces. As a result, the strategic security of the United States by 1988 could be more precarious than it was in 1980.

At the same time, the administration has not been sufficiently vigorous in making an issue of the Soviet invasion and genocidal policies in Afghanistan. That invasion involves ultimately not Afghanistan alone but also Pakistan and Iran and eventually even access to the Persian Gulf. It thus raises not only a moral challenge but a serious geostrategic threat to vital U.S. global interests. The United States has been lax in dramatizing this issue publicly and ineffective in developing a wider international program of support for the mujahideen. So much more could be done—and should be done—to dramatize this issue and to press the Soviets to disengage. Yet one often gets the impression that some of our top policy makers view the Afghan war as a regrettable obstacle to an improvement in the American-Soviet relationship rather than as a critical geostrategic test in the global U.S.-Soviet contest.

More recently, many in the administration have become obsessed with the staging of a Reagan-Gorbachev summit. They are thus repeating the same mistake made early on by the Carter administration which ultimately made the United States appear more eager for a summit than the Soviet side. But President Carter, despite his desire for a summit, did not yield in a spy case similar to the arrest and detention of the *U.S. News and World Report* reporter Nicholas Daniloff, and on the eve of the Vienna summit he announced his intention to deploy the MX. President Nixon even went so far as to bomb Haiphong shortly before going to Moscow. Not only has President Reagan's excessive eagerness diminished the American bargaining power; but the administration's embarrassing weakness during the Daniloff affair has done costly damage to the president's reputation for resolve.

As a result, Reagan is likely to encounter in Reykjavik a Soviet leader as self-confident as Khrushchev was in Vienna in 1961, three months after Kennedy's Bay of Pigs fiasco. The restoration of presidential credibility is thus essential. But a largely cosmetic agreement in Reykjavik will not be enough to restore Reagan's tarnished reputation as a resolute leader. To recoup, the president will now have to do something more tangible— perhaps by approving an initial SDI deployment—than just denying, unconvincingly, that he has yielded to Soviet blackmail.

The next president will also probably confront several dangerous regional crises. They are not the product of the U.S.-Soviet rivalry, but each of them could eventually produce a superpower collision:

The Middle East. For the last six years, the United States has been almost passive in the Mideast. From the role of a creative mediator in the Arab-Israeli dispute, the United States gradually has become a kibitzer, while its funding of Israel has reached levels without precedent in international philanthropy. Neither the president nor the secretary of state has engaged his personal prestige in seeking to advance the peace process, and thus the momentum generated by the Camp David agreement has gradually faded. All that is now needed is some major political upheaval either in Egypt or in Jordan to bring to the surface the full consequences for the United States of a policy that pays lip service to peace but de facto supports a regional stalemate. That stalemate strengthens the fundamentalist forces within all of the conflicting parties, with potentially destructive consequences both for regional stability and for the American national interest.

South Africa. Also, it is probably justifiable to assert that during the last six years the administration has not exercised much leverage to

encourage greater racial accommodation in South Africa. Though I agree
with the administration assessment that it would be a mistake to turn
the white community in South Africa into a beleaguered and besieged
laager, one still cannot suppress the painful suspicion that the white
South African community has drawn self-serving political comfort from
the administration's passive posture. This, in turn, has reduced the
prospects for gradual but substantive racial accommodation.

Central America. Finally, the years ahead are likely to see the fusion
of the current Central American dilemma with the wider systemic crisis
of Mexico, thereby posing an unprecedented security threat to the
continental United States itself. In my recently published book, *Game
Plan,* I foresee the opening of a fourth central strategic front on the
Rio Grande in the worldwide U.S.-Soviet contest—the other three fronts
involving the fate of Eurasia. That development would in itself be a
historical setback for the United States.

This danger surely implies a need for greater urgency in resolving the
issue of Nicaragua decisively, even if that should require the imposition
of a U.S. air and sea blockade to prevent the flow of Soviet arms and
Cuban military advisers. In Mexico, it might call for a shift from a
policy of palliatives that perpetuate various systemic ills to a policy of
more direct financial and political pressure designed to generate, before
it is too late, the desperately needed reforms of the system as a whole.
Our present policy seeks to deal with the problem on the cheap by
supporting the contras, much like President Kennedy tried to solve the
Cuban problem with support for Cuban refugees, and by keeping Mexico
on the dole. It runs the risk of a Bay of Pigs writ large and is unlikely
to compel the Mexican elite to face up to painful truths.

These national security dilemmas are likely to be compounded by
growing economic and political difficulties. The new president in 1989
will inherit a national deficit and a trade imbalance without historical
precedent. Until now, the inflow of foreign capital has mitigated this
deteriorating condition. However, if the United States were to lose some
of its magnetic attraction as a politically safe and profitable country for
investment, the resulting economic pinch could produce a situation for
which the word "ominous" would be a cautious understatement.

To be sure, it would be rash and unfair to argue that any president,
even one as popular as Reagan, should have resolved all these deep-
rooted and complex matters in the course of one or even two terms of
office. But our ability to cope with these matters would have been
enhanced if during his tenure Reagan had moved discernibly toward
greater bipartisanship on national security issues. Such a move would
have made dealing with a fractious and intrusive Congress easier and

maybe even would have mitigated some of the anti-governmental bias on the part of much of the national press.

Reagan assumed office with a truly impressive national mandate. In a praiseworthy precedent, his transition team even included a former Democratic presidential candidate, Sen. Henry Jackson. Had Reagan then moved to fashion a bipartisan foreign and defense policy—for example, by appointing Jackson to secretary of defense just as President Truman did Republican Robert Lovett or as Kennedy did by naming Douglas Dillon as secretary of the treasury—a giant step toward true bipartisanship would have been taken.

A future president, inevitably weaker than the formidable Ronald Reagan, is bound to suffer even more from our partisan polarization over foreign policy. And these divisions could even widen as the 1988 campaign approaches and as the United States confronts sharper dilemmas in the area of foreign policy. Demagogic partisanship will probably be too tempting for many politicians to resist. How then will the next president be able to fashion a strategic doctrine responsive to the imperatives and the potential of new weapons? How will he be able to sustain a coherent geostrategy in the historic rivalry with the Soviet Union? How will he master the regional conflicts that are likely to mushroom in intensity?

To frame these questions is not to slide into despair but to signal sharpening dilemmas that should, and perhaps still can, be diffused. The fact is that Ronald Reagan has two years left as president, and he has enormous personal popularity to deploy and to exploit. That is why he should bite the bullet now on the central strategic issues, notably by moving toward some initial strategic defense deployment.

Reagan should not ignore the fact that the next Democratic president would surely kill the SDI, while the next Republican president would be too weak to pursue it. Second, the president should concentrate on the geostrategic dilemmas in the U.S.-Soviet relationship, such as Afghanistan, and not be seduced by the deceptive mirage of a summit for the sake of a summit. Third, he should energize American policy on the key regional problems, such as the Middle East and South Africa, which are otherwise likely to become increasingly destructive. Fourth, he should take whatever steps are still possible to generate a more truly bipartisan decision-making process, while injecting greater discipline and order into his NSC machinery.

Ronald Reagan's legacy is still, in considerable measure, his to be shaped. But history could be harsh and his successor quite ungrateful if U.S. decision-making during the next two years placed a higher emphasis on political cosmetics than on power politics.

CHAPTER THREE

■

U.S. Military Strategy

A LONG-TERM STRATEGY for the United States must contain the following three elements: (1) it must be derived from a correct diagnosis of the U.S.-Soviet conflict and be based on a realistic assessment of the Soviet challenge; (2) it must provide an effective response to the most pressing strategic threats and exploit the principal vulnerabilities of the adversary; and (3) it must actively explore opportunities for an equitable accommodation and generate the necessary incentives for a positive response from the adversary.

BASIC GEOPOLITICAL PREMISES

1. The U.S.-Soviet rivalry is a long-term contest. It is a classic historical conflict between two major powers and is not susceptible to a broad and quick resolution, either through a victory by one side or through a grand act of reconciliation.

2. The U.S.-Soviet contest is global in scope, but its central focus is the struggle for Eurasia. The Eurasian landmass constitutes almost half the world's land surface and contains the bulk of the world's population and economic wealth.

3. In the contest for Eurasia, there are three central strategic fronts.

The first front, Europe, is critical because it encompasses the most vital and industrialized section of Eurasia and controls the principal outlets to the Atlantic Ocean. Today, the European peninsula of the Eurasian landmass is also the most highly militarized region in the world.

Delivered as introductory remarks to testimony before the Senate Armed Services Committee on January 13, 1987.

The second front, the Far East, represents the world's fastest growing economic region and controls Soviet access to the Pacific Ocean. U.S. trade with the countries of the Pacific Basin now exceeds U.S. trade with the countries of Western Europe. This second front emerged after the Soviet-supported North Korean invasion of South Korea and the resulting U.S. military intervention.

The third front, southwest Asia, contains almost two-thirds of the world's known oil reserves and contains the principal outlets to the Indian Ocean. The third front, therefore, is catalytic in nature. A Soviet victory in the Gulf region would give Moscow tremendous leverage on the other two fronts. It is also the most volatile of the three central strategic fronts. This front emerged with the Soviet invasion of Afghanistan and the subsequent U.S. commitment to the defense of the Gulf region embodied in the Carter Doctrine and reaffirmed by the Reagan administration.

4. There is a danger that a fourth central strategic front may soon emerge in Central America. The Soviet Union realizes that in a superpower conflict in Central America or the Caribbean it would be at a massive geographical, logistical, and economic disadvantage to the United States. It therefore has pursued its geostrategic goals in the region with caution, advancing its interests with tactics not so aggressive as to precipitate a direct clash. Should the internal problems of Central America merge with a larger domestic explosion in Mexico that inflames the U.S.-Mexican relationship, the Soviet Union is almost certain to exploit it, thereby opening up a fourth central strategic front in the U.S.-Soviet conflict.

5. The Soviet Union is unique among major national powers in history because it is a one-dimensional power. Moscow's only claim to the status of a world power is its military might. In all other respects, it is not a truly competitive rival of the United States. While the United States is plunging headlong into the technetronic age, the Soviet Union is still struggling desperately to make its relatively conventional industrial economy more efficient and modern. That difference is crucial for the historical outcome of the U.S.-Soviet conflict. Unless military means prove historically decisive—with Moscow exploiting its military leverage to attain Eurasian preponderance—social creativity will probably determine which side prevails.

STRATEGIC POLICY

These are the basic geopolitical premises that the United States must address. They call for a long-term U.S. strategy with a military, a geopolitical, and a negotiating component.

Military Component

Once Soviet military power is checked, the Soviet Union ceases to be a historically threatening rival. But that is no mean task. My best estimate of trends in Soviet military capability vis-à-vis the United States is as follows:

1986	1996
Strategic Forces	
No assurance that the United States would be unable to inflict massive destruction on the Soviet Union in the event of a Soviet first strike	A reasonable possibility that a Soviet first strike would be able to disarm the United States to such a degree that a retaliatory response would be fragmentary
Conventional Ground Forces on the Three Central Strategic Fronts	
Probability of Soviet success in a purely conventional engagement on the first and third fronts, offset by the possibility of nuclear escalation	Probability of Soviet success with a higher degree of assurance, and a lower likelihood of U.S. nuclear escalation
Conventional Ground Forces in Long-range Force Projection	
High vulnerability to conventional attrition by U.S. RDF because of inadequate logistics and vulnerable supply lines	Progressive improvement in capabilities, but probably continued inferiority to U.S. RDF
Naval Forces in Strategic Conflict	
Secondary role in strategic conflict	Gradual shift to a significant strategic SLBM and SLCM capability
Naval Forces in Central Conventional Conflict	
Soviet capacity for serious, but not conclusive, disruption of U.S. ocean control and of U.S. sustaining efforts on behalf of U.S. forces engaged in conventional conflicts on any one of the three main fronts	No basic change
Naval Forces in Remote Local Conflict	
Soviets unable to sustain long-range deployment of ground forces in the event of limited conventional naval collision with the United States	No basic change but progressive expansion in radius of Soviet capability

In the light of the above, on the strategic level, the objective of U.S. policy must be Mutual Strategic Security. That requires the maintenance of a strategic balance that makes a first strike for either side militarily futile and societally suicidal and that sustains extended deterrence.

To best deter a nuclear war, the United States must adjust its strategic doctrine and its deployments away from mutual-assured destruction and toward greater flexibility in war-fighting options, so that it will be able to respond at any level of a possible conflict.

U.S. strategic forces should have both offensive and defensive components. U.S. strategic offensive forces must be modernized, but their configuration and numbers should be contrived not to pose a threat of a disarming first strike to Soviet strategic forces. But in light of Soviet modernization plans—which in the mid-1990s will provide Moscow between 8,000 and 10,000 first-strike warheads—it is also necessary to deploy a limited strategic defense. That defense should be oriented toward the protection of U.S. strategic forces and command and control systems. It should be composed of a space-based screen to destroy Soviet missiles in the boost phase and a land-based terminal defense to intercept incoming warheads. While it would be an imperfect defense, it would achieve the critical objective of injecting a degree of randomness into any Soviet planning of a first-strike nuclear attack. As a result, no Soviet military planner could ever advise the Soviet leadership that Moscow could prevail in a conflict at the strategic level. That, in turn, would give the United States the needed strategic confidence to compete with the Soviet Union at other levels.

The alternate means of seeking Mutual Strategic Security—namely, through the proliferation of mobile strategic systems—is less desirable both militarily and in terms of cost. Leaving aside the probable domestic U.S. difficulties over the deployment of numerous mobile systems, the fact is that in a competitive proliferation of mobile systems the Soviet side is likely to have a major advantage, both in quantitative deployments and in strategic deception. Moreover, competitive deployment of mobile strategic systems is likely to breed greater insecurity than the deployment of a prudent mix of offensive and defensive systems.

On the conventional level, the United States must address a perilous strategic paradox: U.S. conventional forces are weakest where the United States is most vulnerable, along the southwestern Eurasian strategic front, and strongest along the far western Eurasian strategic front, where its allies have the greatest capacity for doing more on their own behalf and where the risk of a U.S.-Soviet clash is lowest.

Consequently, the United States should undertake a gradual—and certainly only partial—reduction in the level of U.S. forces in Europe. A total of perhaps 100,000 troops could be gradually withdrawn. That would leave over 250,000 U.S. troops deployed in Europe, a number that represents a clear deterrent to the Soviets and a substantial commitment to the defense of NATO. Budgetary savings from these reductions should be allocated to a significant expansion of U.S. airlift capability. Manpower withdrawn from Europe should be absorbed into an enlarged Rapid Deployment Force through the creation of additional light divisions for potential use on the southwest Asian central strategic front or in Central America.

Geostrategic Component

The first priority for U.S. policy is to hold the three central strategic fronts.

In Europe, the United States should encourage the development of a politically and militarily integrated Western Europe, less dependent on the United States but still tied to it by a strategic alliance. NATO should increasingly become a European regional alliance, though with an active and major U.S. presence in it.

In the Far East, the United States should promote an informal geopolitical triangle through wider economic, political, and partial military cooperation among the United States, Japan, and the People's Republic of China. Japan should be encouraged not to increase its defense spending, but rather to increase its economic assistance to developing countries in which Japan shares a security interest with the other industrialized democracies. Recipients of this strategic economic assistance should include Egypt, Pakistan, the Philippines, and even the democratic states of Central America. In the future, the combination of Japanese defense spending and strategic economic aid should reach about 4 percent of Japan's GNP, which would represent a spending level comparable to those of West European countries.

In southwest Asia, the most important priority for the United States is to step up the political and military pressure on the Soviet Union in Afghanistan. It is imperative that the United States increase, quantitatively and qualitatively, the level of military assistance sent to the Afghan resistance and also promote a wider international awareness of the war through public denunciations of the Soviet occupation and through efforts to facilitate television and radio coverage. The United States should also press in U.S.-Soviet bilateral meetings for a disengagement of Soviet forces. It should advance a diplomatic formula that calls for the external neutralization and the internal self-determination of the country. The former would restore Afghanistan's previous status as a neutral state, and the latter would allow the Afghan people to determine their own form of government. As a temporary expedient, peace-keeping forces from Islamic countries not unfriendly to the Soviet Union but still independent of Moscow (such as Algeria and Syria) could be stationed in Afghanistan upon the prompt removal of Soviet occupation forces.

In addition, the United States must seek to reinforce the resilience of Iran and Pakistan to Soviet advances where possible. Continued economic and military aid to Pakistan and the eventual restoration of more normal relations with Iran are essential components of the needed U.S. strategic response on the third front.

In addition, as part of its effort to hold the three fronts, the United States should exploit the weaknesses of the Soviet Union. Moscow is vulnerable at three levels: the systemic weakness of its socioeconomic system, the geopolitical weakness of its imperial system, and the internal weakness of the multinational nature of the Soviet Union itself.

The Soviet objective in Eastern Europe is to dominate its satellites militarily and ideologically and to integrate them into a kind of economic commonwealth. Consequently, the United States should promote the development of an independent-minded and increasingly assertive East European public opinion, not only through radio broadcasts but also through new communications and information technology, such as videocassettes, miniaturized printers, and word processors. The United States should also look with favor on the growing economic cooperation between Western Europe and Eastern Europe because such cooperation would inevitably lead indirectly to closer political ties. That means, for example, that the United States should encourage the countries of Western Europe to provide Eastern Europe with economic options that even the Communist regimes would find attractive.

The internal weaknesses of the Soviet Union stem from the fact that Moscow rules over the world's last surviving multinational empire. The central government dominated by the Great Russians, whose population numbers about 135 million, dominates in turn a dozen other major nations and scores of smaller nations. Those include 55 million Soviet Muslims, 50 million Ukrainians, and 10 million Balts. The multinational character of the Soviet Union creates fissures and openings—as demonstrated most recently in the protests in Alma-Ata in Kazahkstan. The U.S. goal should be to give sharper political definition to these trends through greatly intensified use of modern means of communication. The techniques that have proven so effective in breaking down the Soviet Union's efforts to isolate Eastern Europe should be more actively applied to the Soviet Union itself. The object of the effort should not be to stoke national hatred or even to foster the disintegration of the Soviet Union. The real opportunity is to mobilize the forces for genuine political participation, for greater national codetermination, for the dispersal of central power, and for the termination of heavy-handed central domination that breeds the expansionist impulse.

Soviet systemic weakness compounds Moscow's vulnerability at both these levels. In virtually every other imperial system in history, the center exerted some kind of an attraction for the periphery, whether in terms of learning, culture, economic wealth, or ideology. That is not the case with the Soviet Union. Its ideology has lost its appeal, with not even the most fervent Third World revolutionary movements aspiring to a future based on the Soviet model. Its imperial realm might be characterized best as an "economic co-stagnation sphere," with the Communist bloc lagging severely behind the West in all indexes of economic well-being and falling further behind in most.

Negotiating Component

As part of the same overall strategy, the United States should engage the Soviet Union in bilateral negotiations. These should not, however, become obsessed with arms control at the strategic nuclear level, as has occurred in the last few years and particularly at the Reykjavik summit.

First, in the short term, the United States should formally propose a schedule for ministerial-level meetings to move forward U.S.-Soviet negotiations during the remainder of the Reagan administration.

Second, on the strategic level, the United States should in the course of the next two years seek a five-year interim agreement that provides for serious reductions in the overall arsenals of the two sides. The current proposals at Geneva which call for a restriction of 6,000 warheads, 1,600 launchers, and 154 heavy missiles create the basis for such an agreement. A more comprehensive agreement, however, requires progress on issues of verification and modernization and on finding ways to incorporate limited strategic defense into the arms-control process.

In addition to watertight provisions for verification and for restricting modernization, the United States should press the Kremlin to lift gradually Soviet strategic secrecy. In the age of highly accurate and prompt strategic systems, Soviet strategic secrecy introduces an element of uncertainty and anxiety that is incompatible with strategic stability and that vastly complicates the effort to achieve effective arms control. In this regard, the United States must make a major public issue of Soviet strategic secrecy and insist that its veil be lifted for the sake of mutual strategic security.

Third, beyond any potential five-year interim START agreement, the United States should propose a wider set of negotiations, involving proportional reductions in the strategic and conventional forces of both sides. Such Comprehensive Arms Reduction Talks (CART) ought to have as their objective the shaping of truly comprehensive mutual security, without either side enjoying a one-sided advantage in either strategic or conventional forces. This is of particular importance to stability and security in Europe. It is in the U.S. interest to draw down forces on the central European front, both because a smaller U.S. presence in Western Europe leads to less friction in allied relations and more self-reliance among West Europeans. Also, a smaller Soviet troop presence in Eastern Europe will inevitably lead to greater self-assertion among the East Europeans.

Fourth, the United States should indicate a willingness to resolve the crisis in Nicaragua on the basis of the same formula as in Afghanistan. In both cases, the United States should seek external neutralization and internal self-determination. The external neutrality of Afghanistan and Nicaragua is consistent with the interests of both the United States and the Soviet Union. Neither country should become a base of operations for one superpower against the other. Internal self-determination for Afghanistan and Nicaragua disengages Washington and Moscow from the struggle for power within the two countries, thereby defusing the potential crises. At the same time, it is reasonable to assume that the outcome of genuine self-determination in both countries will produce regimes whose ascendence will be in the U.S. national interest.

Conclusion: The Need for Strategic Policy Planning

One final point. Within the executive branch, there must be more emphasis on strategy. Occasionally, this has been provided by particularly insightful top policymakers. There have also been periods when all the top U.S. foreign policy decisionmakers have been quite unversed either in Soviet-U.S. affairs or in matters of grand strategy. To compensate, the role of strategic planning should be enhanced. The Policy Planning Council in the State Department is not the right vehicle because all too often the State Department tends to confuse diplomacy with foreign policy. Only in the White House is it possible to generate the necessary broad, interagency approach to long-term planning. Hence, within the NSC, a top-level, civil-military geostrategic planning staff should be created to formulate and periodically revise the broad outlines of a long-term policy. U.S. policy is likely to become infused with the requisite longer-term geostrategic content only if the top decisionmakers or their immediate deputies are engaged in this undertaking, only if periodically the president himself is involved, and only if regular consultations are held with appropriate congressional leaders.

CHAPTER FOUR

■

America's New Geostrategy

THE RUMORS OF AMERICA'S imminent imperial decline are somewhat premature. They are, however, quite fashionable. Particularly within some intellectual circles a decided preference has taken hold for Spenglerian handwringing, which barely conceals a measure of schadenfreude over the anticipated end of the imperial phase in the history of this somewhat crass, materialistic, chaotic, libertarian and vaguely religious mass democracy. America's assumption of the imperial role after World War II— with U.S. power and influence projected around the world—was never popular either within America's intellectual class or more recently within its mass media. Hence the anticipatory gloating over the allegedly inevitable demise of the world's current number-one power.

To debate the accuracy of such a prognosis may be futile. The future is inherently full of discontinuities, and lessons of the past must be applied with enormous caution. Some recent scholarly studies have attempted to do so in a searching and comprehensive fashion, and without the dogmatic assumption of any kind of inevitability. This has greatly helped to raise the level of thoughtful discussion. From the political point of view, moreover, there is even some genuine benefit to be derived from the fact that doubts have been raised regarding America's future. Posing the issue so starkly focuses attention on the definition of the actions needed to maintain a constructive American world role, the essentials of American security, the core American interests, and the effects on the foregoing of the inexorable geopolitical and technological changes.

In other words, the intellectual debate over a possibly inevitable decline can become a political deliberation on how to avoid it, how to reinvigorate America's global power and how to redefine it in the context of a changing

This article appeared in *Foreign Affairs* (spring 1988). Reprinted by permission.

world. That can be the objectively positive result of posing the issue. Accordingly, the task of responsible statesmanship is to define more precisely the policy implications of the geopolitical and technological changes for the U.S. relationship with the world over the remaining years of this millennium, bearing in mind that such changes are significantly altering the setting within which U.S. interests and national security must be protected. Out of such an examination one can derive better guidance regarding the very character of America's world role in the years ahead.

In any such analysis three clusters of issues are central, namely: (1) strategic doctrine, which bears on how the United States can best promote its national security; (2) geopolitical imperatives, which determine the central foci of American regional involvements; and (3) the U.S. global role, which pertains to the manner in which America should wield its worldwide influence.

Over the last forty years the United States has relied heavily, indeed, predominantly, on nuclear deterrence to check much-feared Soviet expansion, particularly in central Europe. In the late 1940s and early 1950s, when it in effect possessed a monopoly on the capability to deliver nuclear weapons at intercontinental range, the United States went so far as to postulate the doctrine of massive nuclear retaliation as a response to even conventional Soviet aggression. But as Soviet strategic capabilities grew, adjustments in doctrine became necessary. By the 1960s U.S. strategic doctrine was embracing the concept of flexible response to a Soviet military challenge, though it still lacked to a considerable extent the targeting capabilities and the weapons needed for sustaining such a strategy.

The increased vulnerability of American society to a Soviet strategic attack, however, gave rise to the publicly compelling view that the condition of mutual assured destruction (known as MAD) had now become the basis for reciprocal deterrence. The resulting strategic dilemma was that this transformed deterrence into an essentially apocalyptic threat to commit suicide, a threat that could be credible only to deter a similarly suicidal attack by the enemy. Short of that extreme eventuality, U.S. strategic policy started to lose its credibility in deterring less than a total attack—while concurrent technological refinements have at the same time given rise to altogether novel opportunities for far more selective and strictly military uses of nuclear weaponry. A doctrinal readjustment, with significant force posture implications, was thus becoming due in order to close the consequent deterrence gap.

Over the last four decades, U.S. geopolitical imperatives have been largely preoccupied with the defense of both the far western and the far eastern extremities of the Eurasian continent against Soviet political and military domination. With the recovery of both Western Europe and Japan, which enhanced their capacity for more effective self-defense, and with the felicitous consolidation of a new, stabilizing relationship between the United States and the People's Republic of China, Americans have come to see the Soviet threat as less ominous. At the same time, American geopolitical concerns are being refocused on other critical regions, heretofore not major sources of U.S. security or political concerns.

The American global role has also been undergoing a profound transmutation. Throughout much of the last forty years, American political leadership has rested on a solid base of economic and military preeminence, and much of the motivation for the exercise of that primacy stemmed from a concern that the Soviet Union was seeking to dethrone and to replace the United States in the exercise of that special role. Today, the economic basis of American primacy is clearly much weaker and is likely to become weaker still in relation to the growth of other economic centers. At the same time, however, the Soviet Union has clearly failed as an economic rival. It has been revealed to be at best a one-dimensional power, a challenger in the military realm alone but not a serious rival either socially, economically or ideologically. In other words, the Soviet Union poses a threat to American security and geopolitical interests, but does not represent a challenge to American global primacy as such.

Thus on the strategic, geopolitical and global levels the need exists for significant adjustments in the way the United States participates in the global political process and promotes its fundamental national interests. Let us examine the policy implications that follow in each of the above three broad clusters.

U.S. STRATEGIC DOCTRINE

In strategic doctrine, the United States needs to shift away from its long-standing preoccupation with the threat of a nuclear war between the superpowers or a massive Soviet conventional attack in central Europe. Neither danger can be dismissed as impossible, but a central nuclear war is not likely to be initiated deliberately; America certainly has the means to maintain a military posture that precludes any rational Soviet decision-making process from reaching a suicidally erroneous conclusion. Much the same can be said about the possibility of a massive conventional Soviet attack on Western Europe, given not only the complexities of calculating intelligently the real battle trade-offs between existing NATO and Warsaw Pact forces but also the high risk of nuclear escalation.

It must be hastily added that the reassessment of the level of the threat does not imply in the least any decline in the U.S. interest in the security of Western Europe or any significant U.S. disengagement from the defense of Europe. Indeed, the specific adjustments in strategic doctrine and in force posture that are proposed below focus on the central goal of reinforcing the overall credibility of the American strategic and conventional deterrent, of which Western Europe and also Japan are the principal beneficiaries.

To enhance deterrence in the current and foreseeable conditions, a doctrine and a force posture are needed that will enable the United States to respond more selectively to a large number of possible security threats, ranging from the strategic to the conventional.[1] On the strategic level it must be recognized that technological changes have wrought a revolution in the way nuclear weapons may be used in the future. They are no longer just crude instruments for inflicting massive societal devastation but can be used with precision for more specific military missions, with relatively limited collateral societal damage. The increased versatility of nuclear weapons is the consequence of the interaction between smaller warheads and highly accurate delivery systems. The result is that nuclear weapons are no longer primarily blunt instruments of deterrence but can also serve as potentially decisive instruments of discriminating violence.

As a result, in the future the United States should rely to a greater extent on a more flexible mix of nuclear and even non-nuclear strategic forces capable of executing more selective military missions. The central purpose of the strategy of discriminate deterrence is to heighten the credibility of American threats to respond to aggression by increasing the spectrum of effective responses to such aggression, short of the inherently improbable option of simply committing national suicide. More specifically, this calls for greater reliance on highly accurate but less destructive long-range strategic weaponry, including procurement of the now-feasible non-nuclear strategic weapons. In addition, in order to deny to the potential aggressor the temptation of preemptively destroying U.S. strategic forces, it is also recommended that U.S. strategic forces be based on a prudent mix of both offensive and defensive systems, thus assimilating into U.S. force posture some initial elements of the much-debated Strategic Defense Initiative, marking an important break with the notions of MAD.

Space control is likely to become tantamount to earth control. There are striking parallels between the role of the navy in the emergence of American global power and today's incipient competition for a dominant position in space. The earlier competition among the Great Powers for

---

[1]For more on these recommendations see *Discriminate Deterrence,* Report of the Commission on Integrated Long-Term Strategy, Fred C. Iklé and Albert Wohlstetter, co-chairmen, Washington: GPO, January 1988.

maritime primacy involved rivalry for effective control over strategic space between the key continents. Control over such space was central to territorial preponderance. That is why the United States, in the phase of its geostrategic expansion, placed such an emphasis on the acquisition of dominant Atlantic and Pacific fleets, linked through direct U.S. control over the Panama Canal.

Today the equivalent of that naval rivalry is the competition in space. At the very minimum it must be the U.S. strategic objective to make certain that no hostile power can deny the United States, while retaining for itself, the means for using space for intelligence, early warning, reconnaissance, targeting, and command and control. Modern military operations are highly dependent on space assets performing these functions, and U.S. vulnerability in this area could be crippling. Thus, even short of seeking to exploit space control for offensive purposes against an enemy (e.g., by the use of weaponry deployed in space), the capacity to protect its nonlethal military space assets, or to inflict a denial of the use of space to the enemy, has become essential to an effective U.S. military posture.

On the conventional level similarly important adjustments are becoming necessary. The most probable threat stems from what are called low-intensity conflicts in areas where American forces are not permanently deployed. Thus, the United States must place less emphasis on prepositioned heavy forces in foreign bases and more on lighter forces, supported by enhanced air- and sea-lift capabilities, poised for a prompt long-distance response. This would reduce the risk that in a crisis (such as during the 1973 Middle East war or the U.S. air raid in Libya in 1986) the freedom to use American forces stationed abroad would be restricted by political inhibitions on the part of U.S. allies.

More generally, the United States in the years ahead must take advantage of its enormous capacity for technological innovation to enhance its military flexibility. Over the last several decades the United States has gradually become a military Gulliver, enormously powerful yet clumsy and inert. Technology is certainly not a "silver bullet" for solving a variety of deficiencies. Neither is it a substitute for well-trained and motivated manpower. But it does provide the basis for effective and rapid coordination, for precision in operations, for enhanced intelligence and for prompt concentration of destructive power. America is almost uniquely equipped to exploit these technological capabilities.

These adjustments in our military strategy and posture will have to be pursued in the context of unavoidable budgetary restraint. It follows, therefore, that some standing priorities will have to be revised. It also follows from the foregoing analysis that the targets for budgetary reallocation will have to fall within three broad categories: less emphasis on offensive central strategic nuclear weapons; less concentration on the funding of new major systems for the individual branches of the armed services and more on technological force-multipliers for existing weaponry; and a reallocation of expenditures and heavy forces away from Europe-oriented missions toward greater flexibility and longer-range mobility in conventional responses to conflicts in regions where no U.S. forces are prepositioned.

The underlying purpose of these adjustments will be to sustain a strategy of more selective commitment and more flexible capacity for action. The era of the big stick is over, but the reality of violence in international affairs is still with us. Under these circumstances, while retaining a residual capacity for an all-out nuclear war in order to avoid being blackmailed by its threat, American military power must be designed for more limited, prompt and even preemptive actions in areas clearly defined not only as vital but also as not capable of adequate self-defense. In brief, instead of planning to be able to fight two-and-a-half major wars (as not long ago was the case), the United States must be ready to deter one major war by having the means to fight it while also being able to respond effectively to more varied but less apocalyptic security threats.

U.S. GEOPOLITICAL IMPERATIVES

These needed strategic adjustments go hand in hand with changing U.S. geopolitical imperatives. In the years ahead, three regions other than the far western and far eastern extremities of Eurasia are likely to become the central foci of American concerns. For much of the cold war the major U.S. fear was the possible Soviet domination of Western Europe. It now appears likely, however, that in Europe for the next decade the Soviet Union will be increasingly on the defensive ideologically and politically. The internal communist threat to Western Europe has passed, while the vitality of Western Europe's development stands in sharp contrast to the stagnation to the east. Western Europe's economic and political recovery represents a monumental success for America's postwar policy.

The next phase should therefore involve an increased assumption by Western Europe of the costs of its defense. The U.S. commitment to Europe's security is sacrosanct, but there is nothing sacrosanct about the level of U.S. military manpower in Europe or the proportion of the U.S. defense budget dedicated to Europe's security. Since Europe can and should do more for its defense, and since the United States has to make more of a defense effort elsewhere but cannot afford to do so, it follows that a gradual but significant readjustment in burdensharing is necessary and will occur.

In the meantime, Eastern Europe is rapidly emerging as Europe's region of potentially explosive instability, with five countries already in a classic prerevolutionary situation. Economic failure and political unrest are becoming the dominant characteristics of life in Poland, Romania, Hungary, Czechoslovakia and in non-Soviet-dominated but geopolitically important Yugoslavia. In any one, or even in several at once, a spark could set off a major explosion, given the intensity of popular dissatisfaction. Indeed, there are suggestive parallels between the current state of affairs in the region and the historic Spring of Nations of 1848.

Given the volatile state of the perestroika (restructuring) program in the Soviet Union itself, it is even conceivable that the systemic crisis of Eastern Europe will become a more general crisis of communism itself. Unrest has already surfaced in the Soviet-occupied Baltic republics, in western Ukraine, in Central Asia and elsewhere. Moreover, it could become more acute if current Soviet reform initiatives do not yield positive and tangible results but instead prompt, as is in fact likely, major economic dislocations, higher food prices, inflation and even large-scale unemployment.

In that context, a major eruption in Eastern Europe would almost certainly precipitate not only a Soviet intervention but the end of the perestroika itself. What could happen, therefore, is a matter of some importance to the West as a whole. It is not clear that the West has given sufficient thought to the longer-range implications of East European unrest. Gradual change in the region is certainly desirable, especially change involving the progressive self-emancipation of peoples who have long desired to be part of a larger Europe free of Soviet domination. But a large-scale explosion could have tragic consequences, not only for the region itself but also for East-West relations, by prompting a lasting revival of the most negative attributes of the Soviet system.

As a result the United States and its European allies should focus actively on an effort to forge a more stable relationship with Eastern Europe. A more coordinated Western policy of political and economic engagement should be designed to facilitate the evolutionary dismantling of the Stalinist relics in the region. But such a strategic approach is strikingly absent. Failure to develop one could confront the United States, and its allies, with explosive and eventually very dangerous circumstances.

The region's renewed geopolitical salience is likely to be maximized by growing speculation regarding Germany's future orientation. Already today in Paris and even in London the topic of concerned conversations is focused as much on the future of Germany as on the future of perestroika or the likely outcome of the American elections. Some of this may be dismissed as an outdated obsession with "the German question." But some of it does reflect an intelligent appreciation of the German angst over the country's unnatural division and of the traditional German yearning for a grand deal with Moscow.

Any major alteration in the German-Russian relationship would parallel in its geopolitical consequences the earlier American-Chinese accord that so shook the world and so gripped the Russians with the fear of strategic encirclement. It is, therefore, likely to be tempting to Soviet strategists. Moreover, it can only make Soviet economic planners salivate, for in one stroke a new German-Russian relationship would help to resolve the Soviet cravings for both investment and technological innovation.

Fortunately, however, the scope of any potential Soviet initiative toward Germany is constrained by the scope of the East European systematic crisis. In the present circumstances, releasing East Germany—as the price of seducing West Germany—would deprive the Soviet Union of its key bastion for the exercise of effective Soviet military and political control over Poland, Czechoslovakia and Hungary. A neutralized Germany on the edge of an economically stagnant but politically restless Eastern Europe would be disruptive not only for NATO but for the Warsaw Pact as well.

In any case, because of the region's centrality to East-West relations, Eastern Europe is now likely to become increasingly an object of international anxiety and thus of America's concern. Its economic problems are so deep-rooted, its political structures so weak and its geopolitical moorings so shallow that for the next decade at least the region's problems are likely to be high on the statesman's agenda.

The second major regional focus of American concern will continue to be the Persian Gulf/Middle Eastern area. America's deep involvement in the problems of this part of the world stems from two major developments over the last two decades. One involved the emergence since about the mid-1960s of a tight American-Israeli connection; the second involved the gradual replacement "east of Suez" of Great Britain by the United States. The first has been, by and large, the product of domestic impulses in the United States itself, spurred on by very successful lobbying of Congress on behalf of Israel. The second was the result of the need to fill the geopolitical vacuum left by Britain and by the collapse of its U.S.-sponsored would-be regional successor, Iran.

The consequence was that the region's troubles have become America's burden: America is to prevent the Soviet Union from dominating the Persian Gulf region and also to preserve Israel's security. There is no reason to believe that in the years ahead these obligations will recede, and there is much cause to expect continued or even intensified conflicts in the area as a whole. Protection, mediation and deterrence will remain predominantly American responsibilities.

The Carter Doctrine, deliberately drafted to echo the words of the Truman Doctrine, was subsequently reiterated by President Reagan. It represents an unequivocal commitment to respond, in whatever fashion necessary, to any Soviet effort to gain a geopolitical presence in the Gulf. That Soviet goal, expressly confirmed by Stalin to Hitler in 1940 and implicitly by Brezhnev's invasion of Afghanistan in 1979, can only be denied if America possesses the forces for rapid counterintervention. Only this capability would pose the prospect for Moscow of a direct American-Soviet collision. And U.S. ability to exploit this capability in turn depends on at least a minimal political relationship between the United States and the two geopolitically key barriers to Soviet expansion, Pakistan and Iran.

The creation of the Rapid Deployment Force was meant to meet the first need, and its further expansion has already been justified in the preceding discussion of changes in strategic doctrine. The second requirement was met in part by the extensive American-Pakistani collaboration that developed in the wake of the Soviet invasion of Afghanistan. It is important to register here the proposition that this collaboration should continue even if the Soviet forces are eventually withdrawn from Afghanistan. At that stage, the inclination is likely to arise, especially in the Congress, for a contraction of some aspects of the American-Pakistani relationship, particularly as some of the more contentious but lately repressed issues resurface (such as the Pakistani nuclear program or the question of internal democracy). In addition, there will be the temptation to sacrifice some aspects of the U.S.-Pakistani connection for the sake of a better relationship with India. Yet it is important not to lose sight of the simple fact that an isolated and hence weakened Pakistan could yield the Soviets geopolitical benefits that Soviet arms have not been able to gain in Afghanistan.

Equally important to the stability of the region, and to key U.S. interests, is the independence and territorial integrity of Iran. For the time being, and probably not until the Iranian-Iraqi war wanes or the Ayatollah Khomeini dies, American-Iranian relations will remain antagonistic. But in the longer run some reconstitution of a more normal relationship is in the interest of both countries and thus is likely to take place. For most Iranians, current sloganeering to the contrary, the truly threatening "Satan" is the one to the north and immediately contiguous to Iranian territory. All Iranians know that over the last century and a half the principal hostile designs on their soil and independence have originated from Russia. Rhetorical fanaticism does not obliterate historical memory.

Under these circumstances, some eventual accommodation is likely and will carry opportunities for renewed economic American-Iranian cooperation and perhaps even some military connection. The latter will depend on how the Iranians perceive future Soviet policy and also on the nature of Iranian-Arab relations after Khomeini. One of the major tasks of American diplomacy in this area will be to seek to relieve some of the current antagonism, although the scope for any genuine regional accommodation will probably be quite limited for a long time to come. Much will depend on how long-lasting and dynamic the current wave of Islamic fundamentalism proves to be.

Until then, the more immediate task of the United States will be to make certain that the more moderate Arab states in the region are not destabilized. As events have already shown, this will require both active diplomacy and a significant military presence. There is no reason to believe that the need for either will significantly recede, and thus the American preoccupation with this region is likely to be prolonged, risky and costly.

Much the same can be said of the American involvement in the Israeli-Arab issue, given the incompatible views of the local parties on the Palestinian problem (the West Bank and Gaza) and regarding the Golan Heights. Even if the peace process is revived, it will require extremely absorbing and frustrating mediation. In brief, for America the prospect is a grim one: a continuing and seemingly endless involvement in a messy and dangerous conundrum of ethnic and geopolitical conflicts, in the realization that American disinvolvement from them would create even more dangerous consequences.

The foregoing two geopolitical concerns, as taxing as they are, may yet, and before too long, yield in priority to a third one much closer to home. Unless the United States can soon fashion a bipartisan and comprehensive response to the mushrooming Central American crisis, it is quite likely that in the years ahead the region will pose for the American public the most preoccupying challenge, diverting America from its other global concerns. Fashioning such a response may well become the most urgent foreign priority for the next president, especially since on the other critical strategic and geopolitical issues some ongoing strands of policy exist and some degree of national consensus supports them.

The sad fact is that for the last fifteen years the United States has been attempting to respond to the region's simultaneously nationalist and social revolution, and to the Soviet-communist exploitation of it, by partial measures and through proxies. It has sought solutions on the cheap. Though President Kennedy proclaimed the creation of a communist regime in Cuba to be an intolerable security threat to the United States, his response was to send three thousand Cuban patriots to solve America's problem—and then to abandon them promptly when the going got tough. Two decades later, another president, Ronald Reagan, similarly proclaimed the Nicaraguan Sandinista regime to represent a mortal threat to the United States. He turned to proxies for a resolution of the problem, with the U.S. Congress then abandoning them.

Neither response was worthy of a Great Power, especially when its vital interests were said to be involved. Kennedy failed to exploit the Soviet collapse of will during the subsequent Cuban missile crisis to insist on a neutralized status for Cuba. Reagan failed to define an equally legitimate U.S. goal regarding a neutralized status for Nicaragua. Both shrank from backing such limited objectives with U.S. national power. Instead, their reliance on proxies to achieve more ambitious goals for an otherwise passive America proved in the end to be self-defeating. In Nicaragua, moreover, the Congress failed to back military leverage with the needed economic development aid programs for the region, as recommended by the Kissinger Commission, with the result that the American capacity to use either positive or negative leverage became severely restricted.

It therefore appears altogether likely that in the years ahead political instability, and more assertively anti-U.S. nationalism, will surface more prominently also in other Central American countries. In Panama, instability will pose an immediate threat to a vital security installation. Moreover, just north of Central America and immediately south of the continental United States, Mexico has the makings of a political as well as economic crisis that could impinge most directly on America. Already Mexico's serious financial and demographic problems are increasingly becoming America's nightmares.

Inherent in this mushrooming crisis is an even larger danger: a direct, immediate impact on American society that could prompt a mood of panic and even isolationism. This is why the issue deserves a high priority, and this is also why the most recent conflict on the matter between the president and Congress was so destructive. The disturbing fact was that both sides adopted escapist stances, each avoiding a confrontation with bitter realities. The first chose indirect and evasive means to achieve a forced solution to a problem that went deeper than the presence of Soviet-backed communism. The second preferred to rely on wishful thinking regarding a solution to the real problem posed by the undeniable presence of a Soviet-communist regional challenge. The present political stalemate in Washington does not augur well for the emergence of the needed comprehensive regional strategy, one that combines attainable and legitimate goals with a determination to act effectively on both the geopolitical and the economic levels.

AMERICA'S GLOBAL POSITION

America's capacity to cope on both the strategic and the geopolitical planes will depend ultimately on America's overall global position. The undeniable relative decline in American economic primacy, especially given the American-sponsored recovery of Western Europe and Japan, has already led some to suggest that the United States resembles Great Britain in the early twentieth century. Even more ominously, it is postulated that America is doomed to replicate the experience of other imperial powers, and that the painful process of degeneration is already under way.

It would be historical blindness to disregard warning signs based on past experience. Moreover, there is, alas, some justification for historical pessimism. It is, for example, disturbing to recall that in the initial phase of their decline the Roman, French, and Ottoman empires were characterized by economic inflation and budgetary deficits, by a preoccupation with gold, by costly external (over)expansion, by domestic fatigue and political gridlock, by cultural hedonism and conspicuous materialistic self-gratification, and even by monumental architectural self-glorification. (The manner in which corporate and governmental America splurges on ostentatious monumentalism is strikingly reminiscent of the pompous architectural explosions in Paris, London and Vienna in their late imperial phases.)

But the differences between those circumstances and America's position today are equally important and are perhaps more suggestive of future trends. In almost all cases of imperial decline, economic attrition through war—leading to truly significnt demographic depletion and eventually even to the collapse of the political elite—was the major precipitating cause. This has not been the case with the United States. Even the recent massive expansion of defense spending did not raise its level above seven percent of the GNP. Though prompting for a while extensive social demoralization, the war in Vietnam did not cause massive casualties. In fact, the last several decades have seen a remarkable infusion of new and creative blood into the American social and political leadership previously dominated by the more traditional elite, notably first from the Jewish community and more lately through the remarkable attainments of first-generation Asian Americans. The dynamics of social renewal are still at work in America, with their impulses for creativity, innovation and sheer drive.

Even more important are two major external differences. The relative decline in American global economic preeminence occurred not in spite of America but because of America. It was the consequence of a deliberate and sustained American policy, pursued with strategic constancy over several decades. It was the American goal to further the recovery of Western Europe and Japan, and the current situation is the consequence of the successful attainment of that central goal.

To be sure, it can be argued that the above does not alter the fact of America's relative decline, and that it is the fact of decline that counts and not its origins or motivations. This is undeniably true. But it ignores an important aspect. The change in America's global economic position is neither the consequence of an antagonistic competition nor the result of a hostile rival for global primacy gradually attaining success in displacing America. Instead, it is the outcome of a cooperative policy initiated and sustained by the United States itself. That creates a rather different web of global relations.

Moreover, it leads directly to the other major and perhaps even more important difference. In the past the displacement of a dominant power usually led to the emergence of a replacement power, which then assumed the attributes of wide leadership. A decline and fall of one was part of a cycle involving also a rise and a peak by another. This time the United States does not have a rival that could be a successor. Western Europe simply will not become in the near future a united center of political power capable of filling America's global shoes. Japan's aspirations for military-political power are also modest. Thus, neither of the two principal economic beneficiaries of the progressive redistribution of global economic power are America's political rivals for global primacy.

Neither is the Soviet Union—as this analysis has shown, it is a one-dimensional rival. It is a credible challenger in the military realm alone. But the price paid for that awesome military might is that as a result the Soviet Union is not competitive politically, ideologically, economically or socially. In fact, it is becoming even less of a rival in these domains, and that is the principal reason for the currently desperate efforts of the Soviet leadership at a perestroika.

Since it is unlikely that the Kremlin can greatly diminish its military exertions, it is quite probable that over the next two or three decades the Soviet Union will fade even further. As a result the global economic hierarchy by the year 2010 might be the following: first, the United States (with a GNP just under $8 trillion); second, the European Economic Community (with a similar or perhaps even larger GNP but lacking the attributes of a single political power); third, China (with a GNP of just under $4 trillion); fourth, Japan (with roughly the same GNP); and then only fifth in rank, the Soviet Union (with a GNP of just under $3 trillion).

The Soviet Union thus cannot replace the United States. The most it can do is displace it through the use of its military power, prompting a decisive geopolitical upheaval. But Moscow is simply incapable of becoming the world's financial center or the source of global economic manipulation. This has important implications. Given the fact that the international system cannot operate on the basis of goodwill and sheer spontaneity alone but needs some center of cooperative initiative, financial control and even political power, it follows that the only alternative to American leadership is global anarchy and international chaos. This would have the most destructive political and cultural consequences for those countries that are doing reasonably well in their socioeconomic development.

These considerations, in turn, underline the salience of the point made earlier: the relative decline in America's global primacy is in part the result of America's own policies and was effected cooperatively. This reality enhances the stake that other successful states will continue to have in an America that is able to exercise a constructive and cooperative global role. In effect, the fact that the only alternative to America is anarchy generates the vested interest that both Western Europe and Japan will continue to have in the preservation of some kind of a central American role.

Admittedly, that also implies major adjustments in both the style and substance of that role, as well as some significant efforts at revitalizing the American capacity to act. It is evident that in the years to come the United States will have to exercise its special world responsibilities by increasingly subtle, cooperative and even indirect means. The effective exercise of that role will depend on the cooperative stake of others in a reasonably controlled international environment. The analogy that readily comes to mind is not that of states intimidated by a global policeman but rather that of airliners cooperating with their air traffic controller.

That change has already been occurring, with the United States today sharing to a very considerable extent with West Germany and Japan the responsibility for international financial policy. The annual economic summit, despite its meager output in recent years, provides a further example of essentially indirect policy direction. In the miltiary realm the required strategic changes will also enhance the role of the key European countries in NATO decision-making, with the American role becoming relatively less decisive. Consensual leadership, although still based on a central American role, is thus already becoming a fact.

The positive management of the East-West relationship is also likely to become a more collective affair. It is most improbable that a grand American-Soviet accommodation can take place. The interests of the two sides are simply too conflicting. The notion of a global U.S.-Soviet partnership for peace and development is even more illusory. More probable are partial accords on issues where the two sides do have reciprocal interests, in a setting of both continued geostrategic competition and some cooperation. In contrast our European friends, notably Germany, are likely to move further than the United States in exploring various forms of political and economic collaboration with Moscow.

Nonetheless, it is likely that in the foreseeable future, the Soviet sphere will be preoccupied with a protracted systemic crisis, including major economic upheavals and perhaps even political unrest. Thus, the Soviet Union will remain internally too weak to become a partner for peace and externally too strong to be satisfied with the status quo. Under these conditions the East-West relationship will continue to represent the negative aspect of the global agenda—i.e., how to avoid growing tensions or conflicts—rather than its more positive, cooperative side.

The emergence in the meantime of a greater degree of pluralism in the West's decision-making is all to the good. It is also in keeping with long-standing American aspirations. But such consensual leadership still requires a vital, dynamic and powerful America. All concerned are aware that consensual leadership can otherwise easily degenerate into a gridlock. Thus even America's economic rivals have a fundamentally positive interest in America's economic health.

U.S.-JAPANESE RELATIONS

This is particularly true in the American-Japanese relationship. A greatly revitalized America can be nurtured by policies that exploit the special complementarity of American and Japanese interests, while also providing Japan with the safest route to continued growth. It is really quite striking how much the two countries' needs and interests match. The strengths of one compensate for the weaknesses of the other. Each needs the other; indeed, each is likely to falter without the other. Working together ever more closely, they can assure for themselves unrivaled global economic, financial and technological leadership, while reinforcing the protective umbrella of American global military power.

America needs Japanese capital to finance its industrial renovation and technological innovation; it needs Japanese cooperation in protecting its still significant global lead in creative R&D and in opening up new scientific frontiers for both peaceful and military uses; it needs Japanese participation in securing through enhanced economic development such geopolitically threatened yet vital areas as the Philippines, Pakistan, Egypt, Central America and Mexico. Japan needs American security protection for its homeland; it needs open access to the American market for its continued economic well-being and, through cooperation with America, secure access to a stable and expanding world market; it needs to maintain and even expand its collaborative participation in the vast American corporate and academic research facilities that are so central to Japan's continued innovation.

With Japanese investment in America growing, the Japanese stake in a healthy America will continue to grow. Japan for many years to come will be heavily dependent on American security protection, obtained by an American willingness to spend on defense a share of its GNP more than three times larger than Japan's; hence the Japanese stake in a globally engaged America will remain great. With America heavily indebted, the American stake in a productive and prosperous Japanese partner will also grow—but so will resentments over the trade imbalance and probably also over the increasing Japanese buyouts of American corporations and properties. Conflict between the two thus could grow even as the need for a joint partnership becomes more obvious.

While it is impossible to quantify the importance of the relationship to either of the two sides, over the last several years the American economic situation, given both the trade and the budget deficits, might have become untenable without the inflow from Japan of well over $100 billion. Even that rough figure does not account for the various other tangible and intangible benefits to America of the good political relationship that it has with the new economic giant across the Pacific. It is simply central to America's global geostrategic position.

For Japan, these incalculable considerations are even more important; indeed, they are quite literally a matter of life or death. Japan would simply not be—nor would it remain—what it is without the American connection. At the same time, on the narrow level of military expenditures, it can be roughly estimated that without American protection Japan would probably have to spend on its defense some additional $50 billion a year in order to feel truly secure (while at the same time alienating and frightening by such expenditures many of its neighbors).

It is important to restate these verities, for there is the possibility that in the foreseeable future domestic political pressures, especially in America, could damage the relationship—at the very stage when it is ripe for further development. Only through the deliberate fostering of a more cooperative, politically more intimate, economically more organic partnership—in effect, through the gradual and informal emergence on the world scene of a de facto new player—can these two major countries not only avoid a debilitating collision but also ensure that America continues to play the role the world system requires. In brief, the upgrading of the U.S.-Japanese relationship from a transpacific alliance into a global partnership is needed not only for the sake of the two countries concerned but also for the sake of the stability and prosperity of the international order as a whole.

Seeking a more organic partnership of global consequence will require overcoming the obvious cultural and institutional obstacles on both sides, penetrating the tight insularity of the Japanese society and rising above the inherent shortsightedness of the American political process. It will call for a series of sustained, minor steps toward an ever closer relationship, as well as perhaps one or two major acts designed to lurch the process more significantly forward.

In the first category one might include the deliberate nurturing of a cross-participation of Japanese and Americans on respective boards of directors of major enterprises, mergers by major business institutions or banks, much expanded exchanges of scientific talent, joint investment schemes and widened collaboration in high technology innovation. Some of that is happening already, but much more could be done, especially as the linguistic barriers fade with the greater familiarity with English on the part of the emerging Japanese elites and also with the forthcoming availability of computerized pocket translating devices.

Perhaps even more significant in fostering the needed global partnership—which one can perhaps call "Amerippon"—would be some major, farsighted acts of statesmanship that in themselves would be beneficial to the international community while advancing the special interests of the partnership itself. While such efforts would require a very major initiative and a great act of political will, they are feasible.

One effort could entail a joint, comprehensive strategy for the development of either the Latin American economy as a whole, or for at least its Central American and Mexican portions. Japanese leaders have at times spoken of a possible Japanese initiative on this front. A joint American-Japanese undertaking not only would give the effort greater dimension, but would also significantly upgrade the level of ongoing American-Japanese cooperation. In any case, the need for a major international effort in the region is well established, and the benefits, strategic and economic, to "Amerippon" of a major joint regional initiative—in an area of great potential importance to both—are also self-evident.

An even more ambitious goal might involve jointly setting a target date for an American-Japanese free trade zone. This would involve a commitment by both sides to a relationship that moves deliberately in the opposite direction from protectionism. In today's climate it may appear utopian even to invoke this notion, yet the more farsighted thinkers on both sides recognize that movement in such a direction would greatly enhance the prospects of global multilateral cooperation while directly benefiting the two economies involved. This is why such a seemingly farfetched notion was quietly whispered about during the Japanese prime minister's visit to Washington in early 1988. It would be the logical outcome of a process that deliberately exploits the objective complementarity of the respective interests and needs of the two sides. The result would be not only the creation of the world's paramount economic unit but also inevitably enhanced global political consultations and joint strategizing.

In the years to come no alternative to a leading American world role is likely to develop, and America's partners will continue to want the United States to play that role. But in addition, there will be creative opportunities for a renewed and revitalized American contribution to a more cooperative world system. That makes our historical context rather different from the experience of other major powers whose historical trajectories entered irreversible declines.

To seize these opportunities America will have to be guided by a geostrategic vision that accepts the need for more consensual leadership that purposely shapes a new global partnership with Japan while also coping in the meantime on its own with new geopolitical and security challenges. All of this will call for major adjustments in the American global geostrategy, on a scale perhaps as great as took place in the late 1940s. That is the likely challenge facing America during the last decade of the second millennium. It is also a challenge that can be met.

PART TWO

■

The Making of
National Security Policy

Neither the Constitution nor relevant legislation, such as the National Security Act of 1947, creates an actual framework for the development and management of foreign policy. Thus, every U.S. president invents his own process for making national security policy. This is a vitally important issue because how policy is made determines what policy is made.

Both in academia and in public life, Dr. Brzezinski has been acutely aware of the centrality of the policymaking process. As national security adviser to President Carter, he was responsible for coordinating the development of policy options and the implementation of presidential decisions by the foreign policy bureaucracies. In his memoirs, Dr. Brzezinski assessed the significance of that responsibility in three words: "Coordination is predominance."

In Part Two, Dr. Brzezinski examines three dimensions of national security policymaking. The first is the organization of the policymaking process within a U.S. administration. The second is the conflictual relationship between the Executive and the Legislative within the U.S. constitutional framework. The third is the more abstract dimension of the level of historical awareness within the U.S. public consciousness and the degree of familiarity with history on the part of U.S. presidents. Only by addressing all three dimensions, he concludes, can the United States develop the capability to formulate a coherent and effective foreign policy.

CHAPTER FIVE

■

The NSC and the President

WITH THE 1988 PRESIDENTIAL CAMPAIGN about to unfold in full force, all of the serious candidates for the White House will be asked at some point how they intend, if elected, to manage the conduct of U.S. foreign policy and, in particular, what the role of the National Security Council (NSC) is and how a president should use it. Sensible answers to these questions have become even more urgent in light of the sensational disclosures of misdeeds allegedly committed by senior staff members of the NSC in the Iran-contra scandal. This most recent controversy coincides with the NSC's 40th anniversary. Thus the NSC's Iran-contra role in effect can be seen as the NSC's midlife crisis, with 40 years providing a long enough time both to assess the past and offer some suggestions for the future.

The NSC was set up 2 years after the end of World War II. This was not an accident. By 1947 it was evident that America's engagement in the postwar world would be manifold. American decision makers were conscious that the direction of the war effort in World War II had been improvised and involved a number of ad hoc arrangements for decision making. Key military and political decisions often had been made on the basis of personal arrangements informally structured and responsive to specific circumstances.

The National Security Act of July 26, 1947, provided more formal machinery to deal with America's new involvement in global realities over a longer term. The words "national security" were relatively new in the bureaucratic lexicon and involved a recognition that diplomacy, defense, and intelligence were parts of a larger whole. Each reflected a

This article originally appeared as "NSC's Midlife Crisis." Reprinted with permission from *Foreign Policy* 69 (winter 1987–88). Copyright 1987 by the Carnegie Endowment for International Peace.

separate aspect of America's relationship with the world that henceforth would be integrated into a broader framework subsumed under the overarching term. The NSC's creation also reflected an awareness that only under the president's personal leadership could a broader perspective on global affairs be defined and coordinated as national policy. The locus of decision making had to be inside the White House because the president is the overall operating head of government as well as the head of state.

To formulate policy designed to enhance national security, the act called on the president to draw on the collective advice of the NSC, composed—according to the amended 1947 statute—of himself, the vice president, the secretary of state, and the secretary of defense. Other officials might participate at his invitation, notably the director of central intelligence and the principal military chiefs. The president also appointed a small professional staff with a designated head to prepare the council's work. Soon the term "NSC" came to mean simultaneously—and often confusingly—both the deliberative body, which met occasionally at the president's behest, and the staff of the NSC, which came to be located permanently in the White House.

From the beginning, the NSC's relationship to the president and its dependence on his personal working style determined its evolution. Broadly speaking, two predominant patterns of presidential leadership in the area of national security affairs have emerged. Some presidents have involved themselves directly and intimately in defining national strategy. In addition, these presidents tended to insist that they be involved in the day-to-day implementation of national policy. This can be called the presidential system of formulating national security policy.

Other presidents have reserved for themselves control of the commanding heights of decision making but have deliberately abstained from the day-to-day supervision of policy. These presidents have permitted a dominant secretary of state to assume the preeminent role in the overall strategic direction of foreign policy on the president's behalf. In contrast to the first approach, this one involves a predominantly secretarial system of policymaking.

No conclusions can be drawn about which approach leads to a more effective foreign policy. Each approach has delivered successes and failures; therefore, in and of themselves, the presidential and secretarial systems seem to have little direct bearing on the actual foreign-policy record of any president.

Although not every president has fitted neatly into one or the other model, broadly speaking, John Kennedy, Richard Nixon, and Jimmy Carter embraced the presidential system. They did not permit any member of their cabinets, including the secretary of state or secretary of defense, to play the central role in shaping and managing U.S. foreign policy.

Presidents Harry Truman, Dwight Eisenhower, Lyndon Johnson, and Gerald Ford adhered more closely to the second model. In their administrations the secretary of state tended to be the preeminent player in influencing foreign-policy decisions. The relationship that prevailed between Truman and Dean Acheson, between Eisenhower and John Foster Dulles, between Johnson and Dean Rusk, and especially between Ford and Henry Kissinger made the secretary of state the acknowledged principal foreign-policy adviser to the president.

The presidential decision-making system inevitably elevated the head of the NSC staff into an increasingly important policy player. He became the bureaucratic beneficiary of direct presidential involvement in foreign affairs. That active involvement, particularly if coupled with a personal closeness between the president and his assistant for national security affairs, enabled several such assistants to attain an overall preeminence in guiding U.S. national security policy, notably during the 1970s.

Given the assistant's physical and personal closeness to the president, and given a president's demonstrated interest in foreign affairs, neither the secretary of state nor the secretary of defense is predisposed to challenge directives received from the assistant and issued—actually or allegedly—on the president's behalf. Indeed, on occasion the assistant can feel confident enough to dispatch directives in the president's name even without his explicit authorization because the assistant knows he can count on presidential backing in the event such directives are challenged. In contrast, the assistant to a somewhat passive or disengaged president will find his directives likely to be contested. The bureaucracy also is less likely to be responsive to instructions and requests from the NSC staff in such an administration. In brief, the less actively engaged the president, the less bureaucratic strength accrues to his assistant for national security affairs.

THREE PHASES OF THE NSC

Over time the NSC as an institution has passed through three broad phases, each generating its own distortions. The first phase, which lasted from 1947 until roughly 1960, involved the institutionalization of the NSC process. This process started under Truman, especially after the outbreak of the Korean War in 1950. Until then, Truman had largely ignored the NSC, assuming the chair during the years 1947–1950 in only 12 out of the mere 57 scheduled sessions. In fact, Truman let it be known that he viewed the NSC as an instrument foisted on the president by Congress—abetted by the ambitious Defense Secretary James Forrestal—as a means of limiting discretionary presidential authority.

Once the war started, Truman personally presided at 62 of the 71 formal NSC sessions held between 1950 and 1952. Far from limiting the president's power, the NSC became the body within which presidential policy—combining the president's constitutional responsibility for the conduct of foreign affairs with his discretionary authority as commander in chief—was devised through consultations with a small group of advisers. In addition to the NSC's members, the CIA director, the chairman of the Joint Chiefs of Staff, and, as needed, the secretary of the treasury, some domestic advisers, and other officials began to attend NSC sessions. The NSC thus became the critical decision-making organ.

The process of institutionalization went the furthest in the Eisenhower administration. Meetings were formally and regularly scheduled and procedures well organized. The NSC met every Thursday at 9:00 A.M. To head the NSC staff Eisenhower designated a key civil servant with the title of special assistant for national security affairs. This position is lower than that of assistant to the president in the White House hierarchy. Eisenhower faithfully chaired the meetings himself, presiding over 329 of the 366 NSC sessions held during his tenure.

Eisenhower came to the White House determined to rationalize the decision-making process. In his memoirs, *The White House Years: Mandate for Change* (1963), he recalled: "For years I had been in frequent contact in the executive office of the White House, and I had certain ideas about the system, or lack of system under which it operated. With my training in problems involving organization it was inconceivable to me that the work of the White House could not be better systematized than had been the case in the years I observed it." He added elsewhere in his memoirs that "organization helps the responsible individual make the necessary decision, and helps assure that it is satisfactorily carried out."

In keeping with this predisposition, Eisenhower used the NSC not only for making decisions but also for planning policy. For example, shortly after assuming office, he ordered a highly secret review of U.S. policy toward the Soviet Union named the SOLARIUM exercise. Three teams developed alternative strategic concepts. The first essentially would serve as a reinforcement of the ongoing containment doctrine. The second required that the containment doctrine be globalized, drawing more sharply and comprehensively the dividing line between U.S. and Soviet areas of influence. The third team was given a mandate to develop a policy designed to roll back Soviet influence from the spheres that it occupied by 1952. Senior government officials staffed all three teams and reported in summer 1953. The president then personally chaired a series of NSC meetings, reviewing their proposals in detail and trying to translate them into a comprehensive national security strategy. Through a full discussion of several drafts there emerged in October 1953 a document called "NSC 162/2," which provided the doctrinal framework for Eisenhower's policies.

From the first team "NSC 162/2" borrowed the concept of massive retaliation. From the second team, it adopted the notion of additional regional alliances, building on the experience of NATO; this recommendation prompted the creation of the Southeast Asia Treaty Organization and the Central Treaty Organization. The third team tried to amplify the doctrine of liberation, which to some extent already had been previewed in the course of the 1952 presidential campaign.

Eisenhower emphasized that the NSC must be capable of both planning and implementing policy. To achieve the former he created within the NSC staff a body called the Planning Board. It met more often than the NSC itself, preparing policy papers for the formal sessions and refining options for decisions. To supervise policy implementation, a parallel body, the interagency Operations Coordinating Board, also was created. In addition to weekly supervisory meetings, it was charged with preparing a comprehensive report to the NSC every 6 months. Eisenhower recognized that a great deal of policy execution was skewed by the bureaucracy, and he was determined to assert NSC control of the bureaucracy's performance. Both organs operated with formal agendas and generated a large paper trail.

Institutionalization reached its peak under Eisenhower, and in time the NSC process lost its cutting edge. At first it was innovative and truly impressive by systematically defining both goals and strategy. It also provided a regular forum for a formal review of policy options. But to use the words of Johnson's NSC staff chief, Walt Rostow, it increasingly became a paper mill, a process churning out an enormous number of memorandums and reports but putting less stress on policy innovation. Eisenhower apparently realized this, because for innovation in policy he began to reach outside the system for ideas from people he personally trusted. Individuals like C. D. Jackson and Nelson Rockefeller compensated for the bureaucratic stultification.

The second phase in the NSC's evolution lasted from 1960 to 1980. This phase was characterized by a higher degree of personalization, which in time also became excessive. Kennedy's associates disliked the degree of NSC bureaucratization. They were determined that the system should become more flexible and in some ways more personal. The NSC process therefore was deinstitutionalized: The Operations Coordinating Board and the Planning Board were abolished peremptorily, the staff was cut dramatically, and a public figure was appointed to the post of special assistant for national security affairs.

The choice of McGeorge Bundy was symbolic of the change. A well-known Harvard University dean with personal experience in public policy, he was an individual not known to be either personally or intellectually reticent. Kennedy specifically instructed Bundy to play a public "educational" role and to enlighten the press about the president's policy. The special assistant for national security affairs thus came out of the cold. Now he was both seen and heard.

Bundy participated actively in the policy process itself, as he was specifically instructed to give his own policy views to the president. He no longer was to be merely the overseer of a process in which decisions were funneled for presidential resolution but himself became a participant in debate over policy. While the secretary of state remained preeminent on the outside of the U.S. government, on the inside the special assistant was becoming a major player.

Under Kennedy two significant developments took place. First, the NSC machinery was partially dismantled as procedures became more casual. The NSC did not meet regularly under the president's chairmanship, and the NSC process generally faded in importance. Key decisions usually were made on an ad hoc basis, and some bureaucratic confusion was the unavoidable result. Worse, the deinstitutionalized system tended to favor reactive policymaking, to the detriment of strategic planning. Under Kennedy and later under Johnson, the lack of a formal process to anticipate major issues allowed decisions to slip until an adviser recognized that a situation merited presidential attention. This informal decision-making procedure inherently tended to diminish strategic coherence.

Second, the special assistant for national security affairs gained personal prominence and became an acknowledged policymaker. Both Bundy and the equally prominent and visible Rostow decisively influenced national policy on issues ranging from aborting the scheme for a NATO multilateral nuclear force that was favored by the Department of State to the actual conduct of the Vietnam War. Both men were perceived as being closer to the president than was the secretary of state.

A further major step toward personalization—perhaps the critical step—occurred in the Nixon administration. The head of the NSC staff acquired the title of assistant for national security affairs, which meant that Kissinger became a member of Nixon's top staff, one of his most senior aides in terms of White House hierarchy. But the change went much further, even though no one at the time fully realized the symbolic significance of a statement made at Nixon's first White House press conference on January 27, 1969. The newly inaugurated president, speaking about the Vietnam War, said: "This is all going to take time, but I can assure you that it will have my personal attention. It will have my personal direction. The Secretary of State, my Adviser for National Security Affairs, the Secretary of Defense, all of us will give it every possible attention and we hope to come up with some new approaches."

That statement inaugurated a new phase in the relationship between the president and his NSC staff chief. The secretary of state, the adviser for national security affairs, and the secretary of defense all were listed together, in that order, as the president's principal foreign-policy counselors. The NSC's principal staff officer was listed as a coequal policymaker with the president's two leading cabinet members. Also, the assistant for national security affairs emerged suddenly as the president's "adviser" on national security affairs.

This designation was new and apparently had no precedent. According to the Lyndon Baines Johnson Library, the term "national security adviser" was apparently not used during the Johnson administration, and the president never employed the term in public. A check of the newspaper files confirms that it was not used in connection with either Bundy or his successor, Rostow. Nixon himself has said that his choice of the term was not deliberate, which implies that the term was being used informally by the incoming Nixon team. In the official transcript of the president's press conference the title was capitalized. Thus it was given quasi-official status.

Henceforth the national security adviser was no longer merely a policy coordinator who presented to the president policy options favored by department heads. He also advised the president of the policy choices. He had become the president's closest and only personal ("my") adviser in policy deliberations. A possibly unintended symbolic change had become substantive.

The symbiotic relationship between Nixon as the chief strategist and Kissinger as his skilled tactician reinforced this new reality. It gained public visibility with their spectacular opening to the People's Republic of China. But it drew strength from the renewed institutional power within the NSC staff. The staff was revitalized, enlarged to parallel and supervise the key geographic bureaus of the State Department, and organized into a large number of specialized committees, chaired at the subcabinet level by the president's assistant for national security affairs. Nixon's own immersion in big decisions and his strong suspicions of the State Department's bureaucratic impulses helped elevate the national security adviser above the secretary of state, William Rogers, and make the NSC staff the center of strategic initiative.

Carter openly stated that foreign policy would be made by him and not by his secretary of state. In part this was in reaction to Kissinger's perceived domination as secretary of state over Ford's decision-making process. But in large measure it reflected Carter's genuine determination personally to dominate decision making. Accordingly, Carter took the unprecedented step on his inauguration day of issuing a directive concentrating the policy process, especially for arms control and crisis management, within the White House. In these critical areas the national security adviser—my position during Carter's term in office—would chair cabinet-level committee meetings. Moreover, in a step of greater symbolic and protocol significance inside the White House than elsewhere, he for the first time gave the national security adviser—the term continued to be used—cabinet status.

Carter also charged the national security adviser with the responsibility for developing 4-year strategic goals for the new administration. The president discussed the resulting document, which outlined his foreign-policy goals, with his key secretaries. But the NSC staff had thereby acquired the responsibility for policy innovation and began to play the role that Nixon himself had fulfilled.

At the same time, the president made it known that he did not want his national security adviser to take the highly visible role played by Kissinger. He publicly and repeatedly emphasized the secretary of state's role as the president's principal spokesman and adviser. He wanted the secretary of state to be the lead player.

But he soon became disillusioned. In his memoirs, *Keeping Faith* (1982), Carter speaks of the relative absence in the State Department of "innovative ideas" and of "the inertia of the Department." He also conveys disappointment over the fact that, in regard to "the education of the American public about foreign policy," the secretary of state "was not particularly inclined to assume this task on a sustained basis."

The consequence was paradoxical. The national security adviser, as a cabinet member, was fully expected to participate in policy deliberations, and, as the president's assistant, physically worked more closely with the president than did the secretary of state. But in the politicized Washington setting and by much of the national media, he came to be viewed as a usurper of Secretary of State Cyrus Vance's legitimate prerogatives. This perception served to focus public attention on real or exaggerated policy conflicts between the secretary of state and the national security adviser. The secretary of state was seen as the victim of the sudden expansion in the national security adviser's role.

That problem intensified when Carter indicated that he wanted his assistant for national security affairs to make the case for the administration's foreign policy before the media. Even though the exercise of that role came in response to the president's specific instructions—"almost without exception . . . with my approval and in consonance with my established and known policy," as Carter recounted in his memoirs—each initiative the national security adviser took appeared to the public as yet another manifestation of a continuing but improper campaign of attrition against the secretary of state's position and as evidence of the national security adviser's bureaucratic self-aggrandizement. As in the Nixon administration, personalization became excessive and counterproductive politically.

The most recent phase in the NSC's evolution has involved its degradation. Even if initially justified in order to depersonalize somewhat the prominence that the NSC had acquired during the 1970s, President Ronald Reagan pushed the process much too far. The result was that the national security adviser was now neither seen nor heard. Worse, before too long, his presence inside the administration was not much felt.

Reagan's first national security adviser, Richard Allen, was banished to the basement of the White House, with the president's domestic counselor bureaucratically interposed between him and the president. After the administration's first 6 months, even the daily briefings were supplemented in part by written briefings, thereby further reducing the national security adviser's direct access to the Oval Office. The second adviser, William Clark, was a close friend of the president and therefore able to exercise personal influence. But he was not well versed in foreign affairs. He therefore could not translate his access into significant strategic influence. The third and fourth national security advisers, Robert McFarlane and John Poindexter, were professional military men not in a position to assert themselves in open disputes with respect to either the secretary of state or the secretary of defense.

Matters were aggravated by the president's disinclination to impose a clear-cut decision-making system. After rejecting Secretary of State Alexander Haig, Jr.'s blueprint for a system of secretarial predominance, Reagan took a full year before approving a new formal structure for the NSC process. In January 1982 he finally issued a document outlining a new and rather complex NSC structure, which already was viewed by much of the bureaucracy as defanged. Under the new directive, the national security adviser no longer chaired interdepartmental groups, and there was no provision for exhaustive cabinet-level discussion of issues before they reached the president and the NSC.

The president himself adopted a novel style of exercising leadership. His stewardship fit neither the presidential nor the secretarial system. After determining broad strategic directions he did not wish to be actively involved in the day-to-day tactical management of foreign policy. In the field of foreign policy, he became largely a ceremonial president. He emphasized articulation of the national mood, verbalizing a broad sense of direction and performing masterfully the needed protocol functions, but he failed to concentrate authority in a few clearly designated hands.

At the same time, clearly to the surprise of his first secretary of state, he was not inclined to entertain assertive secretarial leadership. Haig apparently had assumed that his relationship with Reagan would be on the model of Truman and Acheson or Eisenhower and Dulles, not to mention Ford and Kissinger. But instead of becoming the vicar of U.S. foreign policy, Haig was himself decapitated—not by the president but by the White House staff.

As the NSC ceased to be either a policymaking or a truly policy-coordinating organ, the president by default emphasized a cabinet system of decision making. Cabinet secretaries gained far greater independence in formulating their own policies than had been the case under either Nixon or Carter. With little centralized discipline and in the absence of either a presidential or a secretarial system, not only was the NSC degraded but also policy was fragmented to an unprecedented degree.

Paradoxically, as the prestige of the NSC declined its size increased and its titles were inflated. Under Nixon the senior staff numbered approximately 50; during Carter's term it shrank to 35 and then crawled back to about 40; under Reagan, it grew to about 70. Under Carter the NSC staff had 1 deputy assistant for national security affairs, 1 coordinator for strategic planning, and 35 associated senior staff members. By and large the same was true under Nixon. In both cases the NSC staff generally was perceived as an elite group, working authoritatively on the president's behalf and not requiring other status symbols or special titles.

By 1986 the NSC table of organization included an assistant to the president for national security affairs, a deputy assistant to the president for national security affairs, 1 assistant to the president who doubled as his special counselor, 3 additional deputy assistants, 10 special assistants to the president for national security affairs, 14 senior directors for national security affairs, 40 directors of national security affairs, and 9 deputy directors. In effect, the Reagan White House had inverted the pyramid.

Loss of influence at the top spurred organizational dispersal at the bottom, or operational, level. A wholly new institution within the NSC, the Crisis Management Center (CMC), developed a staff separate from that of the NSC. Backed by an ample and readily available data base, the CMC was to provide policymakers with good institutional memory for any crisis. Also, after considerable internal bureaucratic squabbling, Vice President George Bush was designated the Reagan administration's crisis manager. This arrangement placed an individual unlikely to have a personal connection with policy matters pertinent to a future crisis in charge of handling such a crisis once it surfaced. Thus another source of bureaucratic confusion within the NSC had been created.

By the time Frank Carlucci took charge in January 1987 of an NSC shaken by the Iran-contra revelations, the table of organization for NSC policy coordination had become a veritable nightmare. There had been 7 NSC committees under Nixon. Under Carter 2 committees had doubled in different functions: The Special Coordination Committee, chaired by the national security adviser, handled arms control, crisis management, and sensitive intelligence; the Policy Review Committee most often was chaired by the secretary of state. But under Reagan the number of NSC committees had proliferated to 25, 5 of which dealt with U.S.-Soviet affairs. In addition, 55 midlevel committees operated, and the NSC also took part in some 100 task forces and working groups on a variety of issues. The result was a loss of control and increasing absorption in bureaucratic minutiae, at the cost of providing strategic direction and imposing policy coordination.

A side aspect of this deformation was the end of the procedure for sustaining staff control from the top down that the Carter NSC had instituted in 1977. All staff members then were obligated to write detailed but concise reports of 1 to 2 pages summarizing their activities for each day. Staff members were expected to itemize all interagency contacts, any contacts with foreign diplomats or the press, and any other information that in their view the national security adviser should know. The reports were submitted to me at the close of business. That same evening I would read the book of 50–60 pages, and the next morning each staff member would receive my personal reactions. This procedure helped preclude unauthorized activity and maintain continuous and disciplined interaction between me and my staff.

THE PRESIDENT AND THE NSC

In the 1950s the NSC was excessively institutionalized. In the 1970s it was excessively personalized. In the 1980s it has been excessively degraded. There is no single remedy for these distortions. Answers are likely to differ from president to president, depending in large measure on his personal style and his preferred system of command. Nonetheless, every president needs a stronger NSC process than the one developed by the Reagan administration during its first 6 years. Most presidents may prefer a somewhat less dominant national security adviser than was the case in the 1970s; and almost all presidents will benefit from more orderly procedures than those of the last 25 years.

The February 1987 Tower commission report of the President's Special Review Board correctly concluded that the NSC's failures in recent years stemmed not from the failure of the NSC system but from the failure to use the system properly. Therefore, legislated remedies in general would unnecessarily intrude into the business of the chief executive. Rather, the need is for greater clarity about the proper relationship between the president and the NSC.

Some presidents may prefer to adopt the secretarial system, deliberately choosing a dominant and strategically minded secretary of state and designating him publicly his chief counselor. But even then the president would need some professional assistance in the White House. He would still want to use the NSC as a deliberative body within which conflicting interdepartmental interests and points of view were aired and resolved.

In all probability, however, most administrations will select the presidential system. First, a majority of presidents find an advantage in being clearly identified as the active shaper of U.S. foreign policy. It is noteworthy that the strong and successful secretaries of state have not complained about the NSC process. Second, authority in security matters inevitably gravitates toward the White House since it is only there that a supradepartmental perspective on foreign affairs may emerge. Last, the awesome dangers of the nuclear age not only enhance the special responsibility of the president but also give his assistant for national security affairs a very specific role in assisting the president in times of a lethal emergency.

From the experience of the three phases of NSC history—institutionalization, personalization, and degradation—some general lessons can be drawn:

1. It would take a major presidential effort, and the appointment of an unusually assertive secretary of state, preferably very close personally to the president, to reverse history's gravitational pull toward the White House. Even if a president opts for the secretarial system, he will need a national security adviser near him who is more than simply a paper-pushing bureaucrat. Over time the secretary of state or the secretary of defense in every recent administration has become a propagator of his own department's parochial perspective, even to the detriment of the broader presidential vision. Every president needs some arrangement that helps him develop policy and strategy, coordinate decisionmaking, supervise policy implementation, provide him with personal advice that keeps his own presidential perspective and interests in mind, and articulate the policies that he is pursuing. These needs cannot be satisfied through reliance on a traditional department. The fact is that if the NSC staff did not exist, it would have to be invented. To lead effectively, the assistant to the president must have some personal substance and particularly must have the capacity to perform as a strategic policy integrator, even if he is not granted a public role that threatens to upstage the secretary of state.

2. Senatorial confirmation of the national security adviser would make sense only if the president, and perhaps Congress as well, were determined to elevate the national security adviser into the key player, designated by law to be the coordinating supervisor of the Departments of State and Defense and the CIA. It is sometimes argued that such an arrangement

would institutionalize conflict between the national security adviser and the secretary of state and that it would destroy the confidentiality of the relationship between the president and his national security adviser. But conflict between the national security adviser and the secretary of state depends largely on the degree to which the president tolerates it. Nor would personal conversations between the national security adviser and the president be compromised by the process of confirmation. The secretary of state, who is confirmed and therefore must testify before Congress, has not been prevented in recent years from becoming a close foreign-policy confidant of the president.

The most telling argument against confirmation is that the national security adviser would be compelled to spend an inordinate amount of time testifying before Congress. He would become accountable to both Congress and the president, thus diluting presidential leadership. The national security adviser in recent years has enjoyed a real operational advantage over the secretaries of state and defense because of his freedom from this time-consuming obligation. The worst outcome would be to have a congressionally confirmed national security adviser—who could then publicly testify on policy—while the president opted to elevate a strong secretary of state into the primary player. Bureaucratic confusion and conflict would be the inevitable result.

3. The presidential system works only if the president imposes it explicitly, making it clear that his national security adviser is a direct extension of the president's own deliberate involvement. The national security adviser can help the president effectively if his position is perceived to be the consequence of the president's will and not of the adviser's own ambition. Under exceptional circumstances the national security adviser also can serve effectively as the administration's public voice, but only if he is known to be speaking at the president's behest, only if the president lays out a clear policy direction, and only if the secretary of state does not contest the role either directly or indirectly by tolerating or encouraging policy dissent from his department. Under these circumstances, a professional senior diplomat would be the best choice for secretary of state.

4. Crisis management under either system must be concentrated in the White House. Few genuine crises are purely diplomatic. Most involve not only diplomacy but also defense and intelligence. If a presidential system is adopted, the national security adviser can direct the process of crisis management; in the secretarial system, the assistant might merely coordinate the process, with the president turning to the secretary for critical advice. But with the key decisions being made within the White House, with information flowing directly into the NSC's Situation Room, and with the assistant located on the spot, any arrangement for crisis

management that does not vest primary managerial responsibility with the assistant for national security affairs is very likely to be gravely flawed.

5. Strategic planning likewise should be located in the White House and is the proper responsibility of the NSC staff. Neither the State Department nor the Defense Department is capable of undertaking such a task on a comprehensive basis, for each carries its own special diplomatic or military perspectives. Some form of strategic planning can be built into the NSC mechanism, perhaps by having senior officials from State, Defense, the Joint Chiefs of Staff, and the CIA participate in developing long-range foreign-policy plans for each administration under the guidance of the national security adviser. Such a process in effect would combine what initially was undertaken by the Eisenhower administration with what the NSC staff did unilaterally in the first 3 months of the Carter administration. This might involve resuscitating, to some degree, Eisenhower's NSC Planning Board.

6. Policy strategy is closely linked to policy coordination. A strategically focused policy is one that coordinates the different branches of government and develops a broader approach—combining strategy and tactics—with regard to specific regional or functional objectives. Effective coordination also means integrating different viewpoints into a clear statement of options with their pros and cons, thereby facilitating the president's ultimate decision. Under either the presidential or the secretarial model, the coordinating function must be performed within the White House, including the development of the necessary paperwork, the staffing, and the agenda for formal presidential-level deliberations.

7. In recent years the NSC's implementing function has been slighted. Probably not since the time of Eisenhower has any systematic reassessment been made of how to supervise the execution of policy. It appears that even the most assertive NSC heads have failed to give enough attention to policy implementation. Kissinger, while he served as Nixon's national security adviser, frequently complained that the State Department was skewing policy through evasive implementation. And I openly admitted that I was unable to assert effective control over the Defense Department's programming. So it seems desirable to recreate within the NSC staff some organ like the Eisenhower-era Operations Coordinating Board to monitor policy implementation and to report back to the NSC. Without such a mechanism, decisions are likely to be contorted by sloppy, uncoordinated, or willfully negative bureaucratic actions.

8. Enumerating the functions properly located within the White House leads to some preliminary conclusions with regard to the proper NSC staff size. There is no magic number, but it would appear that for successful strategic planning and policy coordination 30–40 senior staff members are probably adequate. However, to ensure effective supervision

over policy implementation as well, the size of the staff should be somewhat larger. An optimal figure for the senior staff probably would be about 50 senior staff members, with the largest proportion assigned to ongoing policy coordination and smaller segments to support for strategic planning and the supervision of policy implementation. The president would be poorly served by any drastic staff reduction, for he would be excessively dependent on the bureaucracy of the State Department.

The character of the staff also should be considered. Under Reagan more military personnel has been recruited into the NSC. The president's varied needs suggest that the best staff composition would combine in roughly equal proportions representation from State Department Foreign Service officers, experienced CIA intelligence analysts, able and strategically oriented military personnel from the three armed services, and academics competent in national security issues. The interaction among these groups would most likely generate innovation without slighting the importance of professional experience.

9. Membership on the NSC staff by definition confers a staff role—to plan strategy, coordinate, supervise, and, for the national security adviser, to advise the president. Active and sustained involvement in bureaucratic operations or covert intelligence activity militates against fulfillment of these roles. Fortunately, that danger has been recognized throughout most of the NSC's history, and deviations from that rule have been few, the Iran-contra scandal notwithstanding. A legislated prohibition in the form of an amendment to the National Security Act of 1947 could provide needed reinforcement here.

Nonetheless, under some circumstances the president reasonably may choose to give his national security adviser a special assignment, usually in the area of negotiations. For example, Nixon sent Kissinger on a confidential mission to China in 1971, and Carter assigned me to undertake some special foreign assignments to develop a comprehensive response to the 1979 Soviet aggression against Afghanistan. These foreign-policy assignments—not intelligence activities—were proper exercises of presidential prerogative, and it would be counterproductive and probably impossible to proscribe the president's freedom of action in this respect.

10. Finally, as a deliberative body, the NSC should be used to develop a wider process of informal consultations with congressional leaders. Effective national policy under the American system of government requires broad congressional support. To generate a sense of shared participation in molding national strategy, an informal monthly NSC meeting with legislative leadership appears to be desirable and feasible. These meetings could involve a more comprehensive discussion of long-range national objectives.

Informal NSC meetings need not violate the constitutional separation of powers, for it could be stipulated that no formal decisions would be made then. Such discussions could help infuse into the NSC process a domestic political perspective it currently lacks. Making foreign policy more responsive to the public will help re-energize the NSC into a more effective organ of national security policymaking.

When the next administration begins to organize itself, then, it can only be hoped that its officials heed the lessons of the past. Before, the effective management of U.S. national security policy might have seemed less important. There were fewer fissures in the U.S. alliance system. The financial foundations of American policy were more secure. And the Soviet opponent was less resourceful diplomatically. That world is gone. To maintain its position in the world and advance its interests, the United States needs to maximize the impact of its diplomatic, military, and financial resources. That can only be done if the NSC system is permitted to perform as its creators originally intended some 40 years ago.

CHAPTER SIX

■

Executive-Legislative Tensions in Foreign Affairs

IN THIS SYMPOSIUM, we will be dealing with a most timely and important topic: foreign affairs and the Constitution. Who makes national security policy is not an idle question for academic debate. How we answer that question in practice determines the U.S. capacity to act in the world. That, in turn, affects not only our ability to ensure the survival and security of the United States, but also our capacity to affect the future course of world events.

A number of constitutional questions have direct relevance to the manner in which the United States shapes its foreign policy. Among them are the issue of the power to use military force, the relationship between the first amendment and national security, the issue of the treaty-making powers, and the question of the powers inherent in the executive. The tensions inherent in the Constitution in the area of foreign policy are an especially timely topic given the current tensions between the executive and legislative and among contending factions within the Congress itself over the U.S. role in the Gulf.

This debate highlights what I see as a political dimension in the constitutional struggle over foreign policy. I would like to address a few remarks to this political dimension, for I believe it to be central to any reasonable management of the executive-legislative relationship.

We have to recognize two obvious facts as a point of departure. First, in the last fifteen years, the balance in that movable, dynamic legislative-executive relationship has clearly shifted from the executive branch toward the legislative branch. Congress has become more active, more involved, perhaps even more central in the shaping of national security policy.

Remarks delivered before the Federalist Society symposium on "Foreign Affairs and the Constitution," in Washington, D.C., on November 6, 1987.

This has resulted from a variety of factors, but it is certainly a fact of life.

Second, an inherent ambiguity exists in the Constitution regarding the proper boundaries of the prerogatives of the legislative and executive. Quite simply, the Constitution does not hand down clear-cut guidelines for the process of shaping national security policy. It gives neither the legislative nor the executive branch exclusive powers in this area; these powers are not separated but blended between the two branches. The president has the specific powers accorded to him, such as the treaty-making power; all the powers inherent in national sovereignty not explicitly given to the Congress; and those implied by his role as commander-in-chief. But the Congress has the power to declare war and the Senate to ratify treaties. The legislative branch also has the decisive role in the budgetary process and that clearly affects national security policy. All of this means that the relationship between the executive and the legislative is inevitably a fluid one. Determinant power will shift in one direction and then another, depending on the prevailing political circumstances.

*   *   *

This fluid accommodation is a part of our constitutional tradition and as such is quite normal. But in recent years our flexible arrangements have become less manageable, more polarized, even gridlocked. Today, I would like to comment briefly on the causes of some of our current difficulties.

The first is the collapse of bipartisanship. The delicate, informal, flexible relationship between the executive and the legislative in foreign affairs operates differently in the context of partisanship than in a context of bipartisanship. The United States has been engaged in the world as a major power for forty years, and for roughly the first twenty years we shaped our foreign policy by and large on the basis of a bipartisan consensus. That inevitably affected the nature of the executive-legislative relationship. It made for greater mutual trust. It made for a more automatic, though informal, process of consultations.

Bipartisan consensus also meant that both branches shared certain common assumptions. I emphasize the word *assumptions* because a great deal of our foreign policy operates on automatically shared assumptions, rather than deliberately framed strategy. We do not have a tradition in this country of shaping a geostrategic approach to foreign policy, but rather one of responding to certain basic common feelings. There is no doubt that our Anglophile feelings, for example, had a lot to do with the emergence of the Anglo-American alliance in World War II and the special relationship between Britain and the United States after the war.

That was then extended into the communion that we undertook with Europe.

But after twenty years, bipartisanship collapsed in the Vietnam War. Today, alternative partisan conceptions color a great deal of the dialogue on foreign policy issues. These conceptions are based on increasingly differing assumptions about the world, about U.S. values, about the use of power, about the nature of the threat, and about U.S. priorities.

A partisan approach to foreign policy inevitably affects the executive-legislative relationship, especially if one party controls the Congress and the other holds the White House. When there is a partisan split between these branches of government, policy differences intensify, further complicating the process of making sound policy. It subjects foreign policy to partisan debate and maneuvering and encourages the legislative branch to counterpose itself to the executive branch on the nature of strategic issues.

The second problem that has compounded executive-legislative tensions over foreign policy is our tendency to confuse strategy with tactics. As I noted, we do not have a strategic tradition in this country. We do not have a tradition of articulating explicitly a set of strategic assumptions that clearly define our priorities. We often fail to distinguish central strategic fronts from peripheral fronts in our conflict with the Soviets. We tend to be driven toward a policymaking process in which tactical considerations become dominant. As a result, tactics tend to shape the content of strategy.

For example, consider a current issue much in the forefront of public attention: the Iran-contra debacle. The problem would not have become acute if there had been a deeper awareness of the strategic issues involved. Such an awareness would not have allowed the issue of the hostages in Lebanon to become paramount. It would also have facilitated a greater discrimination in the choice of tactics designed to serve the strategic objective of renewing the U.S.-Iranian relationship. But the preoccupation with tactics became so strong—and the choice of tactics in the end became so bizarre—that the ultimate strategic objective of the enterprise was overshadowed and finally negated.

In the context of the collapse of bipartisanship, this second problem has become interwined with the executive-legislative debate. The United States simply has not cultivated a process and exercise of devising and articulating a national strategy, revising it periodically, and then adapting tactics to serve it. The confluence of these problems has led to the legislating of tactics rather than to the debating of strategy. The executive branch, which is prey to the same preoccupation with tactics, often compounds the problem by emphasizing tactics without thinking seriously about strategic assumptions.

The third problem is the still inadequate and insufficiently serious consultation between the executive and legislative branches regarding strategic matters. Presidents have tended not to engage their colleagues in Congress on that issue, and the executive branch does not even have adequately developed mechanisms to do so.

The National Security Council could serve as a vehicle to promote a dialogue on strategy. One of the NSC's proper roles is to serve as an adviser to the president on the development of a strategic approach to the world and to coordinate the actions of the different executive departments, the State Department, the Defense Department, and the intelligence agencies. That is how the national security adviser should see his role. Yet he is unable to appear before Congress to explain his efforts or his assumptions. If he does so informally, he is often viewed by those in the traditional departments, such as State, as usurping their legitimate role. That, in turn, further inhibits a process of promoting a dialogue on strategy.

I know from my own experience that whenever I appeared on Capitol Hill to meet with members of Congress I could only do so informally under quasi-surreptitious circumstances. That was almost inevitably followed by recriminations from the Department of State on the grounds that this was usurping its role. Yet, at the same time, the Department of State does not shape national security policy. It too often confuses diplomacy with foreign policy. It forgets that diplomacy is only one aspect of foreign policy. Military power, intelligence, covert activity, financial power, and threat assessment are also all part of the process of making a national security policy. Diplomacy is but one component of that policy.

The fourth problem that folds into today's tensions between the executive and the legislative branches is the nature of modern warfare and the nature of the threat to our national security. These have altered some dimensions of executive decisionmaking. The fact is that modern circumstances have compressed the time available for critical decisionmaking. We live in an age in which we are always faced with the potential danger of having to make critical life-and-death decisions under the most incredible kinds of pressures. This inevitably complicates the constitutional responsibilities of the executive branch vis-à-vis the legislative branch.

In the event of a nuclear conflict between the United States and the Soviet Union the president would have roughly four minutes in which to make the most difficult and most critical decisions. If the Soviet Union initiated a nuclear strike at night, the national security adviser would wake up the president roughly three minutes after the launch of Soviet missiles. The president would then have to consult with the national security adviser and, roughly from the fourth to the eighth minutes, review certain rather complex procedures. He would have to engage in a rather critical process of decisionmaking with some other individuals. He would then have to choose among several options and undertake certain decisions whose execution would have to be initiated roughly from the eighth to the tenth minutes.

Clearly, these procedures require literally a few individuals to assume an enormous amount of responsibility. It is a question of enormous sensitivity and utmost importance. It obviously affects how we operate as a nation and how we make policy under the most dire of circumstances. Yet, it cannot be governed by the conventional constitutional guidelines for the declaration and conduct of war. Given the compression of time for decisionmaking, there would be an unavoidable collision between constitutional provisions and actual, real-life situations. Here, concentration of command-and-control authority in the hands of a single person has to be ensured under all circumstances. Without that, our ability to initiate a retaliatory strike—and therefore the credibility of our deterrent threat—would come into question.

The Carter administration was the first in some twenty years to exercise these complex crisis procedures. The executive branch, particularly the president, has to be both versed in and prepared for these critical procedures. There is no time to learn them in the event of a genuine crisis. The survivability of our government under the circumstances of modern warfare requires attention to this matter, not only for the purpose of war-fighting, should that become necessary, but primarily for that of deterrence. In this regard, it seems inevitable that Congress must delegate authority to the president.

The fifth problem complicating executive-legislative relations involves covert action. Today, there are widely divergent perceptions about the role of covert activity in our national security policy. Few dispute that from time to time there is a need for some covert activity. It is a legitimate form of international action designed to obtain desired objectives. It can involve support for foreign trade unions, counteracting disinformation in the foreign press, influencing key foreign decisionmakers, or exercising other forms of persuasion. Some of these actions are relatively harmless and risk-free, while others carry serious consequences and involve great risks to the individuals concerned.

Can such activities be undertaken without consultation with the legislative branch? The answer is clearly no. Some consultations are necessary. But if there is such consultation, can it be achieved with the security needed for the operation to succeed? Unfortunately, my own experience in the White House and recent experience more generally indicates that the chances for success in that context are uncertain. Both the executive branch and the legislative oversight bodies must make certain that leaks will not compromise the policy because leaks place into jeopardy not only the objectives of the operation but also the safety of individuals engaged in these potentially hazardous actions. Moreover, any leak destroys the needed mutual confidence between the legislative and executive branches, thereby complicating the ability of individuals of goodwill on both sides to undertake the needed cooperation for integrating covert action into our overall national security policy.

All of these problems are in a sense crystallized in the War Powers Act. It represented the outcome of a profound struggle over the proper lines of authority for the exercise of military force by the United States. After the end of U.S. involvement in the Vietnam War, there was a pervasive sense in the Congress that the executive had overstepped its constitutional authority during that conflict. That was the political context in which the resolution was passed. Since then, no president has invoked its procedures or has even conceded the constitutionality of its provisions. I believe the issues it raised are genuine political problems that need to be addressed. But the War Powers Act itself may not have been a proper response to those issues and may not now provide proper answers to the real dilemmas we face.

In a recent speech on the War Powers Act, a former top congressional leader recalled, "As that legislation went to the House of Representatives, the Senate, and was handed down to the president, I took exactly the same position as a member of Congress on this issue as I took while in the White House." President Ford, who before becoming president had served as House minority leader for many years, goes on to say: "I believe that the War Powers resolution is unconstitutional. Secondly, it is impractical. And thirdly, it constrains the President's effort in trying to achieve or maintain peace." These are rather harsh condemnations of a piece of legislation that is still on the books.

In making the case for its unconstitutionality, President Ford stresses a key requirement for the War Powers resolution: the fact that after sixty days—if the Congress has simply not approved the president's actions—all troops must be withdrawn from hostilities. President Ford adds: "If the Congress is mired in indecision or in inaction or lacks courage or guts—if you want to call it that—to do anything, it can do nothing and achieves the same result as if they had ordered it by majority vote in both the House and the Senate." President Ford then goes on to cite some constitutional precedents that suggest this kind of legislation is in fact unconstitutional.

I leave it to the lawyers to resolve the constitutional legalities, but I find it rather revealing that a former major congressional leader, who briefly served as the president of the United States, takes such a strong position on this subject. He also argues that the War Powers Act is an impractical law by requiring consultations under circumstances in which these are impossible. President Ford recounts that in dealing with certain crises he literally could not locate the immediate persons with whom, under the War Powers Act, he had to consult before he could act.

The problems connected with the War Powers Act have been particularly evident in the continuing debate over the U.S. role in protecting certain shipping in the Gulf. Many in Congress want President Reagan to invoke the provisions of the War Powers Act. There have even been fitful movements to force him to do so. Yet, at the same time, it is clear that Congress has no consensus about our policy objectives or our tactical requirements. Congress has debated for months—literally months—about the proper role for U.S. military forces in the Gulf. There is a consensus that the United States has interests in the Gulf that need to be protected. But beyond that, Congress cannot agree about the specific form that our role should take. Are our forces simply on a symbolic mission to show the flag? Should we require cooperation from our Arab friends in the Gulf before putting our forces there? Should we protect the reflagged tankers? Should we protect our Arab friends from Iranian attacks? Should we retaliate in the event of Iranian attacks on our own forces? If so, what should the character of that retaliation be? Congress will not give the president a blank check in the Gulf. But Congress cannot formulate legislative language to cope with the myriad and rapidly changing contingencies involved in our mission. Congress, in brief, cannot act as if it were the commander-in-chief.

I mention this to highlight the fact that over the last fifteen years a pattern in executive-legislative relations has developed that does create serious difficulties. These cannot be finally resolved by legislation or formal arrangements. Repealing the War Powers Act would not solve the problem. Alone, that would not automatically restore a proper balance. The difficulty arises not from a deficiency in the statutes. It is instead a political problem. What is needed is a process of political accommodation and adjustment that takes into account the global circumstances of the United States and political realities at home.

*   *   *

It is with this in mind that I would now like to share five suggestions that might be helpful in dealing with these problems. I would like to note that I said *dealing with* and not *resolving* these problems. We are faced with not a puzzle that can be solved given enough ingenuity but with a condition inherent in the complexity of our constitutional arrangement.

The first suggestion involves a deliberate quest for a greater degree of bipartisanship. For the sake of a better executive-legislative relationship in the area of national security policy, it is important and desirable that a more deliberate effort be made, particularly by the president, to move the country back toward bipartisanship. Now, this is not a pious wish, and it is not a prayer. It must be, if it is to be achieved, a political goal. Bipartisanship does not happen by itself. It is not a gift from the gods. It is a relationship that is accomplished through patient, deliberate work.

President Reagan has missed a very major opportunity to move in that direction. When he came into office, he had a unique, broad mandate, particularly in national security policy. His was a special, unprecedented opportunity in the post-Vietnam period. He was the first president, to my knowledge, who had as a member of his transition team a former presidential candidate of the opposite party working on the issue of national security. If the president had appointed Senator Jackson as secretary of defense, he would have taken a giant step toward achieving bipartisanship. That is the way it was done under President Truman and President Eisenhower. They shared power with responsible members of the opposite party with whom a certain degree of shared consensus existed.

I would like to stress that these things have to be done deliberately. I often urged President Carter to work more closely with Senator Howard Baker—and they both tried—but in my judgment our administration did not try hard enough. We did not go the last mile in this regard. We made no effort to draw members of the opposite party into our administration. The first step must be taken by the executive branch, and then the legislative branch must respond. Future administrations must make a truly serious effort to enhance bipartisanship in order to deal with the political problems inherent in the executive-legislative relationship in foreign affairs.

The second suggestion involves a more deliberate formulation of national strategy. We need a strategic process. We need a method for developing a more coherent approach to our national security—one that respects the needed distinction between strategy and tactics. It must also involve joint participation of the executive and legislative branch. We can no longer shape national strategy or deal with strategic questions simply by relying on the decisions of a president, his national security adviser, and his secretaries of state and defense. We are no longer living in an age, as we were in World War II, when foreign policy is the exclusive prerogative of the executive branch. Ad hoc consultations are not enough. What is needed is a process of consultation.

I believe that it would be desirable for the president to use the National Security Council meetings on a roughly monthly basis for enlarged consultations with the top congressional leadership regarding strategic matters. These would not be decisionmaking meetings, thus maintaining the distinction between the executive and the legislative branches. But it would be a way to engage congressional leaders in the process—and the overall national security policymaking process needs their input and involvement.

In these meetings, the president and congressional leaders would take up a discussion of our national strategic objectives. Our leadership could define our goals, identify simple priorities, distinguish between central and peripheral fronts, and shape the guidelines for the exercise of our power and diplomacy. Such meetings could begin to close the pernicious gap between the two branches of our government and could help to establish more generally a sense of shared direction.

The third suggestion involves the appointment of former congressional figures to top-level executive slots in the area of national security policy. It would be useful for our presidents to look at this possibility, which should become an established practice, though not a pervasive one. But it would be helpful if one of the three principal presidential advisers—the secretary of state, the secretary of defense, or the national security adviser—were a well-respected and well-informed former senior member of the House or Senate who shares the president's perspective. Such an appointee would become a distinct informal link with the Congress. Something along these lines is absolutely essential if we are going to redress current executive-legislative tensions—and particularly the present trend toward micromanagement of foreign policy among five hundred and thirty-five putative secretaries of state and/or defense.

The fourth suggestion is that we consider the possibility of having the national security adviser make regular but informal appearances before pertinent congressional committees. Over the years, there have been only two kinds of national security advisers: those who play a useful role and those who are irrelevant. But if the individual plays the role he should be playing, he should be accessible on a limited but regular basis to the Congress in order to help shape the needed executive-legislative consensus. The fact is that the secretary of state cannot truly articulate national security policy because his department cannot produce such policy for him. His department is essentially preoccupied with negotiations and with diplomacy. It has excellent people for that objective. The same is true, with a different expertise, of the Department of Defense. There needs to be someone who works closely with the president, who shares the president's policy and bureaucratic perspective, and who has legitimate authority to speak on behalf of the president with an overall strategic view.

My final suggestion is that it would help if we had a single, joint intelligence committee in the Congress. The existence of two committees with two staffs creates some of the difficulties that have been experienced.

Under the present system, too many people are involved in the process. That makes a shambles of any administration's effort to conduct responsible, serious consultations on intelligence and covert activity. A single committee, with strictly defined rules of procedure both for its staff and its members, would help a great deal to infuse mutual confidence and trust. That, in turn, would make the intelligence agencies of the executive branch much more confident in fully consulting and sharing its views, aspirations, and problems with the legislative branch, as certainly should be the case.

*   *   *

This critique and these suggestions certainly will not resolve the problems inherent in the executive-legislative relationship in the area of national security policy. No comprehensive solution is possible because the problem is inherent in our constitutional structure. But steps in these directions would help to fashion a more favorable political context for executive-legislative decisionmaking—an approach that would be better designed to mobilize public support for our foreign policy and to generate greater strategic consistency in foreign policy.

None of my suggestions is designed to establish the supremacy of one branch over the other. Rather, they reflect the recognition that in our system neither side has ultimate supremacy and that efforts to achieve supremacy by either side would be counterproductive to the U.S. national security process. Our political system works well only when guided by the spirit of compromise; the quest for unilateral domination can only produce enmity or gridlock. I offer these views in the conviction that a cooperative balance is not only clearly desirable but in fact politically feasible—and the point of departure for a remedy to our current dilemmas is in the realm of politics.

CHAPTER SEVEN

— ■ —

Not History But Morality

THE ROLE OF HISTORY IN STATECRAFT is not only a matter of the statesman's personal interest in the subject itself. It is also a question of national consciousness. A people's historical consciousness shapes political attitudes, helps to define national priorities, and contributes to constancy in the exercise of national power. A nation that is motivated by a collective memory is often intractable but also more predictable; occasionally vengeful but also more trustworthy; often narrow-minded but also more capable of endurance. It does not have to rediscover itself because it knows itself.

Political leadership in a historically conscious nation tends to identify itself with the nation's subconsciously endowed personal identity. The nation—its history and geography—is thought of almost as a person to whom both the leader and the citizen are committed and with whom they simultaneously share a kind of union. Typically the name of the country is invoked as if it were a person, beloved, demanding, often threatened by outsiders. National history thus becomes an extension of personal memory, truly motivating political behavior.

For the statesman, the exercise of power in such a context requires that he be in step with both national history and, by extension, national destiny. Policy goals are defined in keeping with the normal rhythm of the nation's historical experience. Even acute historical discontinuities, such as revolutions, eventually tend to become assimilated into the hidden logic of national history. They come to be seen as phases of renewal. But until that happens a revolution in nationally conscious peoples tends also to be extremely unsettling, generating both bitter struggles between alternatives and mutually exclusive concepts of what the nation is, has

---

Published originally under the title "A Nation That Lives Only for the Future," in the *London Times,* March 21, 1987. Reprinted by permission.

been, and should become. But that conflict, too, is about the "true" meaning of national history and underlines history's centrality in national politics.

To be sure, all nations are not equally motivated by history or possess an equally developed historical consciousness. Nevertheless, it would be difficult to understand the intractability of many contemporary regional issues without reference to history. Moreover, the historical dimension is certainly evident in such critical national decisions as the French determination to acquire its own national nuclear deterrent or in the growing internal problems for Moscow over the proper relationship between the Russian-dominated political center and the non-Russian nations within the Soviet Union.

A historical consciousness also conditions both the leader and his people to accept the reality of conflict on the global scene as something quite normal. Hostility, competition, and prolonged contests for supremacy are not viewed as aberrations but as the manifestations of the normality of struggle in the human condition. And because conflict has been the normal condition of the past, it is more than likely to be the norm of the future as well.

These general considerations highlight the unhistorical distinctiveness of America. America is composed of a people united not by a shared past, consciously perceived, but by a shared commitment to the future. America's own past is short, and much of its population does not identify itself emotionally with that past. To be sure, for the South the Civil War still has some waning meaning. I was impressed in talking to President Carter by how much that legacy still meant to him, not in the sense of hatred or bitterness but in the consciousness of a defeat inflicted on a way of life of which his own grandfather had been still very much a part.

For most Americans, however, the two hundred-year history of the United States is not a personally intimate engagement with the past. Indeed, if most Americans were deeply involved with their personal national pasts, they could not be united, as they are, as a people. It is their shared commitment to the future that defines them as Americans. And that commitment is reinforced by a sense of historical optimism about the future and by shared concepts of what ought to be the proper relationship between the individual and the society and the state. It is not an accident that history and foreign geography are so badly taught in most American schools. Fascination with the past is not compatible with the dominant American outlook. Unity focused on the future, not derived from an emotionally shared past, creates the American consciousness, characterized by its rather unique historical amnesia and by its inward-focused future-orientation.

This broader context must be taken into account in addressing the important question of what role has history been playing in the thinking of recent American leaders.

My judgment must necessarily be impressionistic. In assessing the role that historical awareness played in the exercise of power in recent years, I think it is useful to differentiate between three broad categories of historical influence: (1) the impact of contemporary history of the individual involved; (2) the actual interest of the individual in history as a subject in itself; and (3) the leader's direct personal experience as part of a learning process.

In the first category, one is dealing essentially with leaders whose personal participation in truly important events, or at least very close observation of such events, tended to shape their outlook on world affairs. One might quite easily place in this category President Eisenhower and President Kennedy, though obviously the level of personal experience differed a great deal from one to the other. Nonetheless, the centrality of the wartime experience in shaping President Eisenhower's outlook on the world is quite obvious, and conditioned a great deal of his attitude toward Europe, particularly NATO. President Eisenhower's interest in arms control was also derivative of that traumatic experience. President Kennedy's "heroic" style was probably very much influenced by his admiration for Churchill and his self-identification with him.

In the second category, one would be entitled to place President Truman and, to some extent, President Carter. President Truman had a deep personal interest in history as a subject. He was an avid reader of Plutarch's *Lives*. One senses in his approach to decision making a profound respect for the institution of the presidency and a historically grounded awareness of what is meant by responsibilty for the national commonweal. President Carter was intensely interested in learning about the regions or countries with which he had to deal. He appreciated history as part of that learning process, but it has to be admitted that in many cases such historical self-education came late, coinciding with his stewardship of office. Though possessing the keenest of intellects and an extraordinarily inquisitive mind, his pre-presidential intellectual focus was not directed at history as such, and he thus did not approach policy issues with a historical perspective in mind.

President Nixon is an excellent example of the third category. There is no doubt his service as vice president, his frequent travels abroad, and his subsequent self-education in world affairs in the course of the 1960s gave him a keen understanding of global dynamics, grounded in wide-ranging familiarity with contemporary affairs. He displayed an instinctive strategic grasp of central issues, and that, at least to some extent, had to include either an intuitive or an acquired historical feel for the countries concerned.

To be sure, none of the American presidents in recent years can be said to have shared some of the deeper historical motivations and perceptions derived from being part of a nation that is itself historically self-conscious. The absence of this deeper dimension does explain in part why American policy has tended to oscillate from expectations of a wide-ranging détente with the Soviet Union to widespread apprehensions regarding the renewal of the Cold War. The absence of the historical dimension was the root cause of the tempting thought that the Soviet leaders shared with American presidents the same global concerns and a similar desire to terminate the rivalry between the United States and the Soviet Union. Historical amnesia also helps to explain why, at times, America shifts from apocalyptic anxieties to the kind of utopian escapism demonstrated at the Reykjavik summit.

In effect, the grounding of national policy in a historically shaped geostrategy has been uncongenial to most American leaders. It is easier, and more "American," to base foreign policy on idealistic principles, universal in scope and moralistic in content. The thought that an effective national policy has to be derived from an intellectually solid grasp of history, geography, and strategy is not very palatable for most of my fellow Americans.

PART THREE

■

The Carter Legacy

Although allies and friends of the United States often berate the unpredictability of U.S. foreign policy, there is more continuity than change in its fundamental elements. It sometimes may appear that every administration comes into office intent on repudiating the policies of its predecessor, particularly when there has been a change in the party occupying the White House. But the extent of change can easily be exaggerated. While the tone and particular policy emphases of presidents have varied, each postwar administration has reaffirmed the core commitments of policies created immediately after World War II—and has often incorporated in some fashion the particular innovations of its predecessor.

In these speeches, which were delivered when Dr. Brzezinski served as national security adviser to President Carter, he spells out the thrust of the Carter foreign policy. There was basic continuity in the goals of U.S. policy. What was more novel was the greater emphasis President Carter placed on an attempt to explore ways of accommodating U.S. policies to the turbulent change sweeping the world, particularly in less developed countries, and on a conscious attempt to promote human rights around the globe. Dr. Brzezinski viewed human rights as "the historic inevitability of our times"—ideals for which people yearn regardless of their political circumstances or historical traditions. Human rights had become a universal aspiration, though not a universal achievement.

While explicitly critical of President Carter's human rights policy in the 1980 campaign, President Reagan has, in a large degree, continued to abide by it. His administration has exerted strong pressure on El Salvador to rein in forces involved in systematic murder of political opponents. It assisted in easing out the authoritarian governments of Haiti and the Philippines and encouraged transitions to democratic forms of government in South Korea and throughout Latin America. Thus, even under President Reagan, a clear legacy has been left by President Carter in the area of human rights.

CHAPTER EIGHT

■

U.S. Policy
and Global Change

IN SPEAKING ABOUT U.S. POLICY and global change, it is important
to stress at the outset the underlying continuity of that policy. Since
1945, the United States, with its allies, has been engaged in an effort
to create a more congenial international setting for our values, for our
interests, and for our future. But we have done so in the context of an
international political system beset by the pressures of an intense ideological conflict and a remarkable expansion in the scope of its global
political participation. This conjunction—of conflict rooted in ideology,
power, and national ambitions and of a sudden expansion in international
participation—has made for extraordinary turbulence in world affairs.

Nonetheless, our basic commitments have remained unchanged from
one administration to the next. This is especially true regarding collective
security. Our commitment to a common defense remains a central and
constant element in our policy. But the international context in which
we have sought to maintain these commitments has changed. The nature
of that change has often created enormously complex problems. In reacting
to global change, what factors should we stress and why? In an era of
such rapid change, with some of that change involving values clearly in
conflict with our own traditions, is it more important to preserve the
status quo or to try to shape that change in directions that preserve our
interests and enhance our values? Or is it possible to do some of both?

Each administration has answered these questions somewhat differently,
thereby setting for itself somewhat different priorities. Today, while
emphasizing the underlying continuity in U.S. foreign policy, I wish to
share with you some thoughts on how the new Carter administration

Remarks delivered before the meeting of the Trilateral Commission in Bonn, Federal
Republic of Germany, on October 25, 1977.

defines its objectives, and how it responds to continuing as well as to new global dilemmas. In broad terms, the Carter administration has set for itself four basic priorities: (1) to overcome the crisis of the spirit; (2) to help shape a wider and more cooperative world system; (3) to resolve conflicts that left unresolved are not likely to be contained; and (4) to engage governments and peoples in responding to new and key global dilemmas.

OVERCOMING THE CRISIS OF THE SPIRIT

In some regards, the crisis of the spirit in recent years has been specifically American; in a larger sense, it has been part of the broader malaise of the West; in some respects, it is related to the political awakening of mankind, which has had the effect of transforming heretofore seemingly universal Western values into an apparently parochial perspective. As a crisis of historical confidence, and of international relevance to a world that seemingly rejects Western values, its essence has been well expressed by Herman Hesse writing in *Steppenwolf*: "Human life is reduced to real suffering, to hell, only when two ages, two cultures and religions overlap. . . . There are times when a whole generation is caught in this way between two ages, two modes of life, with the consequence that it loses all power to understand itself and has no standard, no security, no simple acquiescence."

In its specific U.S. dimension, the crisis of the spirit was stimulated by the Vietnam War and by the constitutional and moral crisis of Watergate. In Western Europe and Japan, the very pace of the efforts to overcome the traumatic legacies of World War II may still have played a role. Raymond Aron has also recently pointed at the broader implications of this crisis: "A hedonistic civilization, so shortsighted as to devote itself only to the material satisfactions of the day, condemns itself to death when it is no longer interested in the future, and loses thereby its sustaining sense of history."

This is why the new U.S. president put so much early emphasis, even in his inaugural address, on "the new spirit." Faced with a world that was losing faith in the United States, by the widespread global phenomenon of anti-Americanism, the new administration put high on its list of priorities the need to revive both U.S. confidence and the spiritual relevance of the West to emerging global dilemmas. We sensed that, for far too long, the United States had been seen—often correctly—as opposed to change, committed primarily to stability for the sake of stability, preoccupied with the balance of power for the sake of the preservation of privilege. We deliberately set out to identify the United States with the notion that change is a positive phenomenon, that we believe change can be channeled in constructive directions, and that international change can be made compatible with our own underlying spiritual values.

The emphasis we have put on human rights is derived from this perspective. We believe that human rights is an idea whose time has come. Throughout the world, because of higher literacy, better communications, and a closer sense of interdependence, people are demanding and asserting their basic rights. This phenomenon manifests itself— though in different ways and with differing priorities—in the Far East, in southern Africa, in Latin America, in Eastern Europe, and in the USSR. It has asserted itself in recent years in our own society on the racial front, and it is also making itself felt in other advanced industrial democracies. We do not make the acceptance of our view of human rights a precondition for U.S. ties with other societies. But we do believe that these two words "human rights" summarize mankind's social progress and that neither the United States nor the West should be ashamed of our commitment to the advancement of human rights.

In addition, the revival of popular U.S. concern for events beyond our shores derives in part from the special emphasis that the administration has placed on relating our foreign policy goals to deeper U.S. values. The reawakened U.S. concern for human rights thus not only reflects the deep convictions of the president and of most Americans; this concern has also played a significant role in overcoming widespread popular disillusion and cynicism about foreign policy. It has thus enabled the United States again to play a more constructive role across a broad range of international issues.

It is fair to say that the crisis of the spirit in the United States is coming to an end. The changing outlook of the United States on the world today has several dimensions.

A revival of U.S. optimism. This is not the mere expectation of good fortune expressed in Bismarck's remark that "a special providence seems to look after drunks, fools, and Americans." Rather, it reflects confidence in the basic strength of our position in the world and of the moral character of that position.

A reawakening of U.S. idealism. President Carter does not shrink from affirming our basic values at home and abroad. Americans support him in that. We do not seek to impose our principles on others, but we do not intend to be silent about the things that we believe in deeply. Moreover, by reaffirming our commitment to the basic notions that man is entitled to certain basic human rights and that the Western democratic system gives people the greatest opportunity for self-expression, we contribute to the spiritual revival of the West. A West that believes only in material consumption has a message of no relevance to the rest of the world. A West that stands for genuine liberty and self-fulfillment of the individual has a message and the necessary point of departure for a dialogue with the rest of the world about basic human needs—material, social, political, and technological.

A rekindling of U.S. commitment to reform. The current international situation demands a creative effort to devise new habits of conduct and new institutions for dealing with regional and global problems. We accept this challenge with enthusiasm rather than resignation, recognizing that we cannot design solutions unilaterally nor engage the interests and efforts of others without patient and thorough consultations.

TOWARD A WIDER AND MORE COOPERATIVE WORLD SYSTEM

For us, the point of departure for U.S. involvement in the world is our relationship with Western Europe and Japan. The bonds of interest and sentiment that link our destinies have a special character. We share a commitment to democratic procedures, civil rights, the market system, open societies. We confront the common problems of postindustrial societies. We are not merely occasional allies; we are permanent friends. If we are determined to reassert U.S. leadership in world affairs, we conceive of it as shared leadership; no country today can have a monopoly or even a predominance of wisdom, initiative, or responsibility.

Because of this understanding and belief, we set out immediately to bring relations with Europe and Japan to the forefront of U.S. foreign policy. We have sought to consult on the many issues with which we are vitally concerned, first and foremost with our industrial state partners. Our objective in this is not a pursuit of identical policies. But together we must relate our respective national security policies and our economic policies to common efforts to promote reconciliation among nations and more effective international economic cooperation. In dealing with each other, moreover, we must acknowledge a higher standard of mutual concern than normally marks relations between sovereign states. We must accept a greater commitment to consult, and to adjust our national policies in the light of their impact on our key partners.

A secure and economically cooperative community of the advanced industrial democracies is the necessary source of stability for a broad system of international cooperation. We are aware of the pitfalls of constructing a geometric world—whether bilateral or trilateral or pentagonal—that leaves out the majority of mankind, those who live in the developing countries. A global structure that would ignore this reality would be inhumane, for it would reflect indifference to the hardships of others. It would be unrealistic, for we cannot ignore scores of nations with whom we are increasingly interdependent. It would be damaging in the long run, for the problems that we neglect today will come back in a more virulent form tomorrow. We are therefore seeking to create a new political and international order that is truly more participatory and genuinely more responsive to global desire for greater social justice, equity, and more opportunity for individual self-fulfillment. We believe that paying greater attention to this dimension of foreign policy is not only in our self-interest but indispensable to an effective working of the global economy; to us it also represents a return to some of the deepest values and historical roots of our own country, while reestablishing the relevance of the West to mankind's universal condition.

It is in this spirit that the new administration has sought to put our relations with Latin America and with Africa on a new plane. We have abandoned the traditional device of formulating a new slogan to encapsulate U.S. relations with Latin America. Instead, we have emphasized our respect for the diversity of the Latin American nations; we seek to relate to them on a bilateral basis in most cases, on a regional basis when useful, and on a global basis in regard to problems that are more universal. I believe that most Latin American nations respect and welcome this approach. They see in it the rejection of traditional U.S. paternalism and the beginning of more mature and normal relations, similar to those which the United States has with other nations of the world.

Regarding Africa, we have sought to identify ourselves with the just aspirations of black Africans. We have broken with the posture of indifference and insensitivity that at times characterized U.S. attitudes toward those aspirations. In so doing, I believe that we are also making it easier for the United States, as for the West in general, to play a creative role in dealing with some international problems that today confront the African community.

In Asia, where the United States will continue to play a major role, we are encouraged by the progress made in some parts of this vast region. The emergence of ASEAN, the growing prosperity of the Pacific Basin, the constructive character of recent Japanese initiatives are welcome developments that will cumulatively contribute to a healthier international order.

In brief, our approach to developing nations is characterized by our willingness to actively seek solutions to remaining "anticolonialist" issues; by our engagement in the search for answers to the more structural problems of North-South relations; by our desire to collaborate closely with the increasingly influential emerging states; and by our desire to make foreign aid more responsive to the needs of the world's poorest peoples.

At the same time, a wider and more cooperative world system has to include that part of the world that is ruled by Communist governments. One-third of mankind now lives under Communist systems, and these states have to be assimilated, to the extent that they are willing, into a wider fabric of global cooperation. The objective is thus to assimilate East-West relations into a broader framework of cooperation, rather than to concentrate on East-West relations as the decisive and dominant concern of our times. In the 1950s, world affairs were dominated by an intense confrontation between the United States and the Soviet bloc. In the 1960s, world affairs were dominated by growing diversity in the Communist world and by a competitive relationship between the United States and the Soviet Union. And in the early 1970s, many foreign observers became concerned that the next era would be marked by efforts to create a condominium. An enduring thread runs through these generalizations; whether marked by confrontation, competition, or the feared prospect of a condominium, the nature of U.S.-Soviet relations tended to dominate U.S. foreign policy and, indeed, world affairs.

This should no longer be, nor need it be, the case. East-West relations, notably U.S.-Soviet relations, involve and will continue to involve elements of both competition and cooperation. We are quietly confident about our ability and determination to compete, economically, politically, and militarily. But managing a relationship that will be both competitive and cooperative cannot be permitted to dominate all our perspectives. Today, we do not have a realistic choice between an approach centered on the Soviet Union, or on cooperation with our trilateral friends, or on North-South relations. Instead, each set of issues must be approached on its own terms. A world where elements of cooperation prevail over competition entails the need to shape a wider and more cooperative global framework. We did not wish the world to be this complex; but we must deal with it in all of its complexity, even if it means having a foreign policy that cannot be reduced to a single and simplistic slogan.

This is why we will seek to engage the Soviet Union in wider forms of cooperation. As President Carter said at Notre Dame University, we desire a détente that will be both comprehensive and reciprocal. We want to contain the arms race. The arms race is costly and dangerous. We seek to reduce—and to keep reducing—the level of strategic armaments on both sides, to freeze the improvement of weaponry on both sides, and to achieve an agreement in which each side is responsive to more specific strategic concerns of the other. I believe that the next SALT agreement will, in some measure, reflect these three objectives; it will thus provide a useful basis for seeking even more ambitious limits in SALT III, perhaps also paving the way to more comprehensive security negotiations in the European context, beyond the MBFR negotiations.

No architecture for a more stable and just world order would be complete without taking into account the proper role of the People's Republic of China. We recognize not only that peace in East and Southeast Asia depends upon a constructive Sino-American relationship, but that China can help immensely in maintaining a global equilibrium as well. Mutual interest, not sentiment, brought our two countries close together. We must continue working to make our relationship closer still. Normalization in that relationship is necessary, but even short of it both sides should find it useful to develop a closer consultative relationship; each side must understand and take into account the legitimate global concerns of the other. In fact, a deeper consultative relationship can result in an approach to world affairs that is mutually reinforcing and increasingly cooperative.

RESOLVING CONFLICTS

Our third major objective is to focus on three major issues that in our judgment contain the greatest potential for destructive escalation.

The first of these involves the future of the Panama Canal. To most Panamanians and to many Latin Americans, this issue is perceived as a vestige of U.S. colonialism, a perspective widely shared in the Third World as well. I must candidly say that the effort to obtain a new treaty, which would phase out the U.S. presence in the Canal Zone and permit Panama to increase its participation in the operation and defense of the Canal but which would retain for the United States ultimate security responsibility, is not a popular matter in the United States. Yet the new administration recognizes that efforts to maintain the status quo would poison our relations with Latin America and eventually jeopardize our ability to keep the canal open. We are thus determined to demonstrate that the most powerful nation in the world is willing to work with one of the world's smallest nations to fashion a relationship based on partnership and mutual respect. We also hope, thereby, to demonstrate that watertight zones of big power predominance are a historical anachronism, a point that may have some relevance to some other parts of the world as well.

The second major issue is in southern Africa. There we confront the danger that racial conflict might also become before long an ideological war, with external involvement. In cooperation with the African states, we seek in southern Africa to promote a solution based on justice. Majority rule and one man–one vote reflect our fundamental view of man as a spiritual entity that transcendentally is truly equal to all others. We are willing to play a continuing role in solving the problems of southern Africa on terms acceptable to the people who live there. In

Zimbabwe, this means supporting a rapid transition to majority rule; in Namibia, it means assumption of power by an African government resting on the will of the majority. We recognize also that the situation in the Republic of South Africa is much more complex and will take much more time to resolve. We know that the issue of South Africa involves a fundamental conflict of philosophy, history, and self-definition. We are anxious to help create conditions that will make accommodation to a new reality—one more in keeping with the spirit of the times—as peaceful and palatable to those most affected as possible.

We are also determined to do our part to make certain that Africa in general does not become the terrain for ideological conflict. This is why we insist that major powers refrain from interference and from fueling conflicts, whether in southern Africa or the African Horn. The problems of this continent are painful enough without infecting them with ideological issues derived from another age and from other continents.

The third crucial problem on which we will concentrate is in the Middle East. Continued conflict in that region poses a direct threat to international peace, while increasingly radicalizing Israel's neighbors. Such conflict poses a danger as much to Europe and to Japan as to the United States, not to speak of Israel itself. We also perceived that an opportunity existed to move more rapidly toward a genuine peace. The Israelis, who have fought so courageously for their survival and to whose survival every morally sensitive person must be committed, have often stated that territories occupied in 1967 were being held until their Arab neighbors were prepared to undertake full-scale peace commitments. Our administration, therefore, building on the step-by-step arrangements attained by the previous U.S. administration, has sought to elicit and to crystallize growing Arab moderation, thereby making possible direct negotiations between the parties. We hope that a full-scale conference may be convened before too long, and that in the meantime all parties will maintain a posture of moderation, bearing in mind that sometimes excessive precision on details is an enemy of accommodation.

The road ahead, however, will be extraordinarily difficult. Europe and Japan, and indeed most of mankind, share our commitment to promoting a settlement, and in different ways they too can exercise a constructive influence in pleading for the necessary spirit of moderation needed to settle a conflict so pregnant with political and moral complexities.

RESPONSIVENESS TO NEW GLOBAL DILEMMAS

Our final major objective has been to join with others in increasing the level of global sensitivity to two key problems that, in our judgment, have been given inadequate attention in the past. They are nonproliferation and conventional arms transfers.

Our nuclear nonproliferation policy recognizes two needs: to help each nation secure the energy it needs, and to stop the spread of nuclear weaponry. Thus, our policy is not designed to impose artificial prohibitions on the inevitable spread of an essential technology. Rather we have sought to induce nations to take a fresh look at the problems of the plutonium fuel cycle, and to concentrate greater attention on the technical alternatives which we believe exist. The policy rests on a firm economic and technical base that has two key elements. First, the energy plans of many nations— particularly the developed states—are based on what we regard as inflated estimates of future energy demand. Second, we think that global reserves of uranium and thorium are much larger than was previously estimated.

Our analysis of these considerations impels us to the conclusion that the reprocessing and reuse of plutonium, at this time, would be premature. Therefore, last spring, the president postponed reprocessing in the United States for the indefinite future and proposed an international nuclear fuel cycle evaluation in which developed and developing states could jointly examine these and related issues in an effort to reach agreement.

We also wish to raise the level of awareness about the dangers involved in growing conventional arms transfers. These transfers have more than doubled over the past decade. Not only has there been a dramatic increase in the volume of arms, but those sold today are of ever-increasing sophistication. While only a handful of states produce such weapons, the momentum continues to build, despite the enormous burden that is levied on an already faltering world economy. The tragic irony is that the diversion of resources from economic and social development to buy arms may undermine the very security the arms are intended to purchase.

The United States is moving to meet this global threat to the welfare of mankind. We have begun to restrain our arms exports; at the same time, realizing that we cannot deal with this global problem alone, we intend to work with other suppliers to cut back on the flow of arms and the rate at which advanced weapon technologies spread. Equally important, we hope to work with arms importers to reduce the demand for more numerous and costly weapons. While we remain ready to provide our friends with the necessary means for self-defense, we are determined to do what can be done to reverse the spiraling increase of arms exports.

*   *   *

In these four areas, I do not claim that we have succeeded in reaching our goals. But I believe that real progress has been made.

1. Anti-Americanism has waned; there has been a revival of historical confidence *in* the United States and *about* the United States; our com-

mitment to human rights is helping to restore genuine meaning to the
world democracy, and thus the democracies' relevance to the world.

2. We have made some progress in economic cooperation among the
industrial powers, but we need to do more, especially in regard to
economic growth and the avoidance of protectionism.

We have improved somewhat the climate in North-South relations and
placed our relations with Latin America and Africa on a more cooperative
and mature basis.

We have also made progress in our continuing efforts to put U.S.-
Soviet relations on a stable and equitable basis, without generating the
extremes of public euphoria or hostility. Indeed, today we are negotiating
on a wider variety of bilateral issues than probably at any previous time
in U.S.-Soviet relations.

3. We have signed a treaty with Panama and are now seeking its
ratification. We have engaged U.S. prestige and influence in the effort
to obtain fair solutions to southern African problems. We have made
progress in obtaining Israeli and Arab willingness to negotiate on the
three key issues in the Middle Eastern conflict: the nature of peace, the
relation between territorial and security arrangements, and the Palestinian
question. I believe all the parties now realize that the United States is
serious in its desire to promote a comprehensive peace settlement.

4. We have adopted self-imposed restraints on our arms exports through
the obligation to reduce our totals from year to year; we are now engaged
in negotiating self-restraint arrangements with other countries. We have
also succeeded in generating genuine interest in nonproliferation, despite—and perhaps even because of—the friction that this issue initially
produced.

If there is a single common theme to our efforts, it is this: After
World War II our foreign policy, by necessity, was focused primarily on
issues connected with the cold war. This gave it a sharp focus, in some
cases making it easier to mobilize public emotion.

Today we confront a more difficult task, which calls for support based
on reason. We must respond to a wider range of issues—some of which
still involve the cold war—stemming from a complex process of global
change. A concentrated foreign policy must give way to a complex foreign
policy no longer focused on a single, dramatic task such as the defense
of the West. Instead, we must engage ourselves on the distant and
difficult goal of giving shape to a world that has suddenly become
politically awakened and socially restless.

The struggle for the shape of the future thus has strong parallels to
the experience of Western democracies in the last century and a half. It
is that experience that offers a measure of hope for a more rational and
just accommodation on a vastly more complex and larger scale. The

accommodation, which over time can acquire the character of a genuine global community, cannot be blueprinted in advance; and it will only come about through gradual changes both in the outlook and in the objective conditions of mankind. It is our confident belief that liberty and equity can indeed creatively coexist. It is our confident view of the future that democracy—in its many manifestations and with its own multiple stages of development—comes closest to meeting the genuinely felt needs of mankind. It is our confident judgment that our collaboration can enhance the chances that the future destiny of man is to live in a world that is creatively pluralistic.

CHAPTER NINE

■

The Goals of
U.S. Foreign Policy

SINCE THE MARSHALL PLAN IN 1947, there has been a growing recognition that our security depends on more than military power. Although military power is the cornerstone of our security, other kinds of power—economic, social, political, moral—play increasingly crucial roles. That is especially true in the context of a world order that is changing at an accelerating pace. Where U.S. policy has taken this insight as the basis for action—as in Europe and, increasingly, in the developing world—our efforts have met with success. It is a concept of power we ignore at our peril.

The national security of the United States is not only inextricably bound up with the peace of the world. The revolution of rising expectations means that both peace and security depend more and more on the provision of a tolerable quality of life to all the people of the world. In this, the most dynamic era in human history, U.S. national security thus requires the effective and responsible management of change. The world is inexorably changing under the influence of forces no government can wholly control. We seek to manage change skillfully, in ways that meet the legitimate hopes of people for peace, prosperity, justice, and liberty. At the same time, we recognize the fragility of the human institutions conceived to protect these values.

The United States has a special role in helping to manage global change. Our country is not merely an organic projection of the past, it is also a compact with the future. Global change runs deeper and broader today than at any point in human history. That change defies easy definition. For all its complexity, however, its nature can perhaps be

Remarks delivered before the Foreign Policy Association in Washington, D.C., on December 20, 1978.

reduced to two essential themes. First, the world's population is experiencing a political awakening on a scale without precedent. Second, the global system is undergoing a significant redistribution of political and economic power.

These two conditions—of awakening and of redistribution—are the outcome of some very basic transformations that have taken place within our own lifetimes.

Perhaps the most striking change has been demographic. The explosion in population growth has imposed significant strains on the social structure of many parts of the world. Between 1900 and 1950, the world's population grew by 900 million, to a total of 2,500 million people. But between 1950 and the year 2000, by conservative estimates, the world's population will grow by an additional 3,500 million people to a total of some 6,000 million—and four-fifths of them will live in the Third World. Never before in history has there been such massive growth in the number of people, with compounding pressures on social, political, and economic institutions.

As recently as the eve of World War II, colonial empires based in Europe controlled much of the world's landmass and two-thirds of its population. These empires have vanished, giving way to scores of new nation-states. As a result of this political sea change, the total number of nation-states in the world has more than tripled to a total of more than 160. This is the broadest political revolution in the history of mankind.

Economic power, as a consequence, has also become more dispersed. The influence of Western Europe and Japan has grown relative to the United States. The OPEC countries and others, such as Brazil and Mexico, are playing greater roles in the world economy.

In the military sphere, nuclear parity between the two superpowers is complicated by the existence of other nuclear powers. Nuclear proliferation, unless it is averted, poses the spectre of tripling the number of nuclear states in the near future.

All this has been accompanied by an awakening in the political consciousness of mankind. Previously dormant peoples have become active, demanding, assertive. As a result of literacy and modern communications, billions are becoming aware of new ideas and of global inequity. The people of the congested cities of the Third World are increasingly susceptible to political and ideological mobilization. Nationalism is increasingly imbued with ideological content.

In such a context, our national security depends on giving positive direction to this turbulent process of worldwide redistribution of power. We can do this only by seeking to create a stable and cooperative framework. That is why the United States must be actively engaged in world affairs—and this is why the United States to enhance its historical relevance must be committed to positive change. If we create artificial obstacles to change, we will only isolate ourselves—and, eventually, threaten and undermine our national security.

The United States is thus committed to a policy of constructive global engagement, a policy of trying to influence change in directions that are compatible with our interests and values. Under that broad policy, we have crystallized seven fundamental goals for our foreign policy: (1) to enhance military security; (2) to reinforce ties with key allies and promote a more cooperative world system; (3) to respond in a positive way to the economic and moral challenge of the so-called North-South relationship; (4) to improve relations between East and West; (5) to help resolve the more threatening regional conflicts and tensions; (6) to cope with such emerging global issues as nuclear proliferation and arms dissemination; (7) to reassert traditional U.S. values—especially human rights. I will now take these up individually.

1. To be globally effective, the United States must be militarily secure and capable of defending its allies. In Presidential Directive No. 18, issued in the summer of 1977, the president ordered a comprehensive review of the U.S. military posture. At his direction, we will maintain strategic equivalence; strengthen NATO; develop a more rapidly deployable force capable of defending our major interests worldwide (such as, for example, in the Middle East, in the Gulf, or in Korea); maintain an effective military presence both in the Far East and in the Atlantic; and reexamine our strategic assumptions in terms of the changed needs of the 1980s. We need to correct the impending vulnerability of our Minuteman ICBMs by selecting a new ICBM system and adopting a survivable basing mode for it. Less dramatic, but equally important, we will also make improvements in command-and-control arrangements that determine the president's capacity to manage crises and conflicts. Our first purpose remains, as always, to dissuade an opponent from initiating an attack.

We must also be able to prevent regional instability or conflicts from getting out of hand and becoming the causes of a major confrontation. This not only means developing our capacity for projecting military power in measured ways in defense of our vital interests around the world, but making sustained efforts to promote peace based on credible determination to protect our friends.

2. We have sought to reinforce our ties with our allies and build a more cooperative world system. We have maintained and widened our consultation with our allies on every major policy issue, from SALT to the Middle East, from human rights to international economics. The president has participated in three NATO meetings and two economic

summits, and he made the first visit ever by a U.S. president to the headquarters of the European Economic Community. Our intensified emphasis on improving NATO's conventional forces, and our consultations with our allies on the so-called gray areas pertaining to theater nuclear forces, have increased allied confidence. Trilateral cooperation is a reality today. Japan is strongly linked not only to the United States, but to Western Europe as well. We have also widened the scope of our international cooperation to include newly influential states, such as Venezuela, Brazil, Nigeria, Saudi Arabia, Iran, and India.

3. We have striven to improve relations with the developing world. Most Third World countries perceive the United States today as more sympathetic and positive in its attitude. We have made special progress in improving relations with the African countries, which in the past have been suspicious of U.S. motives. In our relations with Latin America, we have abandoned the use of a single slogan to define our policy. Instead, we approach Latin American states in terms of both their individual needs and their wider global developmental concerns. There is a new emphasis on Caribbean development. There is new U.S. support for the ASEAN countries, particularly Indonesia.

We still have a long way to go in fashioning an adequate response to the economic problems inherent in the North-South relationship. Popular and congressional attitudes clearly lag behind the felt need. The United States has not yet set the example that it should. But some progress has been made.

4. We have tried to improve relations between East and West. For the foreseeable future, U.S.-Soviet relations will continue to be characterized both by peaceful competition and, where feasible, cooperation. The SALT negotiations are a particular example of the latter: a mutual effort to reduce the risk of nuclear war and stabilize the U.S.-Soviet strategic relationship. SALT fits into our broader effort to enhance national security, an effort that we pursue not only through improving our own forces but also, where appropriate, through arms control. A decade of SALT negotiations has shown that arms control is the best approach to certain strategic nuclear policy objectives. Another objective—the maintenance of essential equivalence in strategic forces—will be advanced by the agreement now nearing completion.

In this context, we will never constrain through arms control our ability to meet our national security needs. A satisfactory SALT agreement will allow us to maintain the effectiveness of the U.S. strategic arsenal as a deterrent against nuclear war, based on a credible retaliatory capability in the event that such a war should ever break out. It will maintain the stability of the strategic balance between the United States and the Soviet Union, and it will provide for adequate verification.

While encouraged by the progress of these negotiations, we remain guided by the president's statement at Annapolis: "To be stable, to be supported by the American people, and to be the basis for widening the scope of cooperation, détente must be broadly defined and truly reciprocal." This applies not only to bilateral relations but also to the need to exercise restraint in regard to global and regional turbulence. On the basis of such restraint, we truly desire to widen the scope of genuine U.S.-Soviet accommodation.

While seeking U.S.-Soviet détente, we have also attempted to foster greater U.S. ties with Eastern Europe. We do not believe that our relations with Eastern Europe should be subordinate to our relationship with Moscow.

In dealing with a world of change, no development is more significant than the normalization of U.S. relations with China. This one-quarter of mankind is now determined to develop rapidly and to play an active role in world affairs. A strong and secure China can contribute to international stability. For this long-term historical reason—rather than for immediate tactical ends—the president decided to normalize relations with the People's Republic of China, to expand our bilateral ties, and to consult more closely on matters of common strategic concern. Because of the president's historic decision, a new global political reality is now emerging.

5. To resolve threatening regional conflicts, the president has broken new ground. In the Middle East, through a determined, courageous, and occasionally painful effort, he has brought the parties together. The Camp David summit was not only an exercise in political persuasion; it was an act of moral leadership. But momentum generated at Camp David needs to be resumed, pointing the way not only to an Israeli-Egyptian peace treaty but also to the constructive implementation of the critical framework for achieving peace in the West Bank.

Peace between Israel and its Arab neighbors is a prerequisite to stability and orderly social change in the strategically important Middle East. Peace in the region can lead to a new pattern of cooperative relations among all our friends in the area. For this promise to be realized, we must continue to work for a broad peace, in keeping with the Camp David agreement on establishing an elected self-government for a transitional period in the West Bank and Gaza as well as on the Israeli-Egyptian peace treaty.

In southern Africa, we are continuing to seek an accommodation on both the Namibian and Rhodesian issues. Our efforts have gained the appreciation of moderate African leaders, and we will persist in them.

6. We have sought constructive and cooperative solutions to emerging global issues. For the first time, we have established comprehensive and

consistent criteria to govern U.S. nuclear exports. The international fuel-cycle evaluation program has started its work, and eight working groups are now analyzing every phase of the nuclear fuel cycle in the hope of finding constructive alternatives to reprocessing.

We also seek to cope with the problem of conventional arms transfers, both by limiting the introduction of advanced weapons technology to new areas of the world and by reducing sales. The president set a ceiling reduction of 8 percent from fiscal 1977 to fiscal 1978. We have met that ceiling. A similar 8 percent reduction will be in effect for fiscal 1979. We are negotiating with other arms exporters, including the Soviet Union. We hope to establish a common standard for the major sellers of arms, particularly to Third World countries.

7. Our final goal is the reassertion of traditional U.S. values, particularly the advancement of human rights. States, like men, do not live by bread alone. The vulgar interpreters of Marx (or Adam Smith) notwithstanding, political action is not dictated wholly by material selfishness. Politics is founded ultimately on concepts of the good, the just, and even the sacred, and on theories of the future that embody these ideals. This is as true today as it has ever been, possibly more so. Accordingly, the national security policy of the United States seeks to enhance a sense of community with those who share our values. It seeks to encourage respect for the transcendental human aspirations for liberty and for self-definition. The increasing self-assertiveness of mankind on behalf of human rights is a profound historical movement, and the United States would not be true to itself if it were not associated with this yearning.

The effort to make human rights an essential standard of our foreign policy, while not establishing it as a precondition for all ties with other countries, has been difficult and demanding. When our relationship with another government includes economic and military assistance, we are prepared to take tangible steps to recognize good human rights performance or to manifest our concern over human rights violations. Thus, we have made a decision to channel a growing share of our economic assistance to countries that respect the human rights of their people. No nation relishes being identified in the world community as a violator of human rights. This in itself has helped create an atmosphere for human rights progress.

Throughout the remainder of this administration and beyond, the United States will confront both traditional and novel security challenges. But there are two immediate concerns. The first relates to strategic uncertainties. The steady augmentation of Soviet theater nuclear capability, especially in Europe, and the buildup of Soviet conventional and strategic forces cannot be disregarded. Our second immediate concern involves regional instability. An arc of crisis stretches along the shores of the

Indian Ocean, with fragile social and political structures in a region of vital importance to us threatened with fragmentation. The resulting political chaos could well be filled by elements hostile to our values and sympathetic to our adversaries. This could present the West as a whole with a challenge of significant proportions.

We are committed to the shaping of a more cooperative and just world. But this does not mean ignoring concrete national security concerns. The renovation of the international system through wider participation and more cooperation is the proper response to global political awakening, as is the maintenance of allied power and Western will. The United States can play a genuinely creative role in shaping a world community no longer built on the domination of any one bloc or culture—a community that respects global diversity as the basis for a cooperative and increasingly just world order. Such a world of diversity will be in keeping with our values and thus with the security of our nation.

CHAPTER TEN

■

President Carter's
Human Rights Policy

THREE BASIC PROPOSITIONS underlie this administration's commitment to its human rights policy. First, human rights represent the genuine, historical inevitability of our times. Second, human rights are a central facet of U.S. influence in a changing world. Third, there has been progress in the effort to enhance the human condition insofar as human rights are concerned.

In noting human rights as the genuine, historical inevitability of our times, I chose those words very deliberately. We live in an age very much influenced by concepts of historical inevitability. The Marxist idea of a linear historical progression toward a doctrinally defined world revolution has had a powerful impact on global consciousness. Yet, events increasingly are proving this idea wrong. The notion of world revolution is too simplistic a concept for a world as diverse and as pluralistic as ours. It could only have been born in the narrow confines of a nineteenth-century Europe undergoing the early pangs of the industrial revolution. From that narrow environment, it was generalized in terms of universal relevance.

Today, the world is witnessing the increasing self-assertiveness of man, the increasing political awakening of man, and as a result the increasing assertion of the diversity of man. Thus, the vision of the world reaching a stage of uniform sociopolitical organization through a common revolutionary experience is becoming increasingly unreal. Indeed, many of the difficulties that beset interstate relations within the Communist world result from the fundamental error of the basic historical assumption of communism.

Remarks delivered at the White House Commemoration of the thirtieth anniversary of the Universal Declaration of Human Rights, on December 6, 1978.

But what has become evident is that as man or mankind abandons his centuries-long lethargy, he begins to seek actively a meaningful and a just definition of the proper relationship between man and society and between society and government. This is an issue as old as political philosophy, but an esoteric one of interest only to a few for much of the political history of humanity. Only in our age—indeed, in our own life span—has this issue dramatically surfaced on a global scale.

This fundamental question has arisen from a confluence of several factors. The two world wars were tremendous catalysts for this political awakening. The spread of literacy and education has awakened the political consciousness of men and women. The creation of new nations in the developing world has given more meaningful political expression to the quest for individual expression. The cumulative impact of these factors has been to make human rights the most central item on the global agenda.

I recognize that the term *human rights* will have various meanings and connotations in a world as culturally diverse as ours. Yet there is a common theme to the aspirations and the yearnings of people, whether in Latin America, in southern Africa, in the Middle East, in Eastern Europe and the Soviet Union, or in the Far East. In the recent effervescence of political expression in the central square in Peking—at the so-called Democracy Wall—one of the resounding cries was for socialist democracy, for freedom of expression, for a definition of the proper relationship between man, society, and government—in effect for human rights.

This is the wave of the present. The quest for human rights is the central form in which mankind is expressing its political awakening. It is vitally important to recognize the centrality of the search for human rights. Moreover, it is crucially important to be identified with this genuine historical inevitability of our time.

Human rights are a central facet of U.S. influence in a changing world. This country began as a small group of thirteen colonies on the eastern seaboard of the American continent isolated by several weeks' traveling time—by more time than it takes today to get to the moon. But it had one thing in common with another small sector of humanity, the people in Western Europe. In both places, there was an idea percolating in the intellectual world—the idea of personal liberty. It was a fundamentally new idea and an increasingly important and powerful idea. What made the United States unique was that it was the first country ever to come together consciously and shape itself around a central philosophical idea, the idea of independence and freedom for all.

We did not fulfill that idea by achieving our independence and by signing the Bill of Rights. Far from it. The next two hundred years of our history has been an unending quest to make that idea a reality. The

United States sought that end through the struggles for suffrage, through the extension of civil rights, through the breaking of racial barriers, through the elimination of inequality between the sexes, through the increase of political participation by hitherto excluded groups such as trade unions. And the struggle goes on.

The point is that we created a political framework in our society that was congenial to this struggle and that legitimized it. This is the genius of the historical success of the United States. It is also the key to U.S. influence in the world today. We are not just a geographical entity. We do not have, as other nations do, an organic past that we all share. We are instead united by a compact with the future, and it brings us together because we share certain common ideals. This is what ultimately makes us Americans. We are Americans not because we share a past, but because we share a future. We share a future that is associated with certain fundamental philosophical assumptions about the nature of man, and about the proper relationship between man, society, and government.

Today, these ideas carry near-universal appeal. It is therefore just and right to carry high the standard of human rights. It is also well grounded historically and useful politically for the United States to put itself in the forefront of a powerful movement that has worldwide appeal. In doing so we redeem our own essence. We rededicate ourselves to our inner purpose as Americans when we commit ourselves to this end. We also greatly enhance the appeal of our country worldwide.

U.S. foreign policy depends not only on material wealth or financial power—though the importance of both should not be underestimated— but also on spiritual attraction. That attraction, unfortunately, has waned in recent years. President Carter has sought to revitalize the spiritual element of U.S. influence in the world.

His human rights policy has already contributed to overcoming the crisis of the spirit in this society. That crisis stemmed from fundamental divisions about proper courses of action, but was also associated with profound moral and philosophical differences. These generated a sense of pessimism and moral unease. President Carter has accomplished much to overcome this spiritual crisis. We face enormous dilemmas in world affairs, and each day compounds the difficulties. Yet this country approaches them with a renewed sense of historical optimism. That is terribly important. This new confidence has to be differentiated from self-righteousness. There are a great many things wrong with this society. But in spite of these problems, which we seek to correct within the framework of the Constitution, we are associated with a basic yearning. That is a tremendous political asset. In the context of a politically awakening world, a world seeking readjustments in the political and economic distribution of power, to be concerned with human rights is to be concerned with a central human concern and human aspiration. That is a very powerful political combination.

*   *   *

On the practical level we have made progress in the area of human rights. First, we have succeeded in organizing this government to be more sensitive to this issue. It ensures that human rights concerns are considered in the shaping of our foreign policies.

Second, we have tried to increase global awareness of the importance of human rights, particularly among governments that have to deal with us. There is today not a government in the world that does not know that its human rights record will affect its relationship with us. I want to stress that I use these words advisedly: Their behavior will affect, not determine, our relationship. We have to be cognizant of the fact that there are other considerations involved in dealing with other governments, such as regional interests, specific bilateral interests, and security concerns, that may require close and cooperative relations, even if a government is unresponsive on the question of human rights. At the same time, no government can today afford the luxury of believing that we do not care about human rights or that our bilateral relations are entirely immune to the consequences of an indifference to human rights. Thus, in a practical sense, we have made human rights a genuinely important issue on the global agenda.

I have been struck in traveling with the president to different parts of the world by the extent to which even leaders initially skeptical about our policy have increasingly identified themselves with the issue of human rights. These leaders have in most cases genuinely addressed themselves to the question. While some leaders have been hypocritical, even hypocrisy is a bow to virtue. The fact they felt compelled to acknowledge the legitimacy of the idea of human rights is not without significance.

Third, we have seen some tangible progress in the human condition. There are several ways to assess that progress. Various independent groups from time to time evaluate the status of human rights around the world, and by collating some of these reports, we do see progress. That is not simply a result of our efforts. It stems principally from the increasing relevance of the idea of human rights, which we have helped to stimulate. While measurement is difficult, I would estimate that in at least forty countries around the world—in which 2.5 billion people live—there has been tangible progress. In some cases, there has been more progress than in others; in some countries, there certainly has not been enough progress. This positive change has expressed itself in greater respect for human rights, in less oppression of political opposition, in the release of victims of repression, or in a more sensitive attitude toward established legal procedures.

We can be proud of this progress, though we should not take credit for it. We are part of the process. We live in a time that is often short of hope. The rise of human rights as an issue is one of the more important, reassuring developments. It tells us something about what a human being is. It tells us that ultimately the human being, regardless of the social, economic, or cultural conditions, yearns for something transcendent, for some self-definition of his uniqueness, for something that dignifies him as a spiritual being. If this represents the future of the human condition, it ought to be a source of tremendous pride and reassurance to us as Americans.

PART FOUR

■

Defense and
Arms Control

As national security adviser, Dr. Brzezinski was both the author of the presidential directive—PD-59—that reoriented U.S. nuclear strategy away from the doctrine of mutual assured destruction and one of the key presidential advisers during the negotiation of SALT II. In these essays and speeches, he addresses the relationship between U.S. defense policies and superpower arms control.

Dr. Brzezinski has often observed that "arms control is part of our national defense policy, not a substitute for it." In the first speech that follows, delivered during the Carter administration, Dr. Brzezinski defended the SALT II agreement against its critics and explained how the accord fit into overall U.S. defense planning. After the failure of the Carter administration to win ratification of SALT II in the Senate, both arms control and the strategy of nuclear deterrence fell into disrepute with substantial segments of the U.S. public. In the subsequent entries, Dr. Brzezinski analyzes both these perspectives.

On the one hand, many Americans came to see the idea of arms control as a spent force and to believe that agreements per se ran against U.S. interests. In the second entry, Dr. Brzezinski argued that while the rapid evolution in strategic weapons technology would perhaps create insurmountable obstacles to concluding a comprehensive and verifiable arms-control agreement, arms control could serve a useful strategic purpose if directed toward limiting the weapons on both sides that were accurate and powerful enough to be used in a first-strike attack against strategic targets. While the Reagan administration has recently devoted great effort toward concluding a new comprehensive arms-control agreement, ratification in the Senate will hinge largely on whether its verification provisions can cope with emerging strategic technologies and

111

can reduce the vulnerability of U.S. strategic forces to Soviet first-strike weapons.

On the other hand, other Americans came to see the strategy of nuclear deterrence as immoral. In this section's final two entries, Dr. Brzezinski addresses the strategic implications of the biblical commandment "Thou shalt not kill" and criticizes those who issue a utopian call for the creating of a world without nuclear weapons. He argues that nuclear weapons, as part of human reality and consciousness, cannot be eliminated but that U.S. strategic policy must be informed by moral considerations in order, not only to be acceptable as a policy to the people of the United States, but also to be credible as a military deterrent to the adversary. Moreover, he concludes that deploying a limited defense of U.S. strategic forces would be both morally desirable and strategically stabilizing.

CHAPTER ELEVEN

———————— ■ ————————

SALT and National Security

ON SEPTEMBER 26, 1979, FORMER PRESIDENT FORD delivered an address detailing his view on the SALT II Treaty and U.S. defense policies. In essence, President Ford says that SALT II is a good treaty and that he does not raise major objections to it. He did make some criticisms. There were two surprising things about these reservations. First, the foundation for this agreement was negotiated during the Ford administration. Second, an issue-by-issue comparison between the SALT II Treaty and the last SALT proposal of the Ford administration shows that on essentially every issue the outcome in the SALT II treaty is on the same track or better than the last proposal of the Ford administration. This significant fact underlines the firmness with which the Carter administration negotiated the SALT II Treaty.

I would now like to take up Mr. Ford's criticisms point by point.

• Mr. Ford is particularly critical of the treaty's protocol and its limits on ground and sea-launched cruise missiles. But the concept of such a protocol originated in the Ford administration and was embodied in the last proposal submitted to the Soviets in 1976.

• Mr. Ford criticizes the SALT II limits on new types of ICBMs. But this is an important restraint on Soviet missile programs. The Ford adminstration failed to propose any such limits.

• Mr. Ford takes issue with the way SALT II limits new missiles. The agreement permits only one new type of ICBM, with a new type defined on the basis of a family of several missile parameters, such as size, all of which we can adequately verify. In addition, some modernization of existing types of ICBMs is permitted, if changes do not exceed 5 percent,

Remarks delivered before the School of International Affairs Alumni Association in Washington, D.C., on September 27, 1979.

plus or minus, in terms of these parameters. Mr. Ford criticizes the 5 percent tolerances as "too narrow" to permit adequate verification. This is a perplexing position. The most important and difficult to monitor of the parameters—throw weight and launch weight—are included in the SALT II ceilings on light and heavy ICBMs. These were negotiated in the Ford administration. One cannot claim that a 5 percent tolerance is too narrow when one's own proposals called for zero tolerance on increases in the throw weight and launch weight of the SS-19 and SS-18.

The Carter administration introduced these important limits on new types of ICBMs because new systems were the major source of the Soviet buildup under SALT I. Moreover, it introduced important warhead limits on ICBMs and other ballistic missiles. In contrast, under the last Ford proposal, the Soviets could have deployed both unlimited numbers of new types of ICBMs and unlimited warhead levels.

• Mr. Ford criticizes the SALT II language on the issue of telemetry encryption. But his administration did not even raise this issue with the Soviet Union. We believe that the present resolution of this issue is satisfactory. The Soviets acknowledge that telemetry is relevant to verification and agree that the encryption of telemetry relevant to verification is banned.

Others have attacked the SALT II Treaty for different reasons. There is the issue of the Soviet advantage in modern, heavy ICBMs. The previous administration tried to erase that advantage and could not. We tried to change it. When the Soviets resisted on the grounds that these terms had been agreed to at Vladivostok by the Ford administration, we significantly decreased its importance by limiting heavy ICBMs to ten warheads, the same number permitted on the MX, and by banning new types of heavy ICBMs. Thus, the Soviets could not exploit the potential for placing twenty to thirty warheads on these missiles, as would have been allowed under the Ford SALT proposals. We also obtained a ban on heavy mobiles.

There is also the Backfire bomber issue. It is acceptable for Backfire not to be counted as a strategic system limited by SALT II—in the context of a production freeze on the Backfire and assurances that Moscow will not upgrade the aircraft for intercontinental missions. In fact, while the last Ford administration proposal would have frozen the Backfire bomber production rate only for the shorter period of the treaty protocol, we have frozen it for the entire period of the treaty.

We took a sound framework, developed during President Ford's administration, and expanded its scope in a number of important ways, plugged the gaps, and then negotiated the details with the Soviets in a firm and steady fashion. The outcome injects much-needed predictability and rules into the strategic competition and establishes a solid foundation for the building of future, more comprehensive agreements.

President Ford is a strong supporter of the SALT process. "We should," he says, "firmly reassert our commitment to the SALT process." This we have done, in a manner that unmistakably enhances our security. SALT is a critical issue—too critical to become embroiled in partisan politics, Republican or Democratic. SALT should be decided on its merits.

Without SALT, we could be entering an era of unpredictability and instability. Strategic arms competition would be heightened. We would be less secure in the knowledge of whether we are spending enough for our defenses. Failure to ratify SALT will also have a negative impact on our international position. Besides being unnecessarily expensive, a new arms race in the absence of SALT would mean less stability and more uncertainty about the direction of Soviet strategic planning. It would mean more nuclear weapons in the world. A new arms race in the absence of SALT II would unnecessarily hinder the president's commitment to bolster our military forces and strengthen NATO. Without SALT, our defense policy will lack a framework, and the work of a decade will be forfeited.

We should not confuse SALT's importance with the debate on our defense policy. SALT is the framework for stability and predictability in our defense posture.

From the beginning of this administration we have recognized that the Soviet Union has been steadily increasing its efforts to improve its military capabilities. Such Soviet actions are, in fact, the basis for our original decision to increase, together with our allies, overall defense spending by 3 percent each year in real terms. While our critics say they would have been for strong defense if they had remained in office, defense spending in constant dollars declined in seven of the eight years of the Nixon-Ford administration. For the past decade, there has been a steady decline in the level of the defense budget in real terms. We began to reverse that trend in the first three budgets of the Carter administration, and President Carter is the first president since World War II to succeed in raising defense spending for three straight years in peacetime.

Our security is also built around the efforts of a coalition of nations including our NATO allies. The president has placed great emphasis on leading our allies toward increased defense efforts that will improve our collective security. We are moving toward agreement on a major modernization effort for long-range, theater nuclear forces. Moreover, the allies are following our lead toward increased defense spending.

We must choose our defense priorities rationally. Given the limits on our resources and the hardships imposed on the U.S. people by inflation, we should spend our defense dollars on carefully chosen programs that provide real defense capability. The United States is not rich enough to simply throw money at unrealistic solutions to those problems.

• Would it have been realistic or wise to buy the B-1 bomber despite the fact that it would be unable to perform its mission effectively long before it had reached the end of its service life? The answer is no. The cruise missile is the best near-term means of modernizing our strategic bomber forces. Current and future generations of cruise missiles will cause enormous problems for Soviet air defense for many years to come. This decision, however, does not foreclose a future for the penetrating bomber. Studies are now underway in the Defense Department to identify possible replacements for the B-52. If a penetrating bomber is needed to preserve our security, one will be built.

• Would it have been wise to commit the country to a major and expensive program for modernizing our ICBM force before a workable solution had been identified? Again, clearly not. The basic problem is the improving Soviet capability to destroy our silo-based missiles. We needed to find a replacement system that meets our defense needs while not undercutting the future of SALT. Several administrations struggled unsuccessfully with this problem. This administration found a solution with the MX system based in the racetrack mode. It will contribute to the ability of our strategic forces to survive an attack. It will set a standard for the verifiability of mobile ICBM systems on both sides. It minimizes any adverse impact on the environment. It can be deployed at reasonable cost. It is consistent with existing SALT agreements and with our SALT III goal of negotiating significant mutual reductions in strategic forces.

• Would it be wise simply to increase spending across all categories of U.S. military capabilities—or should we instead place the greatest emphasis where we see the greatest problems? The Carter administration has emphasized defense improvements through discriminate spending increases.

In strategic forces, we are beginning full-scale development of the MX in 1980. It will be fully operational in 1989. We are beginning deployment of Trident missiles in our Poseidon submarines. We are also considering construction of a new class of ballistic missile submarines starting in 1984. Finally, we are modernizing our bomber forces with long-range cruise missiles and will have our first full squadron equipped with air-launched cruise missiles by 1983.

We have also placed strong emphasis on arresting the adverse trends in the NATO–Warsaw Pact balance. While President Ford says we are falling behind in conventional force capability, our projections show that the Warsaw Pact conventional force advantage in numbers will not change much through 1985. This is the result of our current efforts to improve this balance.

Our efforts include a 33 percent increase in the number of artillery pieces in Europe, improvement of anti-tank capabilities by deployment of 10 helicopter companies of TOW-equipped COBRA gunships, and deployment of increased numbers of various other anti-tank weapons. We are also increasing our tactical air force to 26 wings and modernizing these forces with the purchase of over 2,900 new aircraft. In addition, we are increasing the effectiveness of these forces with a joint European purchase and operation of the Airborne Warning and Control System aircraft. We estimate AWACS can increase our tactical air forces effectiveness by as much as a factor of five. We are proceeding with the production of the XM-1 tank and deploying A-10s and F-16s in Europe right now. Finally, we are prepositioning additional supplies and equipment in Europe, which will allow us to move 10 divisions to Europe within two weeks' notice, thus doubling the early combat capability we can bring to bear, compared to our capabilities in 1977.

While we are placing emphasis on improved NATO and strategic forces, this in no way means we are ignoring other areas. The president plans a 35 percent increase in shipbulding funding for 1980. We are also making improvements in our ability to rapidly deploy forces to troubled areas outside of NATO. This is primarily a matter of buying the transportation needed to move our forces quickly and thus involves the procurement of advanced tanker cargo aircraft and the improvement of our current fleet of cargo-carrying aircraft.

In sum, we have recognized the need to expand our capabilities to match the Soviets' military efforts. We have taken the initiative in leading the coalition of nations upon which our collective security depends toward greater and more efficient overall defense efforts. We have developed a strong and rational defense program of our own—a program aimed at making the best use of our resources.

Senator Sam Nunn said in a recent speech that our defense problems did not develop in one or two years and will not be cured in one or two years. I agree fully. Our defense problems will be solved with sober decisions taken in the course of building our defense budgets year by year—decisions taken in the light of the latest and best information on how the trends are actually evolving, not on guesses made years before. If the 3 percent real growth increases prove insufficient, the president has given assurances he will do more.

The SALT Treaty is a product of the efforts of our last two presidents and their administrations. They have passed the baton to us, and we have negotiated the present treaty. As we go on, we must be mature enough to do more for our defense; we must compete effectively with the Soviet Union; and we must pursue arms-control agreements, like SALT II, which are in our national interest. We must be mature enough to meet all these challenges at the same time. *That* is the test of our leadership.

CHAPTER TWELVE

■

From Arms Control
to Controlled Security

THE PROSPECTS FOR A comprehensive and complex U.S.-Soviet arms control agreement, building on the foundations laid by SALT I and SALT II, are increasingly slim. Indeed, it is quite possible that arms control as we have known it has come to the end of the road. Once the great hope of those who believed that the U.S.-Soviet rivalry could be limited by joint agreement—with some even seeing in arms control the catalyst for a genuinely friendly American-Soviet relationship—comprehensive arms control is likely to be the victim of the current Soviet leadership and the dynamics of the technological revolution.

The present Soviet leadership, headed by Yuri Andropov, recently has done something quite remarkable in the history of the U.S.-Soviet competition. It has publicly postulated that there will be no arms control talks unless the U.S. is prepared to accept a public humiliation and a political defeat: the dismantling of the relatively few Pershing IIs and cruise missiles so far deployed in Western Europe as a response to the hundreds of SS-20s deployed by the Soviet Union over the past several years. In effect, the Soviet Union has made arms control a hostage to the attainment of a truly major geopolitical objective: the severance of the U.S.-European security connection.

The Soviet demand is thus unacceptable. Even the accommodationists who today dominate the discourse over foreign affairs within a segment of the American body politic reject the Soviet demand. The Reagan administration enjoys widespread backing here and in Europe in refusing to capitulate. The Soviets have thus backed themselves into a no-win situation, an act of unprecedented diplomatic stupidity.

This chapter appeared in *The Wall Street Journal*, July 10, 1984. Reprinted by permission.

In order to extricate themselves, they have lately proposed separate negotiations in Vienna on an anti-satellite weapons agreement. President Reagan was wise in responding affirmatively to the proposal for negotiations, but he is equally wise in anticipating no real progress in them. The primary victim of this situation is arms control—not in its unrealistic utopian version but as a modest and practical way of somewhat controlling the spiral of defense spending and weapons accumulation on both sides. The Soviet refusal to negotiate simply means precious time is being lost, and as a result it will be even more difficult in the future to reach a truly ambitious and comprehensive agreement, a better version of SALT II.

Political paralysis in the negotiations is being outpaced by the dynamics of the weapons revolution. The simple fact is that both the U.S. and the Soviet Union are rapidly moving—while the arms-control negotiations remain stalemated—to acquire increasingly sophisticated weapons systems, making existing ICBMs anachronistic. As pointed out in a recent study in the *Naval War College Review* by James Westwood:

> The 1980s is a time of rapid transition and readjustments to technological changes in missilery. On the horizon are stealth-type bombers launching stealth cruise missiles (ACLM) and precision-guided munitions (PGMs), further obviating the role of ICBMs. Scientific and technological achievements in guidance, navigation, aerodynamics, electronic circuitry and componentry, and in warhead yields-per-warhead-weight appear to be leading rapidly to a downturn, perhaps to an eventual demise of the once-ascendant and now dominant ICBMs of the period 1960 to 1985. This trend holds both in the United States and in the U.S.S.R.

Highly mobile and extraordinarily precise delivery systems are coming into being and are beginning to be deployed. By way of example, the CEP (circular error probabilities) of a Soviet SS-19 has been approximately 1,200 feet; that of a Minuteman III, 700 feet; of an MX, 450 feet; and of Pershing 2, with terminal guidance, about 100 feet. The latest Soviet missiles also involve similarly impressive operational improvement.

It will be increasingly difficult to impose effective and verifiable limits on these weapons. The verification problem is becoming increasingly acute, given the mobility of the new systems and the opportunities for rapid reloading and covert deployment. The question of how to control qualitative improvements plagued SALT II negotiators and, at best, only a partially satisfactory response was developed. Their difficulties pale in comparison to the complexities posed by the emerging new systems. Adequate verification of both qualitative and quantitative limits would require access to storage facilities and even perhaps to production centers.

As a consequence, it is realistic to conclude that for both political and technical reasons, the chances of a truly comprehensive agreement, which can be reliably verified, are rapidly fading.

In that context, we are likely to see renewed attraction to war planners of a first strike scenario. Since the mid-1950s, acquisition by the Soviets of a respectable nuclear capability meant that a first strike—inherently messy and unpredictable in its consequences—was until recently not an attractive option for either side. A messy attack with large and relatively inaccurate warheads (the only kind possible) would still precipitate an almost equally messy counterattack. But with the deployment of extraordinarily accurate systems, a first strike designed to paralyze the opponent's capacity to respond through the preemptive destruction of most of its forces and through the decapitation of its command structure can again become a viable planning option. From an offensive point of view, a sudden attack by highly precise and very numerous nuclear weapons is more profitable than an exchange resulting from a political crisis prompting both sides to gear their forces to maximum alert.

In the years ahead, one can envisage several ways in which nuclear weapons might be used in anger and by deliberation. Four basic variants summarize the range of possibilities: (1) a massive surprise attack; (2) a crisis escalation; (3) a contagion from non-superpower conflicts; (4) a terrorist attack. Of those, in the years ahead probably the fourth is the most likely since it involves a relatively simple operation, and it can be undertaken by a limited group of individuals with little concern for society and motivated by their own peculiar brand of rationality.

But while the employment of a nuclear device in a terrorist attack may be the most likely, for the U.S. a surprise attack poses the greatest danger. It could in one stroke create circumstances beyond our capacity to foresee either its social or historical consequences. Of course such a sudden-attack scenario remains unlikely, but one can disregard it entirely only at the greatest peril. Given the relative openness of American society, the precise location of key U.S. assets can be much more easily ascertained and effectively targeted than those of the Soviets. That makes the U.S. more vulnerable to such a strike, and it would be escapist to assume that Soviet planners would choose to ignore such an option altogether.

Moreover, a bolt out of the blue could create such initial disbelief among the U.S. decisionmakers that they would be unable to make a prompt response. Even without a special Soviet effort to disrupt or destroy U.S. decisionmakers, a sudden massive attack would put the American leaders under extraordinary psychological pressure, capable of inducing erratic behavior and hesitation. One can hardly imagine how utterly dumbfounding would be the situation in which the president would find himself awakened in the middle of some night, confronted with a life-and-death decision tree (as based on public sources).

Time (minutes)

0	Massive attack launched.
1	SLBMs detected.
2	ICBMs detected.
4–6	Confirmation of attack; uncertainty over scale; U.S. decision process begins.
6–10	First SLBMs detonate in High Altitude EMP attack; SAC launched preemptively; confirmation of scale of attack; final U.S. decision process.
10–12	U.S. decision needed: ride out or respond; first SLBMs detonate over U.S. SLBM bases and National Command Authority.
12–14	Final window for initiating response; launch under attack.
16–20	Delta SLBMs launched from home ports hit SAC.
20–30	ICBM attack initiates possible X-ray pin-down and begins impact on targets.

How in these circumstances would the president perform? How effective would be the chain of command? How rational would be the choices made in response to initially unbelievable information? Could incoming information regarding the nature of the attack be rationally related to the needed response? We are dealing here with truly sensitive and disturbing operational as well as psychological questions.

The advent of increasingly numerous and accurate systems is making it possible for planners of a strategic attack to envisage a first strike that leaves the opponent strategically crippled, capable of only a spasmodic, disorganized and strategically aimless response—or none at all. Given the stakes, this still does not make a first strike attractive from a moral or even political point of view, but the fact is that the military attractiveness of this option is gradually increasing again.

Accordingly, with the stalemate in arms control, the enhanced capacity of strategic offense must be offset—and it is likely to be offset by greater reliance on the part of both sides on defensive strategic systems. The *Times* of London put it correctly when it stated editorially on June 13:

The Soviet Union is now naturally worried about the consequences of a burst in American spending on missile defense. It casts doubt on Soviet plans for offensive systems since the possibility of any missile defense—even an incomplete one—would radically alter the cost calculation of offensive systems. In the long run a defensive program would enhance arms control by reducing the potential gains from building offensive weapons. . . . It is ironic and paradoxical that the age of deterrence has so confused the strategic mentality of many commentators that their reaction to a purely defensive system is to suggest that it increases danger.

The fact is that strategic defense has become feasible not in the sense that it can safeguard society but because it can increasingly complicate the planning and execution of an effective first strike. In other words, strategic defense can somewhat negate the offensive advantages of increasingly sophisticated first-strike systems, restoring the element of deterrence simply by creating again greater uncertainty as to the consequences of first strike.

For the U.S., it is an especially attractive option for it permits us to exploit the advantages of high technology, an area of U.S. superiority. This provides us with genuine potential for offsetting the military advantages gained in recent years by the Soviet Union, and would put pressure on the Soviet Union, to return to serious arms control negotiations.

But even with such negotiations, the development of some defensive strategic capability will remain desirable. It is often said that an imbalance might arise when one side sees the other side acquiring a relatively invulnerable shield while itself remaining vulnerable. Preemption might therefore become tempting. In fact, that is not likely to happen. The acquisition of a defensive strategic capability is not like purchasing an umbrella, which one can unfold against the rain upon leaving the store. It is bound to be a protracted trial-and-error piecemeal process, with both sides experimenting, deploying partially, and adjusting their capabilities. Neither one, at any point in the next 15 to 20 years, will feel it is truly invulnerable to the other side, even though over time the respective vulnerability of each side to a first strike by the other will gradually decline.

Through such a process, a measure of reciprocal stability will be acquired and security of both sides will gradually be enhanced (though the process will not yield the kind of restraint in defense expenditures that many have associated with the hoped-for arms control). But the time has come to lay to rest the expectation that arms control is the secret key to a more amicable American-Soviet relationship or even to the enhancement of mutual security. The maintenance of such security will remain an ambiguous and protracted process requiring unilateral actions by both sides, and increasingly so in the area of strategic defense.

CHAPTER THIRTEEN

■

The Strategic Implications of "Thou Shalt Not Kill"

IT IS AN HONOR TO SPEAK at a forum dedicated to the memory of a theologian, John Courtney Murray, who reflected seriously on the subtle interrelationship between morality and rationality in a complex world. It is in that intellectual context that I wish to address a question central to our national security and even to human survival: the inter-relationship between nuclear strategy and moral concerns. In so doing, we must face up to the intrinsic complexities of formulating strategy in the nuclear age and also to the reality of evil in the human condition. Any discussion that skirts either of the foregoing becomes truly irrelevant.

But before plunging into this admittedly perplexing subject, I wish to make two preliminary points germane to my case. The first pertains to myself and the second to our historical context. In other words, they bear on both the subjective and the objective considerations that affect my message.

First, I speak not as a theologian but as a geostrategist of sorts—that is, a person who is concerned with the exercise of power among competing states in a world in which power still tends to be decisive for historically significant outcomes. But at the same time I do not wish to imply that I am a morally neutral person—a moral eunuch, so to speak—because I do believe that values are involved in the interaction of states and in the exercise of political power. I believe, moreover, that there are states and ideologies that are morally superior—even if admittedly imperfect—to other states and ideologies. Hence, moral choices are involved in the interplay of states, and historical outcomes are infused

Remarks delivered to the John Courtney Murray Forum in New York City, on May 1, 1986. A different version appeared in *America,* May 31, 1986. Reprinted, with slight changes, by permission.

with moral consequences. Outcomes in the interplay of power are not morally neutral. Finally, I believe that moral choices should also affect the means used in international competition, including even the exercise of force. Our use of force should be influenced, to the extent possible, by moral considerations.

Morality requires means proportional to the ends, but also means capable of achieving these ends. I fully accept a statement made some months ago by a colleague of yours, the Reverend Alexander Webster. He said that "an ostensibly ethical policy that is in fact impractical and that cannot achieve its stated end is, in traditional Thomistic moral theology, immoral. One cannot logically or morally will an end and not will the necessary means to that end."

This brings me to a further confessional point: I am not a pacifist. I believe that pacifism would dictate the victory of evil in our world and that to think otherwise is escapist. I cannot improve here on Pope John Paul II's statement on World Day of Peace in 1981:

> For Christians know that in this world a totally and permanently peaceful human society is unfortunately a utopia, and that ideologies which hold up that prospect as easily attainable are based on hopes that cannot be realized, whatever the reason behind them. It is a question of a mistaken view of the human condition, a lack of application in considering the question as a whole; or in still other cases a matter of calculated self-interest. Christians are convinced, if only because they have learned from personal experience, that these deceptive hopes lead straight to the false peace of totalitarian regimes.

The practice of pacifism in our historical age would mean that Auschwitz would have become, not a monument to an evil past, but our reigning reality. The Gulag, too, would define our contemporary human existence.

The second preliminary point pertains to our historical context. Here, too, morality and practicality intersect. We have to face the fact, painful though it may be, that we cannot get rid of nuclear weapons. These weapons are part of our consciousness, of our knowledge, of our memory. They are an integral and organic part of our living reality. There is no way we can get rid of them without getting rid of ourselves. Even if all nuclear weapons were totally dismantled, a war between states that possess the knowledge of how to construct them would see these weapons resurrected and used in order to avert defeat. Nuclear weapons are here to stay.

We should also recognize that nuclear weapons have certainly contributed to an unprecedented degree of restraint in the intense, conflictual rivalry between the United States and the Soviet Union. In any other age, these powers would have come into direct conflict many times in the course of the last four decades. The existence of nuclear weapons has made both sides more prudent, more restrained. Eliminating nuclear weaponry without resolving the political conflicts that pit the United States and the Soviet Union against each other would simply remove a major restraint on their conduct. It would make conventional war between them more likely, and eventually in the context of a conventional war would precipitate the redevelopment and actual employment of nuclear weaponry.

If the reality of nuclear weaponry is unavoidable, and if we wish to be neither "red nor dead," we must maintain some form of credible deterrence as a restraint on conflict—that is, as a means to avoid war without a political capitulation. But for deterrence to be credible to the adversary, we must adopt a posture that makes our determination to use nuclear weapons persuasive. In other words, we must not adopt a strategy for the employment of nuclear weapons that raises doubts about our ability and willingness to follow through if somehow, somewhere, someday deterrence fails.

Deterrence, however, is not entirely devoid of moral content. Because deterrence involves the exercise of power in a world in which evil is a reality, it cannot be shaped in terms of abstract morality alone. It should certainly not be determined by posturing moralism. I do not wish to inject a note of denominational hostility by noting that the recent statement by the Methodist bishops struck me as precisely the kind of posturing that needs to be avoided. But at the same time, as John Courtney Murray has argued, morally sensitive reasoning on this subject is necessary. It can help us define a response that is strategically viable and not morally abhorrent.

With these considerations in mind, I would like to turn to the issue at hand. The categorical injunction "Thou shalt not kill" represents a moral imperative for individuals. However, for states it has to be observed in the context of the doctrine of the just war. That doctrine justifies, under certain conditions, the use of violence, but does not sanction any kind of violence. In this context, "Thou shalt not kill" means thou shalt not kill mindlessly, indiscriminately, vindictively, or needlessly. These requirements are particularly relevant in the nuclear age, since it has become feasible to kill mindlessly an entire society, without discriminating between combatants and noncombatants, either out of vengeance or because of crude, mechanistic military inflexibility.

*   *   *

The strategic issues our country needs to address in order to maintain its national security in the 1980s and 1990s are best examined in terms of three central questions:

1. What will it take to maintain stable strategic deterrence—that is, to prevent war or political intimidation through the use of force?
2. What will it take for the United States to be able to engage in stable crisis bargaining—that is, to prevent war and yet avoid political defeat in the event of an international crisis?
3. What will be the requirements in terms of strategic doctrine and strategic deployments of the politically effective and morally sensitive management of a nuclear war—that is, a war that is not an automatically suicidal conflict, thus preserving some basic options even in the context of initial hostilities?

To answer these questions appropriately, we must answer the last question first. Only by determining what requirements would have to be met to manage a war effectively can we provide a meaningful answer to the question regarding the requirements of stable crisis bargaining. If we could not manage a war effectively or could not bargain stably, we would have either to preempt or concede in the event of a major crisis. Moreover, only if we have answered the questions regarding the requirements both of managing the war and of stable crisis bargaining can we meet the requirements for maintaining a sufficient and stable deterrent that preserves the peace and avoids conflict.

Bearing these difficult questions in mind, we must examine the likely strategic context of the next decade. Until recently, nuclear weapons were essentially blunt instruments of mass destruction. They could be used to inflict massive devastation, either through a sudden surprise attack or in a retaliatory response. In the 1950s, only the United States could inflict massive damage on the Soviet Union, though more recently each has the capability to destroy the other.

Yet, in recent years, the technological capabilities of nuclear weapons have altered this picture significantly: Nuclear weapons have now become instruments capable of being employed in a preemptive first strike designed not so much to destroy the opponent's society as a whole but to eliminate the opponent's strategic forces. The result of a successful first strike would be to render the victim defenseless. The aggressor could then compel his adversary to capitulate without precipitating a counterstrike that would result in mutual suicide.

Two developments have created this potential risk. The first is the revolution in the accuracy of intercontinental ballistic missiles. This is measured by what is called the "circular error probability," or CEP. The CEP of a missile is the radius within which warheads targeted at a certain point will actually land. Each new generation of missiles has had a smaller CEP. In other words, each generation of missiles has been far more accurate than its antecedent. The Soviet SS-19 has a CEP of 1,200 feet, and the SS-18, which is a newer missile, has one of 850 feet. The U.S. Minuteman III, which is our principal land-based ICBM, can land a warhead within 700 feet of its target; the MX can do so within 300 feet; and the medium-range Pershing II, with terminal guidance, within 100 feet. So the radius has shrunk from 1,200 feet to 100 feet.

These refinements represent a truly revolutionary development. One analyst has pointed out that in some ways it is more revolutionary than the transition from conventional to nuclear weapons because improving a missile's accuracy by a factor of 100 increases its effectiveness against hardened military targets about as much as multiplying the energy released a million times. Thus, modern nuclear weapons are becoming the means, not only for inflicting mass destruction, but also for striking precisely enough to disarm the opponent.

The other critical postwar development has been the massive and ongoing buildup of the Soviet strategic arsenal. Since 1970, the Soviet Union has deployed four new types of intercontinental ballistic missiles, while the United States has produced only one new type of submarine-based missile. In 1984, the Soviet Union produced 350 intercontinental and submarine-launched ballistic missiles, while the United States turned out only 80 submarine-launched ballistic missiles. Furthermore, intelligence estimates suggest that by the mid-1990s nearly all of the Soviet Union's present strategic systems will have been renewed, modernized, and thus will likely have a much smaller CEP.

Particularly disturbing is the fact that the Soviet buildup has focused primarily on those weapons that could give Moscow the capability to launch a disarming first strike against U.S. strategic forces. By the mid-1990s, it is estimated that the Soviet Union will have between 8,000 and 10,500 first-strike warheads—which will be enough to allocate three or four to every significant military and political target in the United States. In addition, Moscow has been taking steps that might lead to the covert deployment by the early 1990s of a substantial antiballistic missile defense system. It also has a large-scale civil defense program. The Soviet Union has built shelters capable of protecting approximately 175,000 members of the top Soviet political elite from a nuclear attack. Thus, it might someday become possible for Soviet military planners to design an attack that would leave the United States crippled, capable of only a spasmodic, disorganized, and strategically aimless response—which would also be attrited by Soviet missile defenses.

None of this is meant to suggest that the leaders in the Kremlin would launch a first strike even if they were to acquire the theoretical capability to do so. The execution of a first strike would be such a complicated undertaking, with many operational uncertainties and enormous risks. It is improbable that any Soviet leadership would embark on this course in cold blood. However, the more menacing danger is that such a military imbalance would undermine U.S. strategic confidence and thus give the Soviet Union greater flexibility for using its strategic and conventional power toward achieving its geopolitical goals through intimidation. If the United States were to be strategically paralyzed, deterrence would not prevent a political defeat because the Soviet Union would be strategically free to act.

These circumstances have the following implications for effective and credible deterrence: To deter an attack, the United States must be able to blunt a Soviet strategic strike, to retaliate selectively and not only massively, and to use its strategic forces in exchanges short of a total, apocalyptic, and single response. In other words, unlike the conditions of the past, flexibility and selectivity are needed, in addition to strategic survivability. Only at that point will it be possible for us to have a strategic force that actually deters because only then are we likely to have a force that meets the probable threat at all the possible levels of nuclear escalation.

To put it most bluntly and directly, to bargain effectively during a crisis and to maintain stable strategic deterrence we must be able to do more than fight a nuclear war in which both sides in effect commit suicide. We must also be able to engage in responses that prevent the other side from succeeding in a disarming first strike. Such a response requires a U.S. capability, gradually or selectively, to destroy some of the adversary's nuclear forces and to impose a direct cost on his leadership and command structure. Only then can we actually deter and thus avoid war.

*   *   *

How do we seek that objective? What are the strategic implications of "Thou shalt not kill"? In our search for an answer, a recent book by Professor Joseph Nye of Harvard, entitled *Nuclear Ethics,* outlines some useful general guidelines: (1) self-defense is a limited but just cause; (2) we should never treat nuclear weapons as normal weapons; (3) we should minimize harm to innocent people; (4) we should reduce the risks of war in the near term; (5) we should reduce the reliance on offensive nuclear weapons over time.

His suggestions are helpful in evaluating the following four choices in determining what kind of strategy is likely to be most effective in maintaining stable deterrence during the coming decade.

The first choice is arms control. No doubt the moral imperative "Thou shalt not kill" in the strategic age is best sought by reciprocal arms control. It is obviously the most appealing option and is acceptable both to those whose analysis of the world emphasizes the constancy of conflict and to those who lean even toward pacifism. But what does arms control mean and require? The sad fact of the matter is that the technological complexity of modern weaponry, the growing difficulty of verifying compliance, and the intertwining of political issues with strategic issues makes a comprehensive agreement very difficult to reach. Much more possible are partial and limited arrangements, but these will not by themselves adequately deal with the strategic dilemmas we confront.

The second choice is to maintain deterrence through the doctrine of Mutual Assured Destruction (MAD)—a doctrine that rests on the proposition that peace is best maintained by the threat of mutual annihilation. But MAD requires that we face up to some unpalatable political and perhaps morally abhorrent decisions. In the face of the probable and ongoing Soviet offensive and defensive strategic buildup, MAD requires us to deploy vastly increased offensive forces, above those that we now have, in order to cope with the anticipated problems of the future. Because it is possible that a significant portion of our current deterrent could be attrited through a surprise Soviet attack, we will have to increase such forces greatly and, presumably, to target the Soviet population rather than military assets. Are we prepared as a society to do that? Suppose a conflict erupts with a limited Soviet nuclear strike? Are we really then prepared to commit national suicide by responding to a limited strike through a massive U.S. strike that could only precipitate a massive Soviet counterstrike?

Ultimately, in the long-run MAD fails because its inherent threat is not credible; in addition it is morally dubious. An incredible threat raises the dangerous prospect that our deterrent simply may not deter. The failure of deterrence would leave us with a totally immoral and ineffectual course: to subject all of the civilian population in the Soviet Union to massive suffering and physical annihilation while also perishing ourselves. We must therefore ask ourselves whether this is the best way to maintain deterrence as a practical policy and whether this is truly the most moral choice.

In the last several years, a third choice has been offered by President Reagan: a strategic defense to protect our population—to destroy missiles and to save people. This approach has a great deal of moral attractiveness to the public at large. But we must remind ourselves that this objective is at best obtainable some decades from now; even its most enthusiastic supporters do not claim otherwise. Moreover, beyond the question of actual feasibility, there is a further practical problem. A total population defense against ballistic missiles makes sense only if we can defend against all forms of lethality. Otherwise, such a defense protects only against one way of dying. Unfortunately, the military reality of our times is that people can also be killed quite effectively by nuclear weapons carried by other means, such as cruise missiles and bombers. A defense would only protect the whole population if it countered all potential ways of inflicting megadeaths—and that is simply beyond the range of feasibility.

The fourth choice—which I favor—involves a strategic posture that combines offensive and defensive forces. It would include the deployment of a limited strategic defense designed to protect our strategic weapons and command-and-control centers against a sudden attack. This would be combined with a limited deployment of weapons accurate enough to inflict selective damage on Soviet strategic capabilities. But the numbers of these weapons would be held below a level capable of executing a disarming first-strike attack on the Soviet Union. The limited strategic defense would be designed to make our strategic retaliation survivable, but the scope of that strategic retaliation would itself be limited through U.S. self-restraint. A strong retaliatory capability based partially on highly accurate systems—but mainly on weapons too inaccurate to destroy hardened military targets in the Soviet Union—would not threaten Moscow with the prospect of an invulnerable United States capable of launching a sudden attack to render the Soviet Union defenseless and totally vulnerable.

Such a posture would enhance our security without generating Soviet insecurity. It could be done unilaterally or through joint agreement. I would even argue that a unilateral step in that direction might induce the Soviets to consider more actively far-reaching, arms-control arrangements. It could thus precipitate a joint agreement that otherwise is unlikely to be concluded.

To move in that direction, we must talk about the Strategic Defense Initiative not as a long-term project designed to provide total population defense. Instead, we should be moving more energetically toward the actual deployment of a limited strategic defense—and this will require a U.S.-Soviet renegotiation of the ABM Treaty. We should raise with the Soviets the question of the continued relevance of the ABM Treaty and also register our determination to give notice—if necessary—of our intention to abrogate it and proceed with the deployment of a limited strategic defense. At the same time it would be important to make clear what limits we are placing on the deployment of U.S. first-strike systems. The scale of such deployments in the 1990s should not pose to the Soviets an unacceptable degree of risk. The weapons themselves would then be targeted primarily on military objectives. That policy is more moral than continued reliance on a posture in which the ultimate hostage to peace is the entire civilian population—a condition that is not only inherently unstable but morally depraved if an alternative exists.

In their pastoral letter on nuclear weapons, the U.S. Catholic bishops suggested that the three primary principles of a just war are discrimination, proportionality, and probability of success. All three criteria would be met to a far more satisfactory degree by a mixed offensive-defensive posture than by our existing nuclear strategy. The combination of a limited strategic defense and a conscious limit on offensive strategic systems indicate that we discriminate, as much as possible, between military objectives and defenseless populations. It would also mean that our deployments are proportional only to the threat and are not defined or determined by the scale of the megadeaths we are compelled to inflict in order to reinforce deterrence through the dangerous doctrine of MAD. It would also hold a greater probability of success, for such an approach is more credible than a threat of mutual suicide, whose credibility is inherently dubious. This new strategy charts out an approach in which the quest for strategic security is imbued with a needed degree of morally sensitive reasoning.

CHAPTER FOURTEEN

■

A World Without
Nuclear Weapons

THE VERY CONCEPT of a world without nuclear weapons is an illusion. Assume for a moment that all nuclear weapons have been destroyed. Unless the means for building them are also destroyed, or placed under some airtight supervision, a number of nations would still be able to produce them quickly. In the event of a war that threatens its survival, would any state able to make nuclear weapons abstain from quickly producing them?

The knowledge of how to produce nuclear weapons cannot be erased. Human consciousness cannot be manipulated like a tape recorder. A world in which nations destroyed their nuclear weapons but knew how to produce them would not be a more secure world. Moreover, some states or even terrorist organizations might choose to cheat. Given the closed nature of the Soviet system, its record of duplicity and deception, and its enormous geographical expanse, the risk that the Kremlin might surreptitiously store some nuclear weapons and their delivery systems cannot be disregarded.

To imagine a world free of nuclear weapons is to imagine a world in which nations truly cooperate in enforcing inviolable restraints on their own knowledge, permit controls over all their scientific facilities and accept verification inspections in all parts of their territory, including their military bases and industrial plants. Anyone is free to dream about such a world, but it may not be wise policy to encourage the public to think it will soon come about.

This chapter originally appeared as "The Danger of Disarming," in *The New York Times Magazine*, April 5, 1987. Copyright 1987 by The New York Times Company. Reprinted by permission.

A world free of nuclear weapons might also become dangerously safe for conventional war. Never in history have two dominant powers competed so intensely—during 40 years so fraught with provocations and indirect conflicts—and yet avoided open warfare. Without nuclear weapons, it is likely that during the Berlin blockade in 1948, or during the Berlin crisis of the early 1960s, or during the Korean War, or during the spread of communism to Cuba, some incident would have sparked a major American-Soviet collision. About 60 million people died in World War II. Making the world safe for the resumption of conventional warfare could hardly be considered a major advance for humanity.

And for a world free of nuclear weapons to be safe, not only would the American-Soviet rivalry have to disappear, all other conflicts involving the United States and the Soviet Union would need to be peacefully resolved. It is sheer escapism to believe the world will soon plunge into such unprecedented bliss.

For years, the Russians have espoused the abolition of all nuclear weapons. Why? It is not cold-war-mongering to suggest that, in preaching for a world free of nuclear weapons, Moscow aims to encourage the progressive disarmament of the West while it remains free to pursue its own buildup. Although Soviet public opinion has no impact on the Kremlin's strategic decisions, public opinion does determine American strategic capabilities—and hence the stability and effectiveness of deterrence.

The competitive sloganeering about nonnuclear utopias that escalated so mindlessly at Reykjavik is likely to divert Western publics from seeking genuine strategic security. That security can be strengthened by gradual and progressive mutual accommodation in arms-control negotiations, and also by unilateral actions. Step-by-step reductions, carefully calibrated to reduce the threat of a first strike, should be our principal negotiating objective. This means seeking not only reductions in overall numbers of weapons but also sublimits on such missiles as the Russians' highly accurate SS-18, which can be employed in a pre-emptive attack. We should also seek to block the introduction of even more advanced and threatening strategic weapons, and to develop on-site verification procedures for all limitations and reductions. The more progress is made in strategic-arms reductions, the more important intrusive verification becomes.

But strategic security need not come only from arms control. We can also adopt, unilaterally, a deployment strategy that is relevant to the likely political and technological conditions of the next decade and the century beyond. Given the increased sophistication of nuclear weapons (particularly the enhanced accuracy that allows for precise strikes designed to disarm the other side), deploying some components of strategic defense, both on land and in space, becomes imperative. Deploying limited strategic defenses, while setting careful limits on the numbers of American first-strike offensive weapons such as the MX and the D-5 submarine-launched ballistic missile, would help stabilize the nuclear relationship by reducing the Soviet threat to the United States without enhancing the potential American threat to the Soviet Union. A limited strategic defense, designed to protect only American military command and control facilities and land-based missiles, bomber fields, and strategic submarine bases, would cost less than Soviet efforts to increase their own first-strike potential in response. Much as the Russians may protest initially, economic and strategic considerations are likely to drive them to adopt a similar posture.

President Reagan has rendered the country, and future generations, a vital service by opening up a public discussion of strategic defense. He should proceed to take the initial steps to integrate the limited strategic defenses now available into our overall strategic posture. An early decision to deploy these defenses would not only enhance our strategic security (without increasing the threat to the Soviet Union), but would exert greater pressure on the Russians to consider meaningful arms-control arrangements. In a world with nuclear weapons, mutual strategic security is much to be preferred to escapist pipe dreams and deceptive slogans.

PART FIVE

■

Trilateral Relations

In the global rivalry between the United States and the Soviet Union, Dr. Brzezinski has written, the central issue is the struggle for predominance over Eurasia. This contest involves three strategic fronts, and two of these—Europe and the Far East—are part of the U.S. trilateral partnership with the industrial democracies.

In these speeches, Dr. Brzezinski examines the state of the key partnership on which Western global security depends. In the first entry, delivered during the last days of the Carter presidency, he reviews the actions the administration had taken to reinvigorate the Western alliance. In the next two speeches, he argues that the cooperative security arrangements fashioned in the late 1940s and early 1950s need to be renewed and renovated in light of the changing global challenges facing the West. In the Far East—a region now as economically important to the United States as Europe—he argues that Japan must redefine its role and increase its contribution to Western collective security through a combination of greater defense spending and greater economic assistance to strategically important Third World countries. He writes that the NATO countries must cooperate, not only to protect their security through a common military defense but also to take political steps to foster positive peaceful change on the other side of the Iron Curtain and in the relationship between the two halves of the divided continent.

137

CHAPTER FIFTEEN

— ∎ —

Western Power and Global Security

HISTORY, LEADERSHIP, AND NATIONAL CHARACTER have established France, beyond question, as *the* organic nation of the Continent. I have always felt that my own country's policy in Europe must be premised on a close relationship with France. And that close relationship requires frank exchanges of views.

It is in that spirit that I speak. I come neither to bury nor to praise the past, but to look ahead. Our agenda transcends the immediate political changes on either side of the Atlantic. Both its risks and opportunities require common responses from the United States and its allies, and those must proceed from a shared strategic assessment of the challenges of this decade and the next.

At the risk of some oversimplification, I would begin by stating two basic premises. First, the rapid and turbulent change that has characterized recent decades will defeat any artificial schemes for a new world order. Second, Soviet power injected into that turbulence is likely to intensify international anarchy. From that anarchy, no one—not the Soviet Union, the West, nor the developing world—will derive lasting benefit. While the Soviet Union is not strong enough to impose a Pax Sovietica on this turbulent globe, it is powerful enough to generate wide chaos.

At times, individuals on both sides of the Atlantic have attempted to focus attention on one or the other of these problems. A policy for the industrialized democracies must, however, deal with both. Given these two realities, our task is as simple to define as it will be demanding to execute. To adjust to international change, we must work together to manage both its tempo and its direction in order to enhance the prospects

Remarks before the Institut Français des Relations Internationales, in Paris, France, on January 12, 1981.

for stability and reduce the opportunities for historically futile and internationally destructive Soviet expansionism.

One would be profoundly mistaken, however, to confuse the symptoms of this abiding global unrest with its causes. The condition of disorder cannot be quickly reversed. Indeed, we cannot deal with it intelligently if we choose to perceive all upheaval as Communist-inspired or, as is the current fashion, a direct product of U.S. weakness or Western disarray. Those analyses are simplistic and misleading. Change is diverse in origin and varied in its practical impact. It arises in large part from the dramatic awakening of people who once were passive subjects but who now are active participants in a political process that has become global but not yet orderly. It owes less to Marxism than to modern science—from penicillin to the transistor radio.

World War II ushered in this era. Between 1939 and 1945, the Eurocentric world order was destroyed. That system developed after the Peace of Westphalia and provided the framework for international rivalry. Its collapse led to the unprecedented political, economic, military, and social changes that have swept the nonindustrialized world. In 1945, 51 nations participated in the formation of the United Nations. In 1959, 92 states were independent. Today, more than 160 countries exist, and the number continues to grow. By the end of this century, 85 percent of the world's inhabitants will live on the continents where this political and social transformation has been most rapid and, inevitably, most chaotic—in Asia, Africa, and Latin America.

Beyond the demographic and political statistics, another factor profoundly complicates the management of international relations: the new dimension of economic interdependence between the developed and the developing worlds. Indeed, a major task for the 1980s will be the creation of more harmonious, more equitable working relationships between the two. We are all increasingly reliant on the developing nations as markets, as suppliers of finished products as well as raw materials, and as outlets for Western capital. But developing nations are no longer passive. They have and will continue to seek a stronger voice in international political and economic affairs. Pressure for structural and systemic change, already acute, is certain to mount.

We must learn to deal constructively and imaginatively with these demands for change. They are the new reality. They present no easy choices. They offer only a number of painful adjustments. But to turn them aside or to turn away from this reality is to foreclose the chance to build a new and stable system, flexible enough to adapt to new demands and equitable enough to survive them.

On the issue of the role of Soviet power in this unstable setting, I do not pretend that we in the West have achieved a consensus. But while

I am confident that we will not commit the serious error of ignoring the legitimate demands and aspirations of the world's majority, I am less confident that we possess a shared understanding of the nature of our major rival—an understanding necessary to create a dynamic Western alliance capable of confronting the historic challenge of managing turbulent change.

Achieving that common understanding is essential to constructing a common policy, and such a policy, in turn, can help to close the dangerous gap that has so long separated the Soviet Union from the community of nations. Many Russians have recognized that gap, few more eloquently than Pytor Chaadaev, writing in 1829 of Russia's destiny: "We are one of those nations which do not appear to be an integral part of the human race, but exist only in order to teach some great lesson to the world. Surely the lesson we are destined to teach will not be wasted; but who knows when we shall rejoin the rest of mankind, and how much misery we must suffer before accomplishing our destiny?"

While our long-term goal must be to help the Soviet Union act as a constructive world power and thus bridge that ancient division between the Soviet Union and the West, we cannot make progress toward that end by pretending it has already been reached. The truth is that our task of helping to shape a new order will continue to be greatly complicated by the rivalry with the Soviet Union. The realities of that rivalry and the realities of Soviet power in our day require clear understanding.

In my view, the Soviet system is entering a phase of protracted internal difficulties. Demographic shifts within the Soviet Union itself are generating new social pressures, especially from the non-Russian Soviet nations. The continuing economic slowdown, while reducing the resources available to meet other pressures, also dramatizes the divide between the increasingly unpopular privileged elite and ordinary Soviet people. Similar trends, which contribute to the erosion of centralized power, are even more marked in other Warsaw Pact states.

As a result, the Soviet system is becoming stagnant and brittle. At the same time, there is the seeming paradox of the alarming growth of Soviet military power. As Soviet ideology becomes increasingly unappealing and as the Soviet economy falters, military power is becoming the main source available to the Soviet leadership for dealing with many domestic as well as foreign problems. Together, these two trends heighten the probability of East-West confrontation and increase the risks of Soviet miscalculation and even war.

Given these realities, it would be escapist to believe that domestic difficulties by themselves are likely to constrain and moderate Soviet assertiveness abroad. The West must be prepared to check that assertiveness. To do so, it will have to sustain and indeed increase its own defense efforts. But that process can and should be accompanied by equally genuine efforts to engage the Soviet Union in cooperation, to take advantage of those internal Soviet weaknesses to promote changes that will bridge the East-West gap. To seek to engage the Soviet Union in such cooperation without the needed additional defense efforts, however, would result in de facto self-neutralization for the Western nations that tried such a policy; to increase defense efforts without seeking to engage the Soviet Union would intensify the cold war.

Since the outset of the cold war, U.S. and allied efforts to check Soviet power passed through two distinct phases. The success of those efforts, in turn, set the stage for the period of attempted détente, the openings made in the 1970s toward constructive, peaceful cooperation. Now, however, we have entered a third phase in terms of the West's security needs and, as a result, in our dealings with the Soviet Union.

The two earlier phases were geographically disparate. The first, in the late 1940s and 1950s, saw the consolidation of Europe through a system of alliances. NATO and the OECD created an unprecedented level of institutionalized contacts across the Atlantic. The second occurred in the Far East, where regional security was consolidated through two so-called limited wars. In Korea, the United States and its UN partners won politically; in Vietnam, the United States lost politically. Nevertheless, security in the Far East has been greatly enhanced by U.S. alliances with Japan and Korea and by the growing strategic cooperation with China. In both the Far East and Europe, we recognized a challenge to our vital strategic interests, and we responded collectively to those challenges.

New challenges and new realities have introduced a third phase. For years to come, we will be centrally engaged with a region as crucial to our well-being as Europe and the Far East: southwest Asia. In the Gulf and the Middle East, we must work to create the conditions of stability against both external and internal forces of disorder.

We must recognize that area as a new zone vital to our security. We must recognize, with equal clarity, its intimate ties to the other central strategic zones. The three regions are interrelated. None is secure unless the others are. The policies we follow in one must be in concert with those in the others. It is with that need in mind that we Americans insist on the indivisibility of détente. East-West relations cannot have one profile in one part of the world and a different face a few thousand miles away. Détente will only be valid and enduring if its precepts are applied and enforced with equal vigor and determination in all three interrelated strategic zones. Western security, indeed, depends on the successful defense of all three.

The third zone, however, presents conditions profoundly different from those the United States and its democratic partners confronted in Europe and the Far East. In this region, the United States is not coming to the aid of war-ravaged economies in urgent need of our help. Nor is it dealing with cultures receptive to Western values and outlooks. The countries located in the third central strategic zone are proud, sensitive nations with recent and often painful colonial histories—all the more painful in some cases for having been indirect in nature.

Moreover, these countries are under a double threat. From within, the stability of the new regimes is challenged by the conflicting pressures of modernization and of the Islamic renaissance. We have seen in Iran what that conflict can destroy. Now, in the Iran-Iraq war, we see another stage of disorder, one that could further contribute to the region's turmoil and that could threaten a number of other states on the Gulf littoral, the source of one-fourth of the world's oil production. From without, these countries face a second threat: expanding Soviet influence. Czarist Russia, of course, was no stranger to the area. Soviet negotiators with the Nazis in 1940 revived the claim to a primary interest in the region. And since 1977, the projection of Soviet military power and influence into the Horn of Africa, South Yemen, and Afghanistan has proceeded on an unparalleled scale.

From recent evidence, as well as from more distant history, it is clear that the Soviets have a strategic concept for asserting their power in the area. It is also clear that their presence, guided by that concept, is neither stabilizing for the region nor compatible with vital Western security interests.

It was in response to this strategic reality that President Carter proclaimed one year ago what has come to be called the Carter Doctrine: "Any attempt by any outside force to gain control of the Persian Gulf region will be regarded as an assault on the vital interests of the United States of America and such an assault will be repelled by any means necessary, including military force." His statement was a new, historic commitment for the United States, one with profound long-term implications for the West as a whole. It reflects the recognition that the central challenge of this decade is likely to be as massive and enduring as that confronted by U.S. leadership in the first decades after World War II and that the Western allies, including Japan, need to participate directly in the required response.

Parenthetically, I want to take a moment to dismiss those critics who complained a year ago that President Carter's commitment to the defense of the Gulf was a piece of diplomatic bluff unsupported by either the means or the resolve to make good on the pledge. Democratic nations, I would point out, do not build up military power in order to expand their commitments. They assume obligations, such as the one to defend the Gulf, and then muster the resources to meet those obligations. That was the pattern that marked the U.S. military return to Europe in 1948 and 1949, *after* we assumed responsibility for the protection of Berlin. At that time, too, President Truman defined a security obligation that our country then rose to meet. Together with you and our other European friends we have continued to maintain that commitment. In doing so, we have mounted a deterrent that—at great expense—has assured Europe's security.

In the new central strategic zone, the challenge is just as serious, but the means for our collective response will have to be markedly different from the military and political alliance we have forged in Europe. The sensitivities of the states in the region, for instance, may doom any premature effort to establish permanent military bases on sites so recently associated with colonial forces. Instead, we are advancing our security relations with these countries in a more nuanced and measured fashion— and, I believe, with considerable success. We have developed a security relationship with Oman and further expanded our close ties with Saudi Arabia. Our access agreement with Somalia and our increased cooperation with Kenya are also contributing to enhanced regional security. We have recently held combined training and exercises with the Egyptians and plan more such deployments in the future. And, of course, the deployment of AWACS to Saudi Arabia in a recent emergency provided, along with the two U.S. carrier battle groups steaming along in the Arabian Sea, the most visible demonstration of our resolve.

These U.S. actions to shape a regional security framework, however, have been unilateral. What is needed is a multilateral response, involving not just the affected states, but our European and Asian allies whose dependence on oil from the Gulf area is even heavier than our own. That involvement need not be purely military or purely local. Nonetheless, for Americans to support their own government's commitment in the region, our allies must show their support as well. They must show it tangibly and with the understanding that the need is more likely to grow than to diminish.

What do I mean by tangible support? In the diplomatic area, I have in mind the relevance of the Middle East peace process to the larger regional stability we must seek to promote. That process has now entered a difficult period, neither for the first nor surely the last time. No one who knows the issues at stake expects their reconciliation to come easily, and no one seeks to exclude European leadership from the process. Our allies can, in fact, be of great practical assistance, especially in spurring the parties involved toward greater progress in responding to the Palestinian issue.

Another tangible measure of support is military. It is not enough to divide labor in theory. It is necessary to do so in practice, first of all within NATO, but also to the extent possible in the Indian Ocean area. While I recognize that the pledge to increase defense spending by 3 percent a year may be a crude measure of enhanced effort, I do not know any better measure that carries the same political symbolism. I do not believe that we can delay efforts to restore the military balance until we have put our economies on sounder footing. We also need to do more together in the Gulf area itself.

Finally, I wish to express a word of caution. On this side of the Atlantic, we have all heard the voices questioning U.S. leadership, alleging critical flaws in its competence, its coherence, and the constancy of its strategic purpose. I do not dismiss such criticism out of hand. Nor do I completely share the harsh verdict of a recent *Economist* article portraying U.S. European allies as "sluggish, self-centered and short-sighted." But I do take these mutual recriminations seriously because they contribute to a growing and dangerous perception in U.S. public opinion, and especially in the Congress, a perception of the United States as being more dedicated to the defense of Europe and to the protection of broad Western interests than the Europeans themselves.

Specifically, our legislators ask—and not without cause—whether it is realistic for European nations to nurture notions of a selective détente, to seek to insulate themselves on an island of trouble-free trade and economic advantage while other parts of the world, vital to their and our basic interests, are menaced by chaos and instability. One of those legislators recently, if ungraciously, asked: "how much longer can EC butter be allowed to grease collectivized farm systems in the Warsaw Pact?" And while Americans were heartened by the unified resolve evident at last month's NATO ministerial sessions in Brussels, some American skeptics perceptively noted that mood is no substitute for either hardware or hard decisions.

Mood unaccompanied by muscle will inevitably undermine domestic support for U.S. defense commitments in the heart of Europe itself. Such a shift of public sentiment could call into question the very nature of the transatlantic ties that, since the end of World War II, have not only safeguarded our basic values but have promoted the strength and cohesion through which we have created the most enviable standard of living in history.

A possible remedy lies in a consciously expanded program of sustained strategic consultations between the United States and its principal allies, including Japan. Accordingly, we should give serious thought to the expansion of our yearly economic summit meetings into a strategic summit. These meetings would address, at the highest political levels, the consequences of Soviet power projection and the mutual security requirements to meet that challenge. A strategic summit would provide institutional recognition of the fact that the problems of Asia, Europe, and the Middle East cannot be separated from each other and that economic, political, and security issues are also inseparable. Such a forum, with such a focus, not only could assess the dangers of an East-West confrontation posed by the pattern of Soviet military expansion but also could help supply the political impetus required for a firm and effective response. The key, of course, is the recognition that we face, along with the dangers of confrontation, a historic opportunity to promote through arms control and closer East-West contacts the constructive processes of internal change within the Soviet system itself.

Both elements are essential. We cannot simply push for relaxation of tensions or arms control without commensurate measures to ensure our own strength. Such an imbalance would lead to a de facto self-neutralization of Western Europe, a primary Soviet objective since the end of World War II. Nor can we dwell exclusively on the adversarial quality of our relations with the East, failing to differentiate between the strikingly varied impulses that flourish there. That policy or posture would merely refuel East-West tensions, dangerously narrow the demarcation between cold war and hot, and diminish the prospects for a pluralistic evolution in the East.

Our emphasis today in the new third zone of vital security significance is not arbitrary. It is where we happen to face the gravest danger. A common danger dictates common conclusions and actions, which in turn can lead to common security. The overarching requirement is to forge a common Western posture concerning this vital area of the world, a posture that will demonstrate Western resolve in dealing with Soviet aggression in Afghanistan and in meeting the impact of events in the Gulf. The basic issue is whether we and our allies share the same historic and strategic vision that enabled us to mount such successful responses to the dangers we jointly confronted earlier in Europe and the Far East. Do we now have the political will to take decisive, albeit difficult, measures on behalf of our own vital interests?

I believe that the kind of society we represent will answer that question affirmatively. We confront this historic challenge with historic optimism. History *is* on our side. The idea of human freedom, after all, has become the compelling idea of our time, the way it was two hundred years ago in both our republics, then a very small segment of the Western world. The freedom fighters facing seemingly insuperable odds in Afghanistan, the boat people fleeing oppression in Southeast Asia, the independent voters in Africa's newest nation Zimbabwe, the striking workers in Poland—all of these attest to the truth of that statement, to the dynamic reality of liberty's fundamental appeal for all human beings.

Today, tyranny is everywhere on the political defensive. We must keep it so, recognizing that the careful management of change and the creation of conditions that will favor growing stability and safety represent our central strategic task.

History can be instructive in that process. Constructive management of change means, among other priorities, ensuring that our principal adversary is aware of the danger of repeating the strategic error committed by Imperial Germany. Attempting to escape encirclement, the Germany of the Kaisers embarked on a course of expansion and ensured the very reaction it wanted to avoid. Germany's naval expansion, its colonial push, its burst of railway construction, and the military doctrines it adopted ended by bringing into being the Entente Cordiale and its alliance with Czarist Russia. Similarly, in late twentieth-century terms, Soviet lack of restraint—in Afghanistan, in the Gulf, in the Middle East, in Eastern Europe itself—might well generate an alliance between the NATO countries, Japan, and China. Soviet policy could thus create the very encirclement that Soviet policymakers so much fear.

The conduct of East-West détente at such a juncture requires a combination of power and accommodation, one that addresses the central strategic reality of our time. The Western alliance—if it is to remain an alliance—must summon the resources necessary to meet that reality. Only by fusing our commitment to principle with an appreciation of power can the United States and its allies promote genuine, indivisible East-West détente, one that can help shape the more decent and more equitable world system to which all successor nations of the old Eurocentric order justly aspire. No other kind of détente will be viable. No other response will encompass, let alone resolve, the challenges to our common security.

CHAPTER SIXTEEN

■

The North Pacific
and Global Security

AT THE WILLIAMSBURG SUMMIT IN 1983, the industrial democracies issued a joint statement that included the following significant assertion: "The security of our countries is indivisible and must be approached on a global basis." This was a historic milestone: For the first time, it was recognized that the security of Western Europe and that of Japan and the North Pacific are inextricably intertwined. Prime Minister Nakasone deserves praise for recognizing this fact, as do the Japanese people for showing the political maturity that behooves a truly great power—now not only in economic terms but also because Japan has become a major political force in the world.

Given this new recognition, it is appropriate to ask: What is the common security perimeter of the Western democracies and, more specifically, of the United States and Japan? In a formal sense, the answer is defined by U.S.-Japanese security commitments, by the U.S. military presence in South Korea, and by the very obvious U.S. and Japanese interest in maintaining open sea lines stretching from the Straits of Malacca all the way to Japan. That, in turn, means the countries that lie astride these routes—the Philippines, Thailand, Malaysia, and Indonesia—and those that lie behind them—Australia and New Zealand—are also within the U.S.-Japanese security perimeter. Within that perimeter, the U.S.-Japanese-Korean security relationship serves as the iron triangle of military stability in the north.

In a broader sense, however, one also has to think of the informal security perimeter and that surely must include the People's Republic of China. An independent and strong China that is not vulnerable to Soviet

Remarks delivered at the Fletcher-Hokkaido Program 1985 in Sapporo, Japan, on July 29, 1985.

intimidation is a vital factor of stability in the Far East. It inhibits North Korea from acting aggressively against South Korea, for North Korea would be unlikely to undertake an invasion unless support from both major Communist powers was certain. It also contains Vietnam, for Hanoi would be unlikely to further its southwestward imperialism in light of the lessons administered by Peking in 1979. Thus, in an informal sense, the Western security perimeter includes China, and therefore Soviet threats to the security of China would damage U.S. and Japanese interests.

I say this mindful of the fact that there may occur a further improvement in the Sino-Soviet relationship. Yet neither the United States nor Japan should object to a formal normalization of that relationship, especially if the Soviet Union satisfies China's three conditions. More serious would be a political-ideological rapprochement, establishing closer identity between Soviet and Chinese foreign policies. That, however, would inevitably jeopardize U.S. and to some extent Japanese involvement in China's modernization. That modernization is China's principal priority, and it dictates the conclusion that a solid relationship with the United States and Japan is as vital for China as a secure, strong, independent China is for us.

With this context in mind, we must then ask how the United States should define its relations with the different parts of the Far East.

With Japan, our relationship is one of close alliance and global cooperation. Without Japan's cooperation, the United States could not have succeeded in the Korean War. Our 1960 treaty pledges that the United States will come to the defense of Japan in the event of attack. Our two countries engage in continuing dialogues on military planning and intelligence and on political approaches to problems and crises throughout the world. Since the fall of Indochina in 1975, for example, Japan has accepted over 10,000 refugees for permanent settlement. And most recently, the United States and Japan cleared away obstacles to the transfer of high technology that will be instrumental in the development of President Reagan's antiballistic missile defense. Indeed, Japan and the United States are now global partners—as closely tied, as interdependent, and as friendly with each other as the United States is with any European state. This is a fundamental fact of international affairs.

With South Korea, the United States has a relationship of close alliance and regional cooperation. It is expressed by the presence of 39,000 U.S. troops in South Korea and is reaffirmed through the vigorous efforts now underway to modernize the South Korean forces in order to maintain the balance of power. The United States would thus be automatically engaged if South Korea were to be a victim of a military attack. It is also expressed by the supportive stance taken by the United States after the North Korean–sponsored terrorist bombing of the South Korean leadership in Rangoon and the downing of KAL flight 007. Total trade between our two countries reached $15 billion in 1984. And Seoul and Washington have coordinated a response to the recent diplomatic overtures from North Korea regarding unification talks.

With China, the United States has a relationship of comprehensive bilateral cooperation and selective cooperation on global issues. On some foreign policy issues we differ—and our political systems are based on very different concepts. Nonetheless, we consider China to be a friendly country, and we wish it well in its ambitious development program. In thirteen years, total trade has grown from $96 million a year to over $6 billion, and security cooperation has developed from mere expressions of common interest through political cooperation regarding Afghanistan and technology transfer to sale of goods with clear military capabilities as well as some other security relationships. Academic and scientific exchanges did not exist when the normalization process began in 1972. Now more than 150 delegations per month and about 12,000 Chinese students and scholars per year come to study in the United States. The United States today is China's number-three trading partner, and U.S.-Chinese trade is more than three times greater than Chinese-Soviet trade.

Admittedly, none of the above can exclude the possibility that China will confront some internal difficulties in the months and years ahead as it strives both to modernize its economy and to readapt its socio-economic system. We should be sensitive to this possibility and not exaggerate some occasional reversals. We should be mindful that it might be better for all concerned if the evolutionary changes in the Chinese system are not too rapid. Excessively rapid transformation of an existing system is likely to produce a backlash reaction, especially on the part of the entrenched party bureaucrats who fear the political consequences of progressive economic decentralization. The Soviets are eager to exploit and capitalize on any such internal reversals to reestablish an ideological relationship with the PRC.

It is important in this context to try our best to ease China's "growing pains" by maximizing our own engagement in China's economic development. To put it succinctly, I believe that it is in both U.S. and Japanese interests to help the modernization of Manchuria far more than to sponsor and finance the modernization of Siberia. The former is in our shared geopolitical interest; the latter can only enhance Soviet strategic leverage over the Far East.

In the context of these relationships, it is appropriate that Japan play a more important security role than it does currently.

Japanese efforts have been steadily growing. The current five-year defense program does increase defense spending significantly and will improve Japan's security position, particularly in air/sea patrol and defense capabilities. But Japan still spends a disproportionately low amount compared with other Western powers, both per capita and in terms of the portion of GNP spent on defense. While the United States spends 7 percent of GNP and the major powers of Western Europe spend from 2.8 to 5.3 percent, Japan keeps its defense budget at just under 1 percent of GNP. South Korea, from whose security Japan certainly benefits, spends 7.5 percent of its GNP on defense. The average citizen of the United States spends about $1,050 per year on defense, and the average citizen of Great Britain, France, and West Germany spends $375, $270, and $260, respectively. Yet the Japanese only spend about $100 per capita on defense. This imbalance is, of course, the result of the arbitrary "1 percent of GNP" ceiling placed on defense spending. It is interesting to note that for many years before 1976, when the budget ceiling was declared, Japanese defense expenditures stood well above this arbitrarily set figure, reaching as high as 2.9 percent of GNP in 1952. This is inequitable and does no justice to the global role that Japan should be assuming.

At the same time, it would be a mistake for the United States to pressure Japan to increase its defense spending dramatically. A concern both for Japanese internal political stability and for the sensitivities of Japan's neighbors counsels us to urge only a gradual but steady increase in the Japanese defense budget. The feelings of the Japanese people against militarism deserve our respect. They are genuine and not merely a mask for selfishness. They are the product of painful historical experience. I feel strongly that unilateral U.S. statements pressing Japan to double or triple its defense budget in order to bring it closer to the spending levels sustained by the United States or by its West European allies will only intensify existing antagonisms. Congressional resolutions, such as the very recent one asserting that Japan needs to be "strongly encouraged" to complete efforts toward acquiring "1,000-mile self-defense capabilities by the end of the decade," are inappropriate and counterproductive.

Japan will move in this direction on its own, as a natural outgrowth of its global status and growing international stature. The Japanese realize that regional stability cannot be sustained only on the basis of U.S. commitments and that Japan inevitably must play a larger role in fashioning the region's multilateral security arrangements. It is, therefore, unwise for leading figures in Japan to express satisfaction to Americans with the present inequitable distribution of defense arrangements, as was done recently by your leading defense spokesman.

In the interim, when Japan's defense effort remains markedly lower than the rest of the West, Japan can make an indirect but vital contribution to common security by increasing its strategic economic aid to developing countries whose defense is vital to the interests of the Western democracies.

Egypt, the Sudan, Thailand, the Philippines, and Pakistan are among those key countries, and in 1983 Japan gave a total of $803 million in economic aid to them; another $208.5 million went to South Korea. And in 1984, Japan allocated over $1 billion of aid to the Philippines. These amounts should be considered as part of the Japanese defense contribution.

But given the vital health of Japan's economy, it is appropriate for the United States and the West Europeans to expect that the total proportion of the Japanese GNP devoted to its own direct defense and strategic economic aid designed to enhance our collective security should be approximately 4 percent—which would still be much less than the percentage of GNP expended purely on defense by the United States and approximately equivalent to the level for the major countries of Western Europe. This means that Japan should increase its defense and strategic aid programs combined by about $12 billion per year over a three-year period. These resources should be channeled not only to the present recipients of Japanese aid but also to other states in which we share a common strategic interest, such as Central America (because of the Panama Canal, through which much of Japan's trade flows under U.S. protection). This would help us in coping with a serious security problem in a region vital to the United States, just as the United States helps to assure Japan's security not only in the Far East but also in regions critical to Japan such as the Gulf, where the United States alone is assuming the protection of West European and Japanese interests. In Central America, massive poverty is a fundamental fact of life. Japan can help to alleviate that poverty and thus contribute to greater stability in the region. Indeed, in many of the countries strategically vital to our security, poverty and underdevelopment are the critical causes of a security problem. Both the Philippines and Central America provide excellent examples.

A Japanese contribution of such an amount to our common defense through a more comprehensive collective security budget would be an appropriate action and would reduce charges in the United States that Japan is getting a free ride. Accordingly, it should be an urgent goal of the Japanese to reach such a 4 percent level within the next three years. Spread over this period, the annual incremental increases would be only 1 percent of GNP, reaching in three years the approximate total of $50 billion per annum allocated for Japan's own security and for our collective security. Moreover, such aid should be allocated deliberately for strategic purposes, and not merely as a means to enhance Japan's trade. Accordingly, it should be dispersed through close geopolitical and security consultations between Japan and the United States and other Williamsburg participants, though Japan would obviously retain the absolute right of ultimate decision.

While at first glance this figure might seem to many Japanese to be somewhat excessive, our friends should consider that the current defense budget of the United States is $284 billion, even though the U.S. GNP is only two times that of Japan. The current Japanese expenditure on defense is about twenty times less; the proposed collective security budget would still be about six times less, even though Japan's GNP is one-half that of the United States. Moreover, the general purpose forces dedicated to the protection of the Far East alone (that is, not counting U.S. strategic forces, which also protect Japan) account directly for more than $40 billion per annum. The proposed figure for the overall Japanese defense and strategic aid budget—in effect, the contribution to our collective security—would hence be roughly equal in GNP terms to the burden carried now by Great Britain or France or West Germany on defense alone—but still absolutely and relatively much less than that borne by the United States.

Such a contribution by Japan would also alleviate somewhat a growing problem in our relations—which can potentially poison not only our economic relationship but also endanger our otherwise excellent political relations. This problem, of course, is the trade imbalance between the United States and Japan and the growing resentment it fosters among the people of the United States. I know the issue is more complex than presented in the U.S. media or in the Congress. Nonetheless, the dangerous political fact is that it is quite likely that the congressional elections in 1986 will be dominated by an anti-Japanese mood. Demagogic attacks against Japan can be expected from candidates for Congress, labor leaders, and perhaps even presidential aspirants looking forward to 1988.

This, in turn, will increase the vulnerability of our relationship to the strategy that will most likely be pursued by the new Soviet leadership. The policy of previous Kremlin leaders toward Japan has been singularly inept. It has been clumsy and heavy-handed and has consistently rejected all attempts to redress the legitimate Japanese grievances regarding its Northern Territories, on which we support Japan without reservations. But Soviet blandishments have been totally ineffective thus far because, as Professor Hiroshi Kimura has said, the Soviets have simply been oblivious to the fact that since World War II, Japanese have been insensitive to the use and influence of military power.

Soviet policy might now shift. With Gorbachev's new emphasis on seeking to separate the United States from its allies, we can perhaps expect a more sophisticated policy directed at Japan—one that papers over with a more polished style the fact that it is not just differences over the Northern Territories issue but totally different world views that separate the Japanese from the Soviet Union. We can anticipate a diplomatic offensive—even while a Soviet air and sea buildup in the northeast and also in Vietnam continues. In this context, our task must be to ensure that our own disagreements do not provide troubled waters in which Gorbachev can fish.

Thus, with the likelihood that anti-Japanese hysteria could become a dominant theme in U.S. politics and with the danger this carries for our wider political relations, it is imperative that our shared interests in global security be more emphatically asserted—and that tangible steps be taken toward those ends. Let me conclude by invoking the statement that I cited at the beginning of my talk and that must guide our actions: "The security of our countries is indivisible and must be approached on a global basis."

CHAPTER SEVENTEEN

■

Peaceful Change in a Divided Europe

IT HAS OFTEN BEEN SAID that the postwar division of Europe is unnatural. That has become the obligatory incantation for Western leaders speaking on the postwar fate of Europe. In this context, our leaders also decry the division of Germany as unnatural and denounce as unfair the partition of the German people. Last but not least, when visiting the divided city of Berlin, these leaders emphatically and even emotionally demand that the Berlin Wall be taken down. Only a few months ago at the Brandenburg gate, President Reagan himself said, "Mr. Gorbachev, open this gate. Mr. Gorbachev, tear down this wall."

These proclamations extend beyond the ritual denunciations of the division of the European continent. They are also a proclamation of confidence in the future. Virtually all Western leaders confidently predict— and even insist—that the postwar division of Europe will end. Most not only assert that the legacies of Tehran and Yalta must be undone, but also express their faith that they will be undone.

- In 1963, President Kennedy said, "When all are free, then we can look forward to that day when this city will be joined as one. . . . When that day finally comes, as it will, the people of West Berlin can take sober satisfaction in the fact that they were in the front lines for almost two decades."
- In 1964, President Johnson said, "Our purpose is constant—a united Berlin within a united Germany, united by self-determination in peace and freedom. . . . with persistence and constructive efforts

Remarks delivered before a conference on "Arms Control and Conventional Defense in Europe" sponsored by the RAND Corporation and the Atlantic-Bridge organization, in Berlin, Germany, on September 17, 1987.

155

by men of good will everywhere, that hope will be realized some day."

- In 1969, recalling his visit to Berlin twenty-two years before, President Nixon said, "One thing that has not changed is our devotion and dedication to the goal that the German people will again be united."
- More recently, in January 1985, Prime Minister Thatcher said that "real and lasting stability will be hard to achieve as long as the German nation is divided against its will."
- In May 1987, President Mitterrand said, "There is the Europe of the European Community, but there too is a Europe of our old continent—East and West. . . . One must see the whole from the foundations and see beyond the century what will be possible in the future. . . . It is a question of achieving unity and not conflict."
- In June 1987, in a speech commemorating the 750th anniversary of Berlin, Chancellor Kohl said, "The wall, barbed wire, and orders to shoot are showing their inhumanity particularly this year." He added Bonn will not come to terms with that "today or tomorrow" and that the wall "cannot be history's answer to the German question."

In contrast, Communist leaders claim that history in Europe has stopped. For them, the dialectic of history has been supplanted by the paralysis of history. The top Soviet leaders in Moscow and their counterparts in Eastern Europe assert that what transpired in the wartime meetings at Tehran, Yalta, and Potsdam is a permanent fact. They hold that the division of Europe is here to stay, that the political arrangements of today are here to stay, and that the Berlin Wall is as permanent a European fixture as the Roman Coliseum.

These assertions by Communist leaders are clearly unhistorical. History does not halt arbitrarily. Rather, it is an evolving process of gradual, occasionally more rapid, and sometimes dramatic change. Thus, the Western perspective is ultimately the correct one: Continuing change has been the only constant in human affairs.

That brings me to the question I wish to discuss today. Everyone agrees that war is unthinkable. Hence, peaceful change becomes the only option for Europe's future. I wish to address this subject in two stages. First, I will focus on the present manifestations of peaceful historical change and their implications for the transatlantic relationship. Second, I will make some recommendations for the constructive management of peaceful change in regard to the security issue in a still-divided but gradually changing Europe.

*   *   *

Peaceful change has its own laws and dynamics. It often occurs so incrementally that it is virtually invisible. Its progressive effects usually become apparent only retroactively. The essence of peaceful change is that it is seldom neat, precise, or clear-cut, but rather is riddled with ambiguities and contradictions. At the same time it generates hope, it can also inspire fear and concern.

A striking paradox underlies discussions in the West about the future of Europe: Our policies are premised on the expectation of change—on the notion that change is both desirable and inevitable—and yet the very discussion of such change quickly generates fear among Western leaders. Some leaders and commentators even adopt practical positions similar in substance to those of their Communist counterparts. Historical change suddenly becomes undesirable—something to be opposed—and any suggestion that the political and security arrangements born in the 1940s and 1950s should be revised in the late 1980s and 1990s is denounced as destabilizing and even dangerous.

Yet the fact is that today Europe is stirring. The manifestations of peaceful change in Europe are increasingly evident at two levels. First, in both halves of divided Europe, there is a growing political restlessness. In the heart of Europe, we can see a revival of the old concept of Mitteleuropa. Today, the average Czechoslovak, Hungarian, or Pole openly professes that he feels closer to the average citizen of Austria, Germany, or France than to his eastern neighbors.

Second, the leaders of the two superpowers are increasingly preoccupied with events outside of Europe. It is clear that resuscitating the Soviet economy will be Gorbachev's principal priority in the years ahead, while the unending war in Afghanistan, now almost eight years long, is becoming an increasingly painful preoccupation. What is at stake in Gorbachev's efforts at economic reform is nothing less than the status of the Soviet Union as a first-rank power. Moscow is—and knows it—a superpower solely in the military dimension. If Gorbachev cannot breathe life into the moribund Soviet economy, by the next century the Soviet Union could lose its superpower status.

What is potentially at stake in the Soviet-Afghan war is the internal cohesion of the Soviet Union. Already there have been reverberations of the war in the nascent national self-assertion of the non-Russian nations of Central Asia, most evident in the nationalist riots in Alma-Ata in late 1986. If Gorbachev fails to resolve the war either militarily or politically, these Muslim peoples—who have more in common with the Afghan freedom fighters than with their Soviet imperial overlords—will probably become ever bolder in asserting their legitimate national rights. In an age of nationalism, that must be a disquieting prospect for the Soviet leaders of the world's last surviving multinational empire.

Meanwhile, U.S. leaders will have to focus much of their attention on their southern periphery. What is potentially at stake in Central America is the U.S. capacity to project its power and defend Western interests throughout the world. For the United States to be able to keep its global security commitments, including those in Europe, it must be free from the burden of mounting a defense of the continental United States. But if the Soviet-Cuban presence in Nicaragua destabilizes the entire region—or particularly if regional instability fuses with a deepening internal socioeconomic crisis in Mexico—the United States will be forced to retrench, the U.S. public will be plunged into a state of isolationist anxiety, and the United States will inevitably pull back from its forward positions.

Thus, the incremental and evolutionary process of historical change—both within Europe and within the two superpowers—has begun to alter the geopolitical landscape of both halves of Europe. We must recognize that in the decades ahead this process could even accelerate.

*   *   *

We therefore need to reflect on the implications of the foregoing for Western policy, for the German-U.S. relationship, and for the Western alliance. It is not surprising that these gradual changes are both inspiring fear within the Kremlin and prompting a defensive attitude on the part of the Muscovite empire. Any change is detrimental to the rigid and cohesive structures to which Moscow aspires and still seeks today in the Eastern bloc. But we should not share that attitude. We, the pluralist West, should accept the reality of historical change, and through our policies seek to infuse it with a constructive direction.

It is surely not wishful thinking to observe that a Europe that becomes gradually more independent is also likely to be a pluralist Europe. An independent but wider Europe than the one that currently exists will be tantamount to the historical attrition of communism. In Eastern Europe, communism is already finished as an ideology and as a motivating force. No one—in a practical sense, literally no one—takes the ideas of communism seriously as a world view or as a guide to action. Communism as a motivating force is simply dead beyond resurrection.

Even the leaders of Eastern Europe and the Soviet Union know that in every significant respect they are falling behind the West. Average per capita income of Eastern European countries is approximately half that of the major West European countries. But even that underestimates the impoverished state of Eastern bloc consumers since their currencies have little purchasing power in terms of real goods and services. For example, it takes the average East German seven times as many work hours as it does the average West German to earn enough money to buy a refrigerator or a car—and the people of the other East European countries are even more impoverished. Moreover, there is an increasing disparity in the economic growth rates and growth of productivity in the East and West. Most important, in terms of the high-tech competition, the East has yet to leave the starting gate. Even the Soviet Union, which is technologically most advanced, has fifteen times fewer industrial computers per capita than the EEC countries and forty-five times fewer than the United States. In a word, the Eastern bloc is becoming a kind of "Soviet co-stagnation sphere."

None of that is lost on the people—or even the leaders—of Eastern Europe. In Eastern Europe we are seeing the advanced stages of a process of organic rejection by the East European cultures and societies of a system and an ideology artificially transplanted to their countries after World War II. That system was created on the basis of a historical model that was derived from the Soviet experience and that was altogether inimical to the psychology, culture, and history of the East Europeans. As such, it has no historical staying power.

Just as significant, a corresponding process is beginning to appear in the Soviet Union itself: The Soviet past is asserting itself over the Soviet present. Wait until next year! Soviet Russia will be celebrating the 1,000th anniversary of the birth of Russian Orthodoxy. With Soviet communism increasingly moribund as an ideology, one can expect outbursts of Soviet patriotic fervor and even strong demonstrations of renewed Russian Orthodox faith.

In this context, we must seek to encourage the process of change by creating a geostrategic environment in which it will flourish. Such change could become chaotic, anarchistic, and prompt strong reactions that might even temporarily reverse its thrust and direction. Moreover, such changes could precipitate insecurities, which the assembled military might of the Warsaw Pact might attempt to exploit, especially if an opportunity should develop to take advantage of some temporary military edge and of some imprudent weakening in the U.S.-European connection.

*　　*　　*

The point of departure for a strategy in tune with these basic historical trends is for the West to undertake systematic and deliberate efforts to find ways to mitigate the importance of the military dimension of the East-West conflict. In doing so, we must recognize one fundamental fact: The Soviet threat is real. The Warsaw Pact does pose an offensive threat to Western Europe. It is not an accident, after all, that the Warsaw Pact holds all of its exercises in an offensive mode. In addition, its military dispositions and weapons deployments are clearly guided by an offensive strategy—and motivated by an offensive-minded political intent. In a word, the Warsaw Pact does not train or prepare for defensive war because it does not expect to fight a defensive war.

In this area, a significant fact should become more publicly known regarding the Warsaw Pact's war planning and command arrangements: In the late 1970s, the Soviet Union succeeded in imposing on countries in the Warsaw Pact an entirely new system of command that effectively strips these states of national sovereignty. It allows the Soviet military high command—acting on the Kremlin's direction—to assume control over all East European national armed forces even without giving notice to the political leaders of its purported Warsaw Pact allies. In this connection, let me refer you to the information provided by former Colonel Ryszard J. Kuklinski, who served in the high command of the Polish army and who was actively involved in military coordination with the Soviet Warsaw Pact command.

Particularly important in this regard is the document called "Statute of the United Armed Forces and the Organs for Directing Them in Time of War," to which Poland and other Warsaw Pact states acquiesced in late 1979 and early 1980. In time of war or the threat of war, this document provided for Poland's command over its armed forces to pass entirely into the hands of the "so-called Supreme High Command." What's more, on the receipt of a special coded message, Polish and other East European troops could be deployed westward, without their government's sanction or even initial knowledge. In addition, Poland "had agreed voluntarily that that Single Supreme High Command would be exclusively the Supreme High Command of the Armed Forces of the Soviet Union and that its working organ would be exclusively the Soviet General Staff. The Polish side had even agreed to the present and future absence of any Polish representative or even just a liaison mission at that Supreme High Command."

He added,

In sum, in the event of a war peril or war, as much as 90 percent of the Polish army will find itself under the orders of Soviet commanders. . . . All orders and directives of the Soviet commanders will be addressed directly to their subordinate Polish troops, bypassing the Polish high command. In practice, this means an unbounded right of the USSR to dispose of the People's Polish Army without any prior consultation with [Polish] authorities. Being subject to Soviet orders, Polish army personnel lack even a guaranteed national, that is, Polish, jurisdiction, Polish courts-martial. . . . All of the foregoing decisions are, in view of their exceptionally sensitive nature, classified top secret and no one in the Polish army apart from a handful of heads of the [Ministry of National Defense] has the least notion of them.

Even in peacetime, the Soviet Union denies to East European states the right to control their armed forces. Kuklinski stated,

In the early 1980s, [the Soviets] already had under their control practically anything relating to the national defense of Poland and the operation of its armed forces. For example, it is Moscow that determines the long-range numerical size of the Polish army in peacetime and in time of war, its organizational structures, armaments and facilities, state of combat readiness and mobilizational readiness, directions of training, tasks and plans for its use in time of war, etc.

There is no more fundamental attribute of national sovereignty than the control of national armed forces. That the Kremlin has so totally slighted the rights of Warsaw Pact members is a truly sobering revelation of the nature of Soviet war planning and, more generally, of Soviet control arrangements over Eastern Europe.

Bearing the above in mind, we must make it our collective intent to adopt a strategy and a military posture that offsets those of the Warsaw Pact—while at the same time encouraging positive conditions for the political change that we favor. This means, first of all, that we must adopt a strategy that makes certain that Moscow's military planners could never confidently predict to the members of the Politburo that they would prevail in a military clash. But it also means that such deterrence must be achieved in a way that at the same time facilitates the favorable political trends I have already discussed.

That requires several concrete steps. In the years ahead, the United States will have to concentrate more of its resources on its global responsibilities, as recent events in the Gulf have already shown. It is therefore unavoidable that the United States will need to reduce, partially and gradually, the level of its contribution to the defense of Europe. There is certainly nothing strategically or politically sacrosanct about the present levels of U.S. forces in Europe. Their numbers have been both higher and lower in the past. Some gradual reduction certainly would not mean the abandonment of Europe. The U.S. commitment to the defense of Europe will remain as strong as ever strategically and politically, given the fact that large U.S. forces will continue to be deployed in Europe, even with some reductions. Moreover, the U.S. nuclear guarantee will also continue to provide a clear demonstration of that enduring commitment. In brief, in the years ahead U.S. and European security should and will remain organically insoluble and strategically coupled.

But as a practical matter, it is now inevitable that some reallocation of resources and forces will have to take place, especially since the U.S. defense budget will certainly shrink. Moreover, Western Europe has long since recovered from the devastation of World War II, and it is now in a position to do more for its own defense. Surely 374 million Europeans with an aggregate economy of $3.5 trillion should not need to depend for their defense as heavily as they do on 241 million Americans with an income of $4.0 trillion against an opponent with 275 million people and a GNP of only $1.9 trillion.

Thus, a greater European defense effort will be necessary. Fortunately, contrary to the doomsayers in the United States who have argued that any discussion of a possible reallocation of U.S. forces would immediately precipitate a massive stampede in Europe toward neutralism, Europeans have responsibly taken up the question and have started discussing how to strengthen their collective defense effort. Increased Franco-German cooperation, inching toward a kind of special relationship within NATO, can be the basis for such efforts. Toward that end, the recent steps undertaken to form a joint army brigade are an important symbolic action. This has not so far broached the possibility of de facto reintegrating French forces in the NATO command, but that option—in some flexible fashion—may be also addressed in the coming years.

Beyond efforts to strengthen defense, however, we also need to work toward using arms-control negotiations to create an overall political and strategic environment that will encourage positive historical change. After the expected INF agreement, any future proposals for reducing the number of battlefield nuclear weapons must be linked with proposals for reducing the level of conventional forces. The threat of Soviet conventional forces, after all, was the reason NATO deployed its nuclear forces. It is therefore imperative that if we negotiate on one, we insist on concomitant progress on the other.

In that regard, it is widely recognized that the greatest offensive conventional threat is the Soviet preponderance in main battle tanks. The tank continues to be the weapon most suitable for use in massed offensive formations. Further Western arms-control proposals, particularly if they are to address the issue of battlefield nuclear weapons, must focus on that threat.

For example, the West could propose a 50 percent reduction in the number of main battle tanks. Better still, this could be part of a larger plan to create a "tank-free zone" in Central Europe. This zone might include West Germany and Benelux on the NATO side and East Germany, Poland, Czechoslovakia, and Hungary on the Warsaw Pact side. It would require heightened NATO military cooperation with France, for Western tanks withdrawn from Germany would have to be stationed either there or in Britain. But the benefits of such an arrangement should be apparent, both in time of war and in time of peace.

In the event of war, it would undermine Soviet strategy. As an offensive power, Moscow must seek to have its first echelon of forces as near to the central frontier as possible in order to achieve a surprise attack and a rapid breakthrough, which would then be exploited by rapidly arriving follow-on echelons. With a Central European tank-free zone, that plan would become a pipe dream. On the one hand, a surreptitious attempt to move Warsaw Pact tanks to the front in significant numbers would be quickly detected and will provide significant warning time. On the other hand, a massive redeployment of Warsaw Pact tanks in wartime would create attractive targets for advanced anti-tank munitions. Moreover, to reach the front, NATO tanks would have to travel less than half the distance—over superior roads—than would those of the Warsaw Pact. Thus, it would be impossible to achieve the mass necessary for a breakthrough, particularly if NATO strengthens its anti-tank capabilities and devotes resources to creating fixed anti-tank fortifications in key areas.

One might, of course, say that Moscow would never accept such a plan. Three points should be borne in mind in this connection. First, a tank-free zone in Central Europe would be in any case a useful political initiative, even if Moscow reacts negatively. It would blunt the Soviet efforts to denuclearize Western Europe and to promote a nuclear-free zone because it would focus Western public opinion on the real issue that deserves high attention. Second, it was also said in the West that the Soviets would never accept the zero-zero INF option—and yet eventually Moscow did. Third, paragraph two of the recent Jaruzelski conventional arms-reduction proposals clearly hints at the possibility of focusing on tanks as a specially destabilizing conventional weapon. In brief, if the idea has merit, we should not be deterred from proposing it simply because we fear an initial rebuff.

In peacetime, the consequences of a Central European tank-free zone will be heightened stability and security in Europe. Warsaw Pact countries, particularly the Soviet Union, will have to pull back more tanks farther than will NATO. Furthermore, the pullout of Soviet tanks from Eastern Europe will further beneficially assist progressive peaceful change, as should be clear to anyone in the West who remembers how tanks figured into the events of 1953, 1956, 1968, and 1981. Thus, the overall security for the NATO states on the central front will be increased, while the prospects for desirable political change will also be enhanced.[1]

---

[1]The strategic rationale for and implications to a Central European tank-free zone were set down in greater detail in an annex that was distributed to the participants in the RAND conference and that appears at the end of this chapter.

*   *   *

Finally, I would like to draw some conclusions about the consequences of historical change for the fate of today's divided Europe.

The city of Berlin is symbolic of this continent's tragic history. Within a single century, it has been the capital of Imperial Germany, the dominant European power, a global colonial power, and a center of intellectual creativity; then the capital of a defeated and frustrated country, experimenting unsuccessfully with democracy, struggling with massive inflation, while attracted by cultural nihilism; more recently still, the capital of an ideologically aggressive and brutal state that dominated Europe almost for half a decade, if not from the Atlantic to the Urals, then certainly from Brest to Brest; and lately the spiritual capital of a divided people, whose majority live under a democratic system and most of whom aspire to live in a democratic Europe. Surely, Berlin's future will be different still.

My central message is that the winds of change are blowing in Europe. The Soviet Union is entering a phase that Gorbachev calls perestroika— or reconstruction. That means Moscow will probably be preoccupied with a protracted internal crisis. Gorbachev openly admits that to be the case. He knows that to be effective in revivifying the Soviet economy his reforms must not only reshape the decisionmaking apparatus but also instill the Soviet people, the party, and government bureaucracies with new working habits and new ways of thinking. More than that, in a remarkable burst of candor, Gorbachev admitted that the Soviet Union even needs a fundamental change in its political culture. As he put it in a mid-July speech before the leaders of the mass media and the so-called creative unions, "We are now, as it were, going through the school of democracy afresh. We are learning. Our political culture is still inadequate. Our standard of debate is inadequate; our ability to respect the point of view of even our friends and comrades—even that is inadequate."

Gorbachev is surely right. But such changes—if they ever occur and if they are ever to succeed—will take place only as a result of a most difficult, disruptive, and probably conflictual political process. I was struck on my recent trip to Hungary and Poland that the Soviet Union has lost even its ability to instill fear in peoples living on its frontiers. While no one harbors any illusions about the clout of Soviet military forces, there is a growing feeling that the Soviet army will not be the ultimate determinant of East European history.

During that visit, I called upon a distinguished clergyman who lives not far from the Soviet frontier in eastern Poland. I wanted to talk to him about conditions in Poland, but he was most anxious to discuss with me a topic very much on his mind . . . what will the Soviet Union look like after communism! I cite this as an example of the viewpoint that is becoming more widespread in Eastern Europe.

In any case, it is evident that Europe, indeed, is stirring. It is in our collective interest to give this change a positive expression. We must exploit these trends and build on the confidence in the fact that the existing territorial status quo in Europe, as confirmed by the Helsinki Agreements, is no longer subject to change. We must seek on that basis to shape progressively a new political reality in Europe. That emerging new reality must not involve territorial wars or revisions of national frontiers. Rather, it must be based on the fact that politics is the realm of perpetual change.

In closing, let me affirm as an American of European origin that the restoration of Europe to a larger global role through the progressive termination of its division is surely a momentous prospect—and a highly positive one. It is clearly in the offing. I therefore am certain the city of Berlin will again be a capital—this time of a free people within the framework of an undivided, pluralist, and democratic Europe.

APPENDIX:
CENTRAL EUROPEAN TANK-FREE ZONE

Since the 1960s, NATO has sought to deter a Soviet attack on Western Europe through the doctrine of flexible response. This calls for NATO to respond flexibly with whatever military forces are necessary to turn back the Soviet assault. Moscow's military planners have therefore had to face the difficulty of countering operational contingencies at the conventional, tactical-nuclear, theater-nuclear, and even strategic-nuclear levels. As a result of the threat of nuclear escalation, it was impossible for Moscow's military planners to be able to predict confidently to the Politburo that a Soviet attack on Western Europe would succeed, despite Warsaw Pact superiority in conventional forces.

Flexible response will continue to be the anchor of NATO's strategy. But four trends have made it necessary for the alliance to explore the possibility of strengthening the conventional component of NATO's deterrent. First, the evolution of U.S.-Soviet strategic parity has made the threat of a U.S. escalation to the strategic level less credible. Second, rising public concerns in Western Europe about the risks of even a limited nuclear war have reduced popular confidence in a NATO strategy based on the threat of nuclear escalation. Third, Soviet military writings have increasingly focused on the possibility of waging and winning a war purely on the conventional level. Fourth, new Western technologies have created possibilities for novel conventional weapons systems that will tip the dialectic between offense and defense in favor of the defender.

For a strategy and force posture of conventional deterrence, there is one bottom-line requirement: NATO must make it impossible for Soviet military

TABLE 17.1
NATO and Warsaw Pact Tank Deployment

NATO		Warsaw Pact	
United States	5,000	Soviet Union	36,000
West Germany	4,895	East Germany	2,800
Britain	1,421	Hungary	1,200
Benelux	1,380	Poland	3,400
Denmark	208	Czechoslovakia	3,500
Canada	59	Romania	200
Italy	1,720		
France	1,627		
Total	16,310	Total	47,100

Source: The International Institute for Strategic Studies, The Military Balance, 1986-87 (London: 1987), pp. 11-92.

planners to tell the Politburo that they are certain of success in an attack restricted solely to the level of conventional warfare.

CURRENT DEPLOYMENTS

Current deployments of main battle tanks available to NATO and the Warsaw Pact for combat along the central front in Europe are shown in Table 17.1. Along Europe's central front, there are 57 Warsaw Pact divisions against 26 NATO divisions. In addition to their greater numbers, Warsaw Pact divisions are more densely deployed along the inner German border.

CURRENT STRATEGIES

Warsaw Pact

The forces of the Warsaw Pact train exclusively in an offensive mode. Offense is regarded as a superior form of warfare, and all defensive operations are intended to be solely tactical in nature. In Soviet strategy, the main battle tank is *the* instrument of offensive warfare. It is the vanguard of advancing armies, with infantry and artillery following in the wake of its victories.

Successive echelons. Soviet doctrine calls for rapid rates of advance against enemy forces. But the massed concentrations of armor necessary for a broad frontal advance would make ideal targets for nuclear weapons. As a result, Soviet strategists have dispersed their forces, creating separate echelons of forces which would reach the front in succession. As soon as the forces in the first echelon have been worn down or have exhausted their supplies, the second echelon pushes through to continue the general advance. Soviet echelons seek to defeat the opponent by dealing successive blows to his forces at the front.

Operational maneuver groups. Composing about 20 percent of Warsaw Pact front-line forces, OMGs are a key element of Soviet offensive planning. They are smaller, independently operating, even semiautonomous forces that seek to pierce the front and conduct operations deep in enemy territory, thereby facilitating the advance of the Warsaw Pact main forces. OMGs will attempt to raid preemptively the enemy's rear area, secure certain key objectives (such as NATO nuclear sites), and undercut the effectiveness of a nuclear response by intermingling NATO and Warsaw Pact forces. Surprise and speed are supremely important for the success of the OMGs.

North Atlantic Treaty Organization

The forces of NATO train exclusively in a defensive mode. Numerical inferiority to the Warsaw Pact compels NATO to remain on the defensive, though offensive counterattacks designed to blunt the Warsaw Pact assault would be undertaken.

Forward defense. Unlike its operational plans for the 1950s and 1960s, NATO's current plans call for its conventional forces to hold the line against advancing enemy forces at the inner German border. In order to succeed in containing the initial offensive, it is essential that NATO have adequate warning time to move forces from western Germany, and perhaps from France, to their assigned sectors at the front.

Follow-on Forces Attack. FOFA was adopted as part of NATO plans in the early 1980s. It calls for members of the alliance to develop the forces to attack the rear echelons of the Warsaw Pact before they enter the main battle. This is to be achieved by capitalizing on NATO's superiority in airpower and by deploying new technologies, such as the Assault Breaker, to destroy enemy armored columns enroute to the front.

CENTRAL EUROPEAN TANK-FREE ZONE

To refocus arms-control efforts on the key threat to peace in Europe—the imbalance in main battle tanks—NATO should consider proposing a Central European tank-free zone. This might also be accompanied by a proposal to cut present tank forces by 50 percent.

Under such a plan, all main battle tanks would be pulled out from West Germany, Belgium, Luxemburg, and the Netherlands on the NATO side and from East Germany, Poland, Czechoslovakia, and Hungary on the Warsaw Pact side. The pertinent countries of NATO would have to undertake new arrangements to store and maintain their tanks in specified depots in France, Britain, and Denmark. Those of the Warsaw Pact would have to reach agreements to place their tanks in similarly specified depots in the western military districts of the Soviet Union, and perhaps also in Romania and Bulgaria.

The objective strategic consequence of a Central European tank-free zone would be to complicate tremendously the requirements of offensive warfare— and therefore to enhance greatly the military stability of Europe.

Conventional offensive warfare cannot succeed without the tank. Infantry fighting vehicles cannot withstand the firepower of fixed defensive positions; and airpower cannot occupy territory. Offensive warfare requires a combatant to combine the capabilities of tanks and infantry, which is readily apparent from the fact that every tank division has infantry units and every infantry division has tank units.

Neither side could claim that a tank-free zone would diminish its military security. A tank-free zone would undermine doctrines of offensive warfare and strengthen defense relative to offense.

First, a tank-free zone would fatally undermine the Soviet offensive doctrine. For an echeloned attack to succeed as envisioned in Soviet doctrine, it is imperative that the first wave be stationed at the front and that it capture the element of surprise. But it would be impossible to move surreptitiously enough tanks into the zone to achieve a militarily significant advantage. Even nonintrusive means of verification could detect the movement of large numbers of tanks through prohibited territory. Neither side could create the kind of massed armored forces that the Warsaw Pact maintains today on the inner German border. The initial phase of war would involve a massive westward redeployment of Warsaw Pact forces. NATO would have plenty of warning time to mobilize and mount its defenses in West Germany. There would be no way that Moscow's forces could achieve the kind of surprise and rates of advance required by its doctrine.

Second, a tank-free zone would strengthen defense relative to offense by leaving defensive forces in place. Both sides would retain in Central Europe their airpower and their short and long-range anti-tank weapons. In effect, each side would have the task of striking follow-on forces without being burdened with the problem of forward defense. In addition, both sides could consider improving their anti-tank capabilities—both in terms of weapons systems and fixed fortifications—thereby rendering offensive warfare even less likely to succeed. Moreover, since military exercises of armored formations would be prohibited in the tank-free zone, offensive-minded military planners could have little confidence that their forces would perform up to specifications on unfamiliar terrain.

It might be objected that, given its offensive geostrategic intentions, Moscow would never accept such a plan. Three points should be borne in mind in this connection. First, a proposal for a tank-free zone in Central Europe would be a useful political initiative, focusing the attention of Western publics on the real threat to peace and thus blunting Soviet efforts to create a nuclear-free Europe. Second, it was also said in the West that the Soviets would never accept the zero-zero INF option—and yet Moscow eventually did. Third, the West should not overlook the fact that even leaders of the non-Soviet members of the Warsaw Pact might find some merit in such a proposal.

Thus, if accepted, a Central European tank-free zone carries the potential of increasing military stability in Europe. For the West, it would create a high degree of confidence in NATO's conventional deterrent, thereby reducing the risk of a slide toward neutralism caused by the fear of nuclear war. For the Soviet side, it would mean that the threat purportedly posed by NATO would also be thwarted. If rejected, such a proposal would carry a profoundly important beneficial effect: It would educate Western publics about the real danger posed by the 50,000-tank armada of the Warsaw Pact and would thereby stiffen their resolve to take the steps needed to counter that threat.

PART SIX

■

Regional Conflicts

There are two regions in turmoil—the Middle East and Central America—that will profoundly affect the outcome of the U.S.-Soviet conflict. Each involves not one but several interrelated political and military conflicts as well as the potential for a wider regional conflagration involving the superpowers. In these essays, Dr. Brzezinski examines the imperatives for U.S. policy in these areas.

Over the last ten years, the Middle East—from Afghanistan to the Horn of Africa—became what Dr. Brzezinski called the "arc of crisis." With the fall of the shah and the Soviet invasion of Afghanistan, southwest Asia became the third central strategic front, in addition to Europe and the Far East, in the U.S.-Soviet contest over the future of Eurasia. As national security adviser to President Carter, Dr. Brzezinski participated in the talks leading to a peace settlement between Egypt and Israel, negotiated arrangements with several countries to provide financial and military assistance to the Afghan resistance, initiated military programs to develop a rapid deployment force capable of projecting U.S. power into the Gulf area, and crafted the Carter Doctrine, which drew the line against further Soviet expansion into the region. In the first three essays, he examines the consequences of the failure of the Reagan administration to press forward with the Arab-Israeli peace process, the imperatives and requirements of the U.S. role in the Gulf, and the guidelines for an effective U.S. policy on the issue of Afghanistan.

In Central America, Dr. Brzezinski writes, a defeat for the United States would represent a major strategic reversal, while a loss for the Soviet Union would mean only a tactical setback. But the task of fashioning a solution to America's dilemmas in the conflicts in El

Salvador and Nicaragua involves profound regional and domestic difficulties. In the last two essays in this section, he outlines the parameters within which the United States must work in order to avoid falling into the trap of pursuing a solution in ways that could carry consequences worse than the problem.

CHAPTER EIGHTEEN

■

America's Mideast Policy
Is in Shambles

FIVE YEARS AFTER Camp David and one year after the announcement of the Reagan Plan for Middle East peace negotiations—both high-water marks of constructive United States engagement on behalf of peace in the Middle East—our Middle Eastern policy is in shambles.

Reacting to events tactically, the United States has been reduced to playing a subordinate role. Militarily, America is acting as an auxiliary to the Lebanese Army, and politically, as a proxy of Israeli foreign policy.

Most tragically, perhaps for the first time ever, uniformed Americans have been dying neither in defense of American national interests nor on behalf of any genuine American policy objectives. The longer-term beneficiary of this disastrous turn of events is likely to be the Soviet Union.

Recently, in justifying what is happening, Secretary of State George P. Schultz declared that "the crisis of Lebanon cannot be isolated from the larger Middle East crisis. . . . Progress toward a peaceful solution in Lebanon will contribute to the broader peace process; setbacks in Lebanon will make the broader effort that much harder." What was strikingly missing from his pronouncement was any acknowledgment of the critically important truth that the opposite connection is even more important: Lebanon cannot be restored without serious and tangible progress in the Arab-Israeli dispute. It was that dispute that destabilized Lebanon in the first place and produced the destructive chain of events of the last year.

The central fact is that Lebanon, as a multi-ethnic and religious compromise, became unstuck as a consequence of the Arab-Israeli dispute.

First the large-scale influx of Palestinians into Lebanon upset the fragile balance within that country between the Maronite Christians and the Moslems. The resulting strife then precipitated the entrance of the Syrians into Lebanon, in part to promote the Moslem cause and in larger part to restore Syrian domination that existed before the creation of the Lebanese entity under French rule. Finally, continued strife in Lebanon, the increased Syrian military presence and the use of Lebanon by the Palestine Liberation Organization for incursions against Israel precipitated the Israeli invasion last year, with its further destabilizing impact on the fragile fabric of Lebanese compromise and the resulting civil strife.

That strife cannot be resolved by a political pastiche designed purely as a solution to the Lebanese problem. It is only a matter of time before the current cease-fire collapses. An enduring solution for Lebanon must somehow take into account the Palestinians' presence which automatically includes the Arab-Israeli dispute into the Lebanese issue. It must also deal satisfactorily with both Israel's and Syria's security problems. It is difficult to imagine the Syrians acquiescing in a permanent solution for Lebanon that results in a pre-eminent Israeli role, including the *de facto* incorporation of southern Lebanon into Israel and that at the same time leaves the Golan Heights permanently in Israeli hands. In one way or another, the future of Lebanon is linked organically to the Arab-Israeli dispute.

Indeed, it was because of the United States effort to resolve that dispute that Menachem Begin and Ariel Sharon quite deliberately sought to preoccupy the United States with Lebanon. Diverting United States diplomatic efforts into Lebanon and involving the United States in a protracted diversionary crisis was the most effective way of derailing the Reagan Plan for a Jordanian–West Bank confederation. Moreover, the more the United States became engaged in Lebanon, the more likely it was that eventually the United States would become a protagonist in the conflict, pitted more directly against the Palestinians and the Syrians.

That is precisely what is now happening. The United States is on the brink of becoming plunged in military activity against the Palestinians and the Syrians. The result of such involvement is likely to enhance the standing of Syria in the Arab world as the authentic voice of Arab nationalism. Even moderate Arab governments unsympathetic to Syria would find themselves under popular pressures in the face of Syria's willingness to stand up to an America perceived by the Arabs as military proxy of Israel.

Our prospective candidates in the 1984 presidential elections, on both the Republican and the Democratic sides, are already beginning to compete in militant rhetoric, the effect of which is likely to further diminish the

United States' ability to act as a mediator in the Middle East and to further transform America into a protagonist.

The historically more farsighted Israeli statesmen probably realize that, in the longer run, Israel's security will not be enhanced by a Middle East that is further destabilized and radicalized. Indeed, not enough thought has been given to the extraordinary opportunities for Israel's prosperity in the event of a genuine Middle Eastern peace. However, the more militant leaders bent on incorporating the West Bank into Israel certainly welcome developments that have the effect of making the United States a direct military antagonist of the Arabs. This not only polarizes the Middle Eastern conflict in a manner that is welcome to them, but also it creates additional openings for the incorporation of the disputed territories.

From a geopolitical and strategic point of view, the most serious aspect of this development is that it is likely to redound to the Soviet Union's advantage. Without becoming directly engaged, but merely by providing military assistance to Syria, the Soviet Union can reap the benefits of growing Arab resentment against the United States and of the continued absence of peace in the Middle East.

I have long held the view that the Soviet Union is not interested in a constructive settlement, and that is why it should not be a party to any American-sponsored effort to promote Arab-Israeli reconciliation.

The Russians' interests are best served by continued turmoil, and they are likely to be served best of all if American policy and military action create the pervasive impression of one-sided support for Israel's maximum objectives.

It is only a matter of time before the United States is deserted by its European allies. None of them has any interest in duplicating America's willingness to take on the Arabs. Already some of them are placing obstacles to American military shipments in support of the Marines. Before too long, we will be alone in this strange adventure.

The situation has so deteriorated, and American options have so narrowed, that it is difficult to envision constructive alternatives. Yet, the situation is likely to be cast into greater turmoil and as a result the Soviet Union, without too much exertion, will find itself increasingly influential. Under these circumstances, we have to consider alternatives, however difficult.

One is simply to withdraw, realizing that such a withdrawal may increase the chances of a head-on Israeli-Syrian collision. But the prospect of war may have a salutary effect on the minds of the leaders in Damascus and Tel Aviv. If war comes, the Syrians know that they risk a military defeat; the Israelis know that casualties will be high. An American withdrawal would have the effect of making the two sides confront the question of whether they prefer war or peace. And, if it is to be peace, both will then have to accommodate and accept some compromise.

Alternatively, the United States should more actively return to a determined pursuit of the Reagan Plan. In effect, what was missing from Secretary Shultz's statement would have to become the central focus of American policy: a concerted and determined effort to find a solution for the future of the West Bank and Gaza in the context of a larger peace settlement. This means using American leverage in the region—military assistance, economic aid, moral suasion—to press the parties toward serious negotiations and to be prepared to impose penalties on those who are not prepared to play ball with us.

If United States power is to be involved, and if American servicemen are to die, it should be on behalf of a desirable objective: a wider and more enduring peace in the Middle East. Focusing on Lebanon alone will never get us there.

CHAPTER NINETEEN

■

Geopolitics and U.S. Strategy in the Gulf

THE SOVIET MILITARY THRUST into Afghanistan, and therefore into the Persian Gulf region, is characterized by two features that give it a genuinely significant and historically unprecedented character. The first is that it occurs in an international setting that can be defined as one of at best strategic parity between ourselves and the Soviet Union. Every other major international crisis since our own deep involvement in world affairs began in 1945 has taken place in a context in which the United States enjoyed strategic superiority. This was true of the first Berlin crisis, where we did not have the forces necessary to defend Berlin, but where the other side knew that we had overall strategic superiority. This was also true of the second Berlin crisis—and its extension into the Western Hemisphere, the Cuban missile crisis. The challenge of the Persian Gulf is one that finds us in the uncomfortable and perilous stance of strategic parity, and that vastly complicates the nature of our response and makes our difficulties far greater.

The Persian Gulf crisis is also unique because no acceptable fallback positions exist in case of a major setback. The comparison with past crises is instructive: Had we lost Berlin, we could still have defended Western Europe, though at a much higher cost and with far greater effort. But it could have, and in all probability would have, been done. Had we lost Korea, we could still have defended Japan, though again at a much greater cost and with far greater effort. The Persian Gulf does not permit the luxury of acceptable fallback positions. If the situation in the Gulf deteriorates further, the consequences will be so grave as to

This chapter originally appeared as "The Offensive Wedge," in *The Washington Quarterly,* vol. 4, no. 2 (summer 1981). Copyright 1981 by the Center for Strategic and International Studies, Georgetown University. Reprinted by permission of the MIT Press.

preclude establishing tolerable lines of defense in other areas. The inevitable consequence of a major Western setback in the Persian Gulf will be the destruction of the entire post–World War II American-built international system. A negative outcome in the Persian Gulf area would mean at best the neutralization of Western Europe, and more likely its transformation into a Soviet dependency. The same holds true for our Far Eastern position in Japan and South Korea.

Hence, the crisis that we confront today in the Persian Gulf is strategically and geopolitically unprecedented in its character, and in my judgment it is the gravest challenge that we have had to face since World War II. To make matters worse, there is no convenient clear-cut response that we can offer, since there are so many different elements to the crisis. First of all, there is the increasing power of the Soviet Union. As recently as three years ago, the Soviet Union was shut off from the region by a strategic tier composed of Turkey, Iran, and Pakistan and protected to some extent by neutral Afghanistan. Today the buffer has become a Soviet offensive wedge and the pivot of the strategic tier—Iran—has disintegrated. The strategic balance has shifted dramatically and clearly in favor of the Soviet Union, and that is bound to have longer-range implications for the region. The entire area is now vulnerable.

Second, of course, is the Arab-Israeli dispute, which carries serious implications for the stability and vulnerability of the entire region. Leaving aside the rights and wrongs of the dispute, it certainly fragments the area, and it has created a whole legion—the Palestinians—who are the carriers of revolutionary ideas and who today play the role that a century ago was played in Western Europe by the Poles and the Hungarians. In other words, the Palestinians today are the primary source of revolutionary intensity and initiative in the Middle East. The perpetuation of the Arab-Israeli conflict makes it more difficult to mount a collective response to the Soviet threat. Secretary of State Alexander Haig was reminded of this fact in the course of his recent trip there, when his interlocutors insisted repeatedly that one could not shape a strategic consensus to deal with Soviet expansionism while downplaying the significance of the peace process and of the conflict between Israel and the Arab world.

Third, there are the uncontrollable forces of modernization, which transform traditional societies that have contemporaneously emerged from the colonial period.

The question facing the United States is how to respond to three challenges that together pose the overwhelming prospect of the dissolution of our influence in the region and a potentially fatal blow to our West European allies. There is relatively little we can do about the third factor (modernization), but we can directly influence the first two (Soviet expansion and the Arab-Israeli dispute).

We therefore have a fairly dense political-military agenda: We must fashion sensitive and subtle arrangements with the countries of the region that recognize colonial history. Our ties must therefore avoid overt alliances with permanently stationed forces. We have in fact moved in that direction, but we need to do more in trying to create collective relationships of a consultative type with those countries upon which we can rely more closely: Turkey, Egypt, and Israel.

All of this must be accompanied by diplomatic initiatives designed to mitigate the dynamic consequences of the persistent Arab-Israeli dispute. Unless there is progress on that front, internal pressures within otherwise friendly countries such as Egypt or Saudi Arabia are going to make our task more difficult. This will become far more difficult after the Camp David deadline of April 26, 1982.

Despite various American initiatives, and the almost universal recognition of the gravity of the situation and of the urgency of American action, I do not believe that either the country or the administration has fully recognized the intellectual and historical magnitude of this task, and they have not yet fashioned a strategy for an adequate response.

There is one concrete step that should be taken in the near future: the transformation of the so-called Economic Summit of the Western World into an Economic Strategic Summit. This would enable Western Europe, Japan, the United States, and Canada to focus more explicitly on the strategic issues of current concern. The next summit might well focus on the strategic political problem of the Persian Gulf and its implications for all the countries involved. The agenda before the summit would be a vast one, but one which we ignore at our collective peril.

Unless such steps are taken quickly, I fear that we will continue—as we have for far too long—to react slowly and incoherently to problems that confront all Western countries. Yet with regular discussions, joint exercises where required, and systematic planning, we may yet manage to overcome the crisis of the 1980s and 1990s.

CHAPTER TWENTY

———————— ■ ————————

Afghanistan and Nicaragua

TO IMPLY THE POSSIBILITY of some political linkage between the regional crises that involve Afghanistan and Nicaragua is not the same as to equate morally the roles that the two superpowers are playing in these crises. Indeed, the contrasts could not be sharper. Though the United States has applied direct economic and political pressure on the regime that it does not like in Managua, its military leverage has been both indirect and limited. The Soviet Union, on the other hand, has directly used its military power to impose on Kabul a regime to the Soviets' liking.

In the case of Afghanistan, the international community confronts a classical foreign invasion, waged with Nazi-like brutality. Scorched villages, executed hostages, massive bombings, even chemical warfare have been inflicted by the Soviet Union on a people who simply do not wish to be governed by communists. It is a staggering fact that Soviet policy has prompted the flight abroad of nearly 25 percent of Afghanistan's total population, not to speak of the several hundred thousand killed and maimed by Soviet military operations that qualify as genocidal in their intent and effect.

Afghanistan is thus a genuine moral cause—and it is scandalous that so much of the conventionally liberal community, always so ready to embrace victims of American or Israeli or any other unfashionable "imperialism," is so reticent on the subject. It needs to be said directly, over and over again, that Soviet policy in Afghanistan is the fourth greatest exercise in social holocaust of our contemporary age: It ranks only after Stalin's multimillion massacres; after Hitler's genocide of the European Jews and partially of the Slavs; and after Pol Pot's decimation of his own people. It is, moreover, happening right now.

This chapter appeared in *National Interest* (fall 1985). Reprinted by permission.

Moral outrage is a proper response—and also the necessary concomitant of a political reaction. But the latter must also involve an appreciation of political realities and, on the political plane alone, even of some parallels between the Soviet involvement in Afghanistan and the American concern over Nicaragua. Both superpowers first welcomed the internal upheavals that took place within their respective small neighbors—and then felt that the upheavals went sour. Each superpower fears, or professes to fear, that internal troubles within its respective neighbor will be exploited by the other from the outside, as part of the superpower conflict.

In Afghanistan, the Soviet Union approved, and perhaps sponsored, the original communist coup. Later, however, that coup produced an increasingly radical communist regime under Amin that appeared over time less and less able to cope with internal anti-communist opposition, and at the same time appeared determined to preserve Afghanistan's external autonomy. In late 1979, the Soviet Union invaded Afghanistan directly, killed President Amin, and installed in Kabul a pliant collaborator—and since then Soviet armed forces have continued, with increasing brutality, to "pacify" the country.

In Nicaragua the United States welcomed the fall of President Somoza. The dominant, though not unanimous, view within the U.S. administration was that the Sandinista victory would produce in Nicaragua a democratic regime, essentially friendly to the United States. The initial U.S. reaction was to extend economic assistance to the new Nicaraguan authorities, and a genuine effort was made to place U.S.-Nicaraguan relations on a more friendly footing. But the effort soon went sour, for two reasons. First, the new Nicaraguan government openly proclaimed itself to be in the forefront of a new revolutionary wave in Central America and covertly became involved in abetting a Marxist revolution in El Salvador. Second, within Nicaragua a steady turn toward a less and less democratic and more and more totalitarian regime became evident.

Moreover, both the United States and the Soviet Union came to see each other not only as abetting but also as directly exploiting the difficulties brought on by their respective historic disappointments. The Soviet Union has charged repeatedly that the United States has been actively supporting the mujahideen; the United States has focused public attention on the role of Cuban military advisers and Soviet military equipment in Nicaragua and on the threat that they pose regionally.

Given all of that, it may not be inappropriate to ask whether at some point it may not be possible to contrive arrangements that both superpowers would find politically tolerable and that over time could prove to be regionally stable. It is evident that any such solution to these two problems is the *sine qua non* for any wider U.S.-Soviet accommodation, in turn creating a somewhat more favorable climate for ongoing arms control negotiations.

The search for such accommodation must take as its point of departure some initially unpalatable propositions. The Soviet Union must become convinced that the United States cannot accept indefinite Soviet subjugation of Afghanistan for the reason that such expansion of the Soviet geopolitical domain would threaten the security of West Asia and the Persian Gulf—areas of genuine strategic concern to the United States. That requires intensified American aid for the Afghan cause—tangibly and politically—as well as a concerted effort to increase the scale of international condemnation of the Soviet aggression. The only possibility for a Soviet reassessment of current policy is if both the military and international costs of that aggression become prolonged and high.

Beyond the specific focus on Afghanistan, it is also necessary to demonstrate some sensitivity for the Soviet concerns regarding the future of the pro-Moscow regime in Managua. After all, it is rather unrealistic to insist that the Soviet Union accept an outcome in Afghanistan of a type that the United States would not be prepared to live with in Nicaragua. In effect, we are dealing here with two situations that may involve not only a political parallel, but also some degree of indirect political linkage. To put it differently, a constructive solution to the Afghan tragedy has to be based on a formula that the United States can also accept in Nicaragua.

Such a formula may be easier to articulate than to implement, but its articulation is the necessary first step toward implementation. In a nutshell it should involve an arrangement for both Afghanistan and Nicaragua that can be encapsulated by the words "external neutralization and internal self-determination." External neutralization means that arrangements would have to be contrived assuring that the country concerned will not become allied with forces hostile to the adjoining superpower, nor will it engage in political or military activities that adversely affect the regional interests of the pertinent superpower. Internal self-determination means that political arrangements within the given country correspond to the freely expressed views of the population concerned, and that such political accommodation at least initially is reinforced by some external forces acceptable to, but not controlled by, the adjoining superpower.

Such a definition of an acceptable outcome should come close to meeting the professed concerns of the two superpowers. Obviously, if the real Soviet motive is the domination of Afghanistan, or if the U.S. motive is to topple directly the Sandinista regime, the above will not do. But "real" Soviet motives—which probably in fact are real in the sense that the Soviet Union does desire to dominate Afghanistan and uses its professed motives only as an excuse—can be altered by a policy that not only offers a negotiated outcome but also is prepared to increase the costs of the continued aggression. Hence the need is to pair a willingness to settle with continued aid for the Afghans.

But there is a further requirement as well. It is to give substance to the formula "external neutralization and internal self-determination." To achieve the external neutralization of Afghanistan, the United States must be ready to participate in a five-power guarantee of the genuine neutrality of Afghanistan. This would involve the Soviet Union, China, Pakistan, and Iran as well as the United States. (One might also consider India's participation.) Such a five-power pact would be explicit in its assurances and commitments, perhaps bearing in mind the Austrian model. Upon the conclusion of such a pact, Soviet forces would have to be withdrawn from Afghanistan in their totality, and on the basis of a relatively short time-table (e.g., three months). Otherwise such a guarantee of neutrality would be meaningless. Some additional arrangements, which would include the deployment of an international peace-keeping force in Afghanistan, would be necessary to assure the Soviets that the departure of their forces from this area would not prompt immediate massacres of the pro-Soviet minority elements.

The composition of such a force would be of obvious importance not only to the Afghans but also to the Soviet Union and the United States. An acceptable arrangement might involve the deployment in Afghanistan of Islamic peace-keeping forces drawn from those Islamic countries that have foreign policies not unfriendly to the Soviet Union. From the American point of view, Algerian and Syrian, and perhaps even Libyan, forces should be acceptable, given the strong emphasis these regimes place on Islamic values and the centrality of Islamic religion. From the Soviet point of view, the presence of such forces would provide considerable reinforcement for the neutralization arrangements and would mitigate Soviet paranoia regarding any possible exploitation of anti-Soviet sentiments by American intelligence services or other forces that the Soviets may view as hostile.

The formula of external neutralization and internal self-determination could be applied similarly in Nicaragua. External neutralization would involve the removal of all foreign military and secret police personnel, notably from the Soviet bloc, and the end of the importation of military equipment by the Managua regime from countries hostile to the United States. Moreover, a regional guarantee based on the Contadora participants could ensure a genuinely neutral status for Nicaragua. At the same time, with direct Contadora monitoring, the political process within Nicaragua would have to be genuinely opened up to participation by all parties concerned, with new elections at some point providing for the free and uninhibited expression of Nicaraguan popular will. Should such elections return President Ortega to power, the United States would be obligated to accept the outcome, provided that both external neutralization and political self-determination within Nicaragua continue to be respected. An American pledge, formally reinforcing the regional guarantee of Nicaraguan neutrality, might also be an appropriate part of the arrangement.

To be sure, nothing may come of the above, if the Soviet Union is both determined to control Afghanistan and not particularly interested in any serious improvement of relations with the United States. But that hypothesis can be tested in action. That will require continued pressure on Nicaragua by the United States, making it evident that the United States is not prepared to accept the status quo, including the reinforcement of the Soviet presence in the Central American isthmus. It will also require continued support for Afghan resistance as well as intensified efforts to dramatize to the world the genocidal scale of the Soviet "pacification" policies. But finally it will also require a willingness to talk to the Soviet Union about both Afghanistan and Nicaragua, holding out before the Soviet leaders the prospect of regional accommodations that could pave the way also to some further improvement in the American-Soviet relationship. A negative Soviet response to a concrete proposal along these lines would speak loudly for itself.

CHAPTER TWENTY-ONE

■

Strategic Implications of the Central American Crisis

THIS ESSAY TOUCHES ON FOUR ASPECTS of our current dilemmas in dealing with the outbreak of insurgencies in Central American countries friendly to the United States. It will examine the Central American problem as (1) an issue in the American-Soviet relationship, (2) a military issue, (3) an issue in hemispheric and regional relations, and (4) a domestic issue in American politics.

The Central American problem poses for the United States a particularly anguishing dilemma. All countries, democracies included, deviate from time to time from the norms to which they are committed. That certainly has also been true of the United States in its international conduct. But in Central America the United States has deviated from its internal norms more consistently and for a longer period of time than in any other part of the world. American political and economic domination of this region has been extensive, and by and large has involved forms of behavior and consequences not altogether compatible with the norms to which we subscribe.

If that were all one could say on the subject, remedies would be self-evident: They would be derived from the principles that guide us, and the self-corrective mechanisms of the American system would probably move us in the right direction. In this manner, very basic changes did transpire in the United States–Mexican relationship in the 1930s. At the time, the Mexican government expropriated American property, but the United States was able to adjust to that.

What clearly makes the Central American problem much more difficult for us is its relationship, whether we like it or not, to the American-

This chapter appeared in Joseph Cirincione, ed., *Central America and the Western Alliance* (New York: Holmes and Meier Publishers, 1985), pp. 105–110. Reprinted by permission.

Soviet rivalry. The existence of Cuba and the Marxist cast of much of the Central American revolution automatically makes the Central American problem part of the larger American-Soviet confrontation. That complicates not only the political ramifications of the problem, but indeed even ultimately the moral judgments regarding that problem. One can no longer confine oneself to the relatively simple and categorical statement that I made about the American deviation *from its internal norms.* Instead, one is compelled to ask also what would be the long-range consequences of unfavorable developments, if such events were associated with the larger American-Soviet confrontation.

Insofar as the U.S.-Soviet rivalry is concerned, for the Soviet Union the Central American issue is at best a secondary front. It is a relatively minor objective at this stage; it does not constitute a central area of competition with the United States. To be sure, for the Soviet Union there are certain benefits to be derived from the existence of the problem and—from the Soviet point of view—from a deterioration in the situation. The United States would be likely to be more isolated internationally, and that would clearly be in the Soviet interest. Indeed, if things go in the wrong direction, the Central American problem could produce a crisis in the Western alliance for the United States. In addition, for the Soviet Union, there is the more specific interest in preserving revolutionary gains, which means making certain that neither Cuba nor Nicaragua is jeopardized.

The Soviets are clearly aware that there is a fundamental asymmetry between the American and the Soviet stakes in the region. Without defining specifically such terms as victory or defeat, one can nonetheless postulate that for the Soviet Union something amounting to historical victory in this region would be a genuine strategic triumph. However, a Soviet defeat in the region would be only a tactical setback. Conversely, for the United States a victory in the region is only at best a tactical success. But a defeat for the United States in the region is a strategic calamity. That means that Central America is a serious problem for us— and a very complicated problem—but is essentially a low-risk opportunity for the Soviet Union.

That brings me to some comments on the military dimension of the issue. From the military point of view, the problem is clearly much more manageable for us and, in contrast, more complicated for the Soviets. In stark contrast to the Vietnamese conflict, one has to conclude that the scale of the problem, its operational conditions, and the opportunities for operational leverage are much more advantageous for the United States than for the Soviet Union. Insofar as the scale of the problem is concerned, the size of the territory is smaller, the insurgency problem is smaller, the external backup and the capacity for the insertion of external enemy forces are infinitely smaller than was the case in Vietnam. Insofar as operational conditions are concerned, the distance from the United States in contrast to the distance from the Soviet Union is infinitely to the advantage of the United States in Central America, whereas it was not in Vietnam. There exists the Southern Command, and a very elaborate military infrastructure has lately been developed by the United States through a deliberate buildup in the last several years in Central America. The region is clearly accessible to the United States and relatively inaccessible to the Soviet Union, Cuba notwithstanding. In terms of operational leverage, the area is clearly susceptible to effective military interdiction, and indeed, if necessary, is susceptible to direct pressure and action on the source of the problem (however that source may be defined).

However, there are some indications that the United States in its military strategy is tempted to pursue an approach reminiscent of its engagement in Vietnam. The rather interesting strategic critic of the Vietnam War, Colonel Harry Summers, in a recent review of our strategy pursued in the Vietnam War, makes a number of suggestive points. He writes, "Our adoption of the strategic defensive was an end in itself, and we had substituted the negative aim of counter-insurgency for the positive aim of the isolation of the battlefield." He goes on to say,

In Vietnam such an adjustment was never made. Instead of focusing our attention on the external enemy, North Vietnam—the source of the war— we turned our attention to the symptom—the guerrilla war in the south— and limited our attacks on the North to air and sea actions only. In other words, we took the socio-political task (nation-building/counter-insurgency) as our primary mission, and relegated the military task (defeating external aggression) to a secondary place. The effect was a failure to isolate the battlefield, but because of the confusion over objectives this fact was not readily apparent.

These comments point out some of the military dilemmas that confront us and do have some bearing on the kind of security policy that we are pursuing. However, any consideration of the logical implications of these assertions has to be assessed in the context of the hemispheric or regional issue in the Central American problem. The hemispheric and regional aspects of the problem clearly rule out, from the political point of view, a direct military intervention by the United States.

The United States in a larger sense is now in the process of readjusting its traditional relations, both with Central America and with Latin America. Certainly the Panama Canal treaties are a reflection of the greater willingness of America as a society to temper the one-sided character of its previous relations with Central America and to readjust that relationship on a more equitable basis. More generally, the relevance of the Monroe Doctrine has come to be questioned as a guiding principle for American policy, and more and more Americans realize that the Monroe Doctrine was interpreted altogether differently by North Americans and by our Latin American friends. By the United States, it was viewed as an altruistic declaration of commitment to joint security; to most Latin Americans it was a document spelling out the justification for the Yankee imperialism.

Since that adjustment is now underway, and has been underway for some decades, it is clearly more difficult to countenance a solution that relies primarily or even exclusively on the use of military force, even though the objective conditions for the use of force are more favorable than in many of the cases of postwar American involvement. The Central American issue nonetheless inflames passions throughout the continent and could divide us from that continent on a massive and highly counterproductive scale. Moreover, it is quite evident that there is a fundamental dichotomy between our perspectives on this problem and the perspective of some friends and other potentially affected countries in which we have a vital interest.

It is enough just to read some key passages from speeches by President de la Madrid of Mexico and President Reagan to see how wide a gap in perspectives exists. During President de la Madrid's May 1984 visit to the United States, he said:

We are convinced that the Central American conflict is a result of economic deficiencies, political backwardness, and social injustice that have afflicted the countries of the area. We cannot therefore accept its becoming part of the East-West confrontation, nor can we accept reforms and structural changes being viewed as a threat to the security of the other countries of the hemisphere.

In contrast the President of the United States put it entirely differently:

For the United States the conflagration in Central America appears too close to ignore. Like a fire in one's neighborhood, this threat should be of concern to every nation in the hemisphere. . . . Complicating the situation and making it even more dangerous has been the intervention of a totalitarian coalition which has undermined what we had hoped would be a democratic revolution. These totalitarians have been pouring gasoline onto the fire by pumping massive supplies of weapons into Central America and encouraging tyranny and aggression. Thousands of Cubans and Soviet bloc military personnel have accompanied this flow of weapons and equipment into the region. Responsible governments of this hemisphere cannot afford to close their eyes to what is happening.

This striking gap clearly should make any American policy maker extremely careful about relying primarily on the military dimension in dealing with the problem. If such reliance were to lead primarily to military solutions, however surgical in their character, the entire fabric of American–Latin American relations would be endangered. In the shortest term, American-Mexican relations would be badly strained, thereby complicating even our own ability to help Mexico cope with its internal problems. Clearly the ability of our own polity to deal intelligently with Mexico's internal problems is in the vital security interest of the United States.

All that, in my judgment, underlines the importance of United States sensitivity to such formulas as those advocated by the Contadora group in order to project an American willingness to compromise and to adjust and to project also some American recognition that the diagnosis offered by the Mexicans contains at least 50 percent of the truth.

But beyond that there is the further problem of our domestic politics and how they impinge on the shaping of policy. One can begin by contrasting the early phases of the Vietnam War and the current political situation. The Vietnam War started in the setting of bipartisan support in the United States for the engagement, and it was only the war that destroyed bipartisanship in the United States, not to speak of bipartisan support for engagement in the war. The Central American conflict, and the need to shape a policy responsive to it, have started in a setting of partisan conflict and of intense partisan division. The question is: Will the awareness of the stakes eventually generate a bipartisan response?

The initial moves in that direction, such as the Bipartisan Commission's report, have not been promising. It did not generate bipartisan support for United States policy. The contrast between President Reagan and President de la Madrid continues to be replicated domestically. When one reads the discussions of the Central American problem on the two sides of the political fence, one can hear echoes almost word for word of the sharp disagreement between Reagan and de la Madrid. The Democratic party puts primary emphasis in its analysis of the problem on its socioeconomic roots, and presents it almost as a crisis generated by the imperatives of social reform. The administration in office clearly puts primary emphasis on the externalities of the conflict, merging, if you will, the possible consequences of a hostile victory with the causes of the problem.

Inherent in all this is the longer-range danger that domestic division and national fatigue will make the maintenance of an effective and balanced policy in that region impossible. It could indeed make Central America, which has not yet become the political equivalent of Vietnam, a highly divisive issue which then propels the United States into seeking urgent remedies by one or another extreme.

In the light of the above, my own bottom line involves the following set of propositions. First, the United States cannot afford to lose because of its rivalry with the Soviet Union. Whether we like it or not, that rivalry is a reality. A loss would have widespread ramifications for ourselves, for others, for perceptions of international affairs that intangibly merge (and inevitably so) with the realities of international politics. Second, if the United States cannot afford to lose, it similarly cannot afford to win militarily and preemptively because of conditions in the hemisphere. Third, the United States simply must stay on course, essentially on the two levels of its current engagement, which is to some extent military and to some extent socioeconomic. Fourth, to stay the course the United States must apply pressure directly on Nicaragua, since a prolonged conflict would be domestically too divisive. It must do this also because the absence of direct pressure on Nicaragua means that the United States has little choice but to put primary emphasis on military counterinsurgency in El Salvador itself—as earlier in South Vietnam—at the expense of the longer-range social, economic, and political problems that should be our priority in El Salvador.

In brief, we have to exploit some of the military advantages we have in the region in order to try to effect positive political changes in Nicaragua internally and to affect the external conduct of Nicaragua and perhaps Cuba. Through such pressure, the conflict will either peter out, or we will be in a better position to negotiate an accommodation that exploits politically the application of pressure on the adversary. That, in turn, will give us greater opportunity to pursue an enlightened socio-economic political program *internally* in El Salvador. This is not an attractive conclusion to many Americans, but the other alternatives strike me as either unrealistic or as excessively dangerous.

PART SEVEN

■

U.S.-Soviet Relations

As a traditional historical rivalry between leading world powers, the U.S.-Soviet conflict will endure for generations. In these speeches and essays, Dr. Brzezinski examines the character of the Soviet rival and the current dynamics of the superpower competition.

Moscow's bid for world leadership, he wrote in the first entry, is uniquely one-dimensional, relying exclusively on the might of its military power. The other traditional elements of great power status—economic capacity, technological innovation, and ideological appeal—have proven to be beyond the Kremlin's mastery. The consequences of this within the Communist world, taken up in the second and third entries, have been twofold. First, the Kremlin has failed to consolidate stable control over even its most closely linked satellites in Eastern Europe. In this sense, Dr. Brzezinski wrote, "Yalta remains unfinished business." Second, rather than leading to a deepening crisis of capitalism, history has seen the unfolding of a crisis of communism. Around the world, governing Communist leaders are struggling to come to terms with the political, social, and economic transformations of the late twentieth century. All these require enhanced popular participation in social processes—and the crisis of communism involves finding a way to stimulate that participation without threatening the prerogatives of power of the Communist party. In the final entry, Dr. Brzezinski examines the prospects for the U.S.-Soviet relationship in the Gorbachev years and the U.S. response to internal and external dilemmas of America's rival.

CHAPTER TWENTY-TWO

■

A World Power
of a New Type

I WANT TO EXAMINE with you in this article the distinctive nature of the Soviet Union as a world power and to try to assess the special character of the Soviet challenge to the international system. The basic theses of my analysis can be stated briefly at the outset:

1. That the expansionism of the Soviet imperial system is a unique organic imperative produced by the sense of territorial insecurity on the part of the system's Great Russian national core;
2. That as a result of the Great Russian stake in the imperial system a transformation into more pluralistic forms is not likely in the foreseeable future;
3. That the political priorities and bureaucratic distortions of the Communist system confine the Soviet Union to the role of a one-dimensional military world power;
4. That the Soviets—who now have military global reach but who lack political global grasp—feel themselves both too strong internationally to accommodate to the *status quo* and too weak domestically not to fear it;
5. That as an organically expansionist but one-dimensional military power, lacking the capacity to effect a genuine revolution in the world system, the Soviet Union is confined to the essentially negative role of disrupter of wider and more cooperative international arrangements;
6. That a major disruption of the international political system could occur as a consequence of Western failure to offset Soviet military

This chapter appeared in *Encounter* as "Tragic Dilemmas of Soviet World Power," December 1983. Reprinted by permission.

power, while not coping effectively with the mushrooming crises in the strategically and geopolitically central zones of the Middle East and Central America.

A UNIQUELY ORGANIC IMPERIALISM

The Soviet Union is the political expression of Russian nationalism. The Great Russians dominate the multinational Soviet Union, populated by some 270 million people; and through the power and resources of that Union, they dominate in turn a cluster of geographically contiguous states numbering approximately an additional 115 million people. In effect, about 135 million Great Russians exercise political control over a political framework spread over much of the Eurasian continent.

This is not to say that the system is one of simple "national oppression." The Great Russians rule as much by cooptation as by suppression. The historical record of Russian imperial preponderance is replete with examples of successful cooptation, corruption, and integration of foreign elites; of the gradual absorption politically and even culturally of ethnically related peoples; of the creation of a sense of a larger community. Nonetheless, in the background of this process is the reality of Moscow's power, which is applied ruthlessly whenever a given nation chooses to resist domination and especially if it seeks to detach itself from the Russian-dominated larger whole.

The distinctive nature of the Russian imperial drive is derived from the interconnection between the militaristic organization of the Russian society and the territorial imperative which defines its instinct of survival. This has often been noted by both Russian and non-Russian historians alike. From time immemorial, Russian society expressed itself politically through a state that was mobilized and regimented along military lines, with the security dimension serving as the central organizing impulse. The absence of any clearly definable national boundary made territorial expansion the obvious way of assuring security, with such territorial expansion then breeding new conflicts, new threats, and thus a further expansionary drive. A relentless historical cycle was thus set in motion: Insecurity generated expansionism; expansionism bred insecurity; insecurity, in turn, would fuel further expansionism.

Russian history is, consequently, a history of sustained territorial expansionism. This sustained expansion from the northeast plains and forests of Muscovy has lasted—almost on a continuous basis—for more than 300 years. It has involved a push westward against major power rivals, resulting in the eventual expulsion of Sweden from east of the Baltic and in the partition of the Polish-Lithuanian Republic. It has involved the persistent drive southward, culminating—in the wake of defeats inflicted on the Ottoman Empire—in the subordination of the Ukrainian Cossacks and the Crimean Tatars and in the absorption of several Caucasian nations and of Moslem Central Asia. It has involved a steady stream of settlers, penal colonists, and military explorers eastward, along the brim of the Chinese empire, all the way to Kamchatka. Such territorial expansion is doubtless—both in scale and in duration—one of the most ambitious examples of a relentless imperial drive in known history.

The Russians have come in this manner to control the world's largest real estate. They do so by inhabiting relatively densely its inner core—the large area known as European Russia—and by settling in smaller but still politically significant numbers in strategically significant colonial outposts in the Baltic region (including Kaliningrad); parts of Byelorussia; East Ukraine; the northeast shore of the Black Sea; large parts of Kazakhstan; and a long security belt spanning the Trans-Siberian Railroad all the way to the Soviet Far East. The empty vastness of Siberia has thus been effectively sealed off and remains available for gradual colonization.

In the process, the Russians have come to dominate the weaker peoples inhabiting some of these territories, by subordinating them politically, co-opting them culturally, and even sometimes decimating them biologically. The non-Russian nations are controlled from the center and prevented from coalescing against the politically dominant Great Russians, who populate the strategically located central inner core of the multinational state.

The Russian imperial system—with its mixture of cooptation, subordination, and strategic settlement—thus emerged in a manner that differs profoundly from the experience of other recent empires. Naval expansion to remote lands, followed by limited settling, was not the method. It was much more organic. It was a process of steady seepage into contiguous territory, with the atavistic instinct of survival dictating the felt need to acquire more land, with "insecurity" being translated into persistent expansion. As a result (and contrary to many journalistic clichés), Russia historically was not so much a victim of frequent aggression but rather the persistent aggressor itself, pressing from the center in this-or-that direction, whenever opportunity beckoned. Any list of aggressions committed in the last two centuries against Russia would be dwarfed by a parallel list of Russian expansionist moves against its neighbors. The vaunted Russian sense of insecurity does exist—but not because Russia was so frequently aggressed against. Rather it exists because Russia's organic expansion has prompted, and was prompted by, territorial acquisitiveness, with its inevitable antagonistic ripple effects.

An additional, and enduring, consequence of such sustained territorial expansion has been the emergence of an imperial consciousness among the Great Russian people. Such a notion of "imperial consciousness" is difficult to define, but difficulty of definition is not a negation of the phenomenon. There is something strikingly imperial in the insistence of the Russians on describing themselves as the "Big Brother" of the other peoples; in the spontaneous determination to build huge Russian Orthodox cathedrals in the very centers of dominated capitals (as in Helsinki and Warsaw—and even to replace the Warsaw *Sobor* which the newly emancipated Poles blew up in 1919 with the monumental Stalin "Palace of Culture" thirty years later); and in the deeply rooted feeling that somehow the non-Russian nations of the Soviet Union and of Eastern Europe must be retained as part of Mother Russia's special domain. Anyone who has seen, or read reports of, how the Soviet ambassadors stationed abroad handle their periodic joint sessions with fellow ambassadors from the Warsaw Pact obtains a first-hand insight into imperial and hierarchical relations.

Great Russian imperial consciousness is a complex web of religious messianism, which has long associated Moscow with "the Third Rome," of nationalistic instincts of survival and of power, and of the more recent universalistic ideological zeal. In addition, territorially expansive insecurity has been reinforced by the Communist obsession with internal and external enemies, reinforcing an already existing paranoiac attitude toward the outside world. This complex web of motivations has helped to generate and sustain a world outlook in which the drive to global pre-eminence, for decades measured by competition with the United States, has become the central energizing impulse. That impulse sustains the predatory character of Great Russian imperialism.

It is this drive toward global pre-eminence as well as the vested interest in the imperial system that inhibits the prospects of a qualitatively significant evolutionary change in the character of the Soviet system. Without Soviet intervention, Czechoslovakia under Dubcek or Poland under Walesa probably would have become social-democratic republics, with Communist totalitarianism effectively dismantled.

But Soviet intervention occurred for the very same reason internal evolution toward greater political pluralism within the Soviet Union will be intensely (and probably even more successfully) resisted for a very long time to come. The reaction against peaceful change in Eastern Europe stemmed from the same impulses which make Great Russians fear any significant relaxation of central Moscow control. A genuinely far-reaching decentralization of the Soviet system, even if only economic, would pose a mortal danger to Great Russian imperial control, and thus, in the Russian psyche, eventually to the security of the Great Russian people. After all, what does "only economic" decentralization mean in political terms insofar as the Soviet Union is concerned? Inevitably, it would have to mean a greater degree of autonomy for the non-Russians, who would be then in a position to translate greater economic self-determination into growing political self-determination.

The majority of the Great Russians feel that is a highly threatening prospect. Any significant national self-assertion on the part of the non-Russians constitutes also a challenge to Russian territorial pre-eminence and could possibly even pose a biological threat to Great Russian national survival. Where would genuine Soviet decentralization, the acceptance of more democratic norms, the institutionalization of pluralism eventually lead? Where, indeed, could one even draw proper lines between the Great Russians and the others, given the demographic intermingling of the recent decades? There would be escalating tensions, eventually even head-on conflicts in a variety of areas: in some of the Baltic republics heavily settled by unwelcome Great Russians; in the culturally co-mingled areas of Byelorussia and the Ukraine; and certainly on the fringes of the Caucasian and Central Asian republics.

The dismantling of the overseas British and French empires did not mean the end of either Britain or France. The dismantling of the territorially contiguous Russian empire could even threaten Russia itself, given the absence of natural frontiers.

The difficulties the French faced in Algeria would be dwarfed on the peripheries of the purely Great Russian lands. Any attempted disentangling along national lines would be messy and bloody, and awareness of that prospect makes almost every Great Russian instinctively wary of tolerating any significant devolution of Moscow's central control. The instinct for survival gives the autocratic, highly centralized, and imperial Soviet system unusual staying power. It neutralizes the kind of inner self-doubt and imperial fatigue that induced the British and French to accede to the dismantling of their empires.

A ONE DIMENSIONAL WORLD
POWER OF A NEW TYPE

Western observers of the Soviet system have been loath to concede that the political centralism of the Soviet system has staying power and that the Russian imperial impulse is vitally inherent to that system. It is certainly more reassuring to believe that both conditions are evanescent: that the system will "mellow" because of either containment or economic development (or a combination of the both) and that its imperial drive will wane with the allegedly inevitable fading of Marxist zeal. The transformation of the system and the waning of its imperial ambitions will thus relieve the West of the obligation of having to face up to the much more difficult dilemma of determining how to coexist historically in the nuclear age with a powerful and closed political system motivated by vague but highly unsettling global goals. But what if the Soviet system does not mellow, and what if its military power continues to grow? Seldom, if ever, do Western observers address themselves to the international implications of this issue except occasionally from an extreme right perspective, focused usually in highly Manichaean and moralistic terms. Yet the issue demands attention and, above all, sober realization that for many decades to come an uneasy historical—but not entirely peaceful—coexistence with a militarily powerful Soviet Union may continue to teeter on the edge of the nuclear abyss.

The point of departure for a realistic appraisal of the relationship must be recognition of the special character of the Soviet system as a world power. The Soviet Union is a world power of a new type in that its might is one-dimensional. As a result, the Soviet Union is essentially incapable of sustaining effective global dominance. The fact of the matter is that the Soviet Union is a global power only in the military dimension, but in no other. It is neither a genuine economic rival to the United States nor—as once was the case—even a source of a globally interesting ideological experiment. This condition imposes a decisive limitation on the Soviet capability to act in a manner traditional to world powers or claimants to the status of world power.

Traditionally, both the dominant world military power as well as its principal rival possessed relatively matching political and socio-economic systems, each with the capability for sustained and comprehensive pre-eminence. From the late Middle Ages on, naval power has been the central instrument for exercising global military reach. The powers exercising it (to the extent that such global reach can be said to have existed in the age of slow communications and limited weaponry) and their principal rivals were—broadly speaking—Portugal and Spain (during much of the sixteenth century); followed by the Netherlands and France (during the seventeenth century); by Britain, and then first France and later Germany (during the eighteenth, nineteenth, and part of the twentieth centuries); and finally by the United States and the Soviet Union (during the second half of the twentieth century). In all cases until the most recent, the contest was between powers at a comparable level of development. The rival was quite capable of also providing wider commercial and political leadership as a supplement to its military pre-eminence. In effect, the rival, in displacing the pre-eminent global power, could both provide and sustain equally comprehensive leadership.

The unusual quality of the Soviet global challenge is that the Soviet Union is manifestly unequipped to provide constructive and sustained leadership in the event that it should succeed in unseating the United States as the number-one world power. The Soviet Union could not provide global financial leadership. Its economy could not act as the locomotive for global development and technological innovation. Its mass culture has no wider appeal (and its leading intellectuals and artists have been steadily fleeing the Soviet Union). In brief, American displacement could not be followed by a Soviet replacement.

The main reason for this condition is to be found in the Russian Communist system itself. Its bureaucratization, centralization, and dogmatization of decision-making have stifled socio-economic initiative to an unprecedented degree. As a result, the Soviet record in all the non-military dimensions of systemic performance ranges from the average to the mediocre. It still takes literally a *political* decision at the highest level for the Soviet economic system to produce some item that is generally competitive world-wide. Soviet economic performance over the years has required social sacrifice altogether disproportionate to the actual output.

Perhaps never before in history has such a gifted people, in control of such abundant resources, labored so hard for so long to produce relatively so little.

Comparative studies of socio-economic development, as for instance by Professor Cyril Black of Princeton, show that today the Soviet Union occupies in world rankings of social and economic indices a place roughly comparable to that it held at the beginning of this century. Black concluded that:

> In the perspective of fifty years, the comparative ranking of the USSR in composite economic and social indices per capita has probably not changed significantly. So far as the rather limited available evidence permits a judgement, the USSR has not overtaken or surpassed any country on a per capita basis since 1917 with the possible exception of Italy, and the nineteen or twenty countries that rank higher than Russia today in this regard also ranked higher in 1900 and 1919. The per capita gross national product of Italy, which is just below that of the USSR today, was probably somewhat higher fifty years ago.[1]

In other words, the extraordinary sacrifices, the unprecedented loss of life, the sustained social deprivation that every Soviet citizen has felt have yielded results comparable to those achieved by other societies at much smaller social cost. Moreover, the pace of Soviet economic development after World War II has been only average, despite the fact that

---

[1]Cyril E. Black, "Soviet Society: A Comparative View," in A. Kassoff, *Prospects for Soviet Society* (1968), pp. 42–43.

initially the Soviet Union had the statistical advantage of recovering from an artificially low plateau generated by wartime devastation. In 1950, the Soviet GNP accounted for about 11 percent of the global product; three decades later it is still 11 percent. No wonder that Soviet propagandists now prefer not to recall Khrushchev's challenge of 1960 "to surpass the United States" in absolute production by 1970 and in relative per-capita production by 1980.

The picture is just as bleak in the social and cultural dimensions of Soviet life. Recent studies point to a decline in male longevity, to the poor state of Soviet health care, to increasing infant mortality, to the spread of alcoholism. Intellectual and artistic life has become stifled; social innovation has been shackled by bureaucratic inertia. In brief, the Soviet Union is not a society capable of projecting worldwide an appealing image, a condition essential to the exercise of global leadership.

The main effect of this poor performance is twofold. First of all, it magnifies the traditional Russian and the doctrinaire Communist suspicions of the outside world. That world is perceived as bent on dismantling Moscow's empire and on promoting an anti-communist counter-revolution. The outside thus continues to look threatening to Moscow, despite the Soviet attainment of the status of a global military superpower. Though the Soviets take great pride in their new military prowess, and have used it to claim coequal status with the United States, in the Soviet perception of the world the United States looms as a giant, with its finances, its communications, and its mass media enveloping the world with many tentacles. American technology (currently, for instance, microelectronics) keeps on providing the American military establishment with new capabilities which the Soviets take more than seriously. In the Far East there looms the potential for a Chinese-Japanese constellation, while in the West there is always the magnetic pull on Eastern Europe of a Europe that has not fully resigned itself to an indefinite post-Yalta division.

All of that enhances Soviet paranoia and contributes directly to the second major effect of the one-dimensional character of Soviet global power. It generates an erratic pattern of accommodation and competition with the United States, in which (on the one hand) the Soviets seek to attain a condominium with Washington, and yet (on the other) fear becoming locked into the role of the junior partner in effect committed to the maintenance of the global *status quo*. That *status quo* Moscow rejects, for it not only would perpetuate American preponderance but— in Soviet eyes—it would serve as the point of departure for policies designed to promote "peaceful evolution" of a contained Soviet Union, i.e. its political subversion.

As a result, the promotion of regional conflicts, the inhibition of wider and more genuinely supernational international cooperation, opposition to what is called "world order," all are strategies that the Kremlin finds compatible with its own one-dimensional global military power. That military power permits Moscow to play a wider role in keeping with the Soviet imperial consciousness; it reduces the fear that regional conflicts could precipitate a head-on collision with the United States; and it enables the Soviet Union to use military leverage to undermine American pre-eminence in areas hitherto considered as U.S. safe havens. Particularly important and effective in this respect is the Soviet ability (in excess of the American) to deliver promptly from its large inventories huge amounts of military equipment to Soviet clients and would-be friends. In effect, a policy of gradual undermining of American global pre-eminence is a key aspect of the historical self-definition of the Soviet Union as a global power.

And that leads to a broader conclusion still: The real danger to the West is not that the Soviet Union will someday succeed in imposing a *Pax Sovietica* on the world. It is rather, that the Soviet Union, as a one-dimensional world power—committed to the disruption of the existing arrangements because such disruption is essential to the displacement of America—will contribute decisively not to a world revolution in existing international arrangements but to greater global anarchy from which all will suffer.

A PARTIALLY REVISED PERSPECTIVE ON THE SOVIET CHALLENGE

Implicit in the foregoing conclusions are some revisions of the prevailing Western view regarding the nature of the Soviet threat. In the immediate post–World War II era, the West was preoccupied with the fear that vast Soviet armies would pour westward, literally swamping Western Europe. Internal high-level American discussions—as recent studies by Professor D. A. Rosenberg show—focused heavily on the question of how the U.S. should respond, given its limited but monopolistic nuclear arsenal. Postwar Berlin became the symbolic linchpin of Western resolve, with the Soviet blockade of West Berlin in 1948–49 providing an American-Soviet test of wills.

Western, and notably American, anxiety mounted further after the communist invasion of Korea, leading for the first time to comprehensive U.S. nuclear war planning and to the creation of the SAC (Strategic Air Command) as the principal means of "Massive Retaliation." In the late 1950s, First Secretary Khrushchev's missile-boasting precipitated more intensified U.S. efforts to offset the allegedly emerging Soviet advantage, resulting by the early 1960s in a considerable U.S. strategic superiority. However, by the late 1970s and early 1980s, with the U.S. homeland fully vulnerable also to a Soviet attack, the Soviet Union was again perceived as being on the verge of obtaining a politically significant military edge (with President Reagan even explicitly proclaiming that the Soviet Union is already strategically superior to the United States).

In fact, during much of the postwar era the Soviet challenge to the West—contrary to prevailing perceptions—was not primarily military, and even now the much more important military dimension of the Soviet threat needs to be seen in a broader political framework. During the immediate postwar years, Stalin did engage in some peripheral probes designed to establish the resilience of the new geopolitical realities; but his challenge was not primarily a military one. Indeed, the West greatly overestimated the existing Soviet military capabilities, in apparent ignorance of the large-scale demobilization of the Red Army. To be sure, the West (and especially America) disarmed most hastily; but the West confronted an East that was socially exhausted and that militarily was also readjusting to a peacetime status.

The primary challenge in those years was in fact ideological-political. The Soviet Union emerged from World War II with unprecedented prestige. It was hailed and idealized in the West (and not only by fellow travellers). Many in the West so desperately wanted to believe that the USSR would remain also a postwar ally that they bent over backward to see the Soviet point of view on the contentious international issues. Moreover, to the populations of war-devastated countries, the Soviet Union projected the image not only of a victor but also of an apparently successful socio-economic system. It was that image that generated the ideological support and invited political imitation. An enormous American effort, above all the Marshall Plan, was required to neutralize that appeal—and it was on this front, and not purely on the military level, that the initial historical confrontation occurred. This is not to deny the importance of NATO or of the Korean War in the containment of the Soviets; but it is to postulate that the political-ideological dimension was critical in the rivalry.

The next crucial phase in the Soviet challenge occurred during the late 1950s and early 1960s. Khrushchev's policy of premature globalism, based on deliberately falsified claims of missile superiority, collapsed during the Cuban crisis of 1962. Khrushchev's challenge was predicated, however, also on a more generalized historical vision in which economic optimism was the decisive element. The Soviet leader's vulgar threat— "We will bury you!"—was not, as it was widely perceived at the time, a physical threat but an historic gauntlet, derived from misplaced confidence that American economic stagnation and Soviet economic dynamism would result in the emergence by the 1970s of the Soviet Union as the world's number-one economic power.

That did not happen. In 1980 the Soviet Union was as behind the United States as it had been a quarter of a century ago. It is now also behind Japan. The vaunted technological space race ended with the American flag on the moon. Today the Soviet economy is widely perceived as being, if not in crisis, then at least non-innovative and confronting increasingly difficult trade-offs. Soviet agriculture is clearly an undisputed failure. The Soviet system has generally lost its ideological appeal and that, too, detracts from Soviet global influence.

By the 1980s, however, Soviet military power had acquired, for the first time, genuine global reach, compensating thus for the lack of systemic appeal. This new condition was clearly gratifying to the Soviet leaders, and anyone who has dealt with them can testify to their pride at the Soviet Union's new status as a global superpower.

But global reach is not the same as global grasp. The Soviet challenge today, as I have already noted, is one-dimensional—and therefore it cannot be the point of departure for either comprehensive global leadership, or even for an enduring global partnership with the United States. The ambivalent condition of one-dimensional power induces an outlook on the world which is a combination of possessive defensiveness and disruptive offensiveness.

To be sure, it is quite doubtful that the Soviet leaders operate on the basis of some broad revolutionary blueprint, or that they even have a systemic long-term strategy. In real life, most decision-makers are so compelled to respond to circumstances and to cope with a myriad of specific issues that they simply lack the time and the intellectual inclination to engage in any systemic long-term definition of policy goals. The Soviet leaders are doubtless no exception. But the Soviet leaders do operate in the context of an orientation in which the retention of what Moscow controls and the disruption of what Washington seeks to organize provide lodestars for more specific tactics and strategies.

It is important to recall here that there is a basic difference between a genuinely revolutionary world-power and a disruptive world-power. Napoleonic France threatened not only the *status quo;* France's socio-economic development was such that France could serve as the center of a new international order that would have emerged if Napoleon had prevailed over Britain and Russia. In that sense, France was a genuinely revolutionary power. To an ominous degree, both Hitler's Germany and Tojo's Japan had also the revolutionary potential for creating a new international system, in the event that German and Japanese arms had won the war.

In contrast, the Soviet Union is limited to a disruptive, but not a truly revolutionary, role. It is confined to that role by the nature of its one-dimensional power and by the character of nuclear weapons. Nuclear weapons eliminate the possibility of a central war serving as the revolutionary cataclysm. Until the advent of the nuclear age, a world power could be displaced by its rival through a head-on military confrontation. Military victory was then translated into premier status by the exercise of the other attributes of national power, such as the economy, finances, science, and national culture. The nuclear age has had the effect of making these other means of exercising world domination also become the more critical instruments for *achieving* such world domination.

Yet it is in these other attributes of power that the Soviet Union is most deficient. Moreover, there is no reason to believe, given the inherent limitations of the Soviet system, that this situation will soon alter to the Soviet Union's benefit. The Soviet Union is thus condemned to seeking global status neither by head-on nuclear collision nor by a peaceful socio-economic competition. The only way open to it is that of attrition and gradual disruption of stable international arrangements so that the U.S. suffers directly and indirectly.

A STRATEGY OF DISRUPTION

The most effective way of pursuing such a strategy of disruption is to achieve and maintain sufficient military power to deter U.S. reactions and to intimidate U.S. friends, while encouraging trends hostile to U.S. interests in those particularly strategically vital areas which possess the greatest potential for a dynamic shift in the global political-economic balance. Today, these areas are, above all, the Middle East and Central America.

Accordingly, what happens in these two strategically and geopolitically sensitive zones will determine the longer-range pattern of the American-Soviet relationship and define the Soviet global role. A progressive deterioration of the political stability of the Middle East, combined with the gradual political re-entry of the Soviet Union into a region from which it has been excluded since 1973, could have far-reaching implications for American relations with both Europe and the Far East. The strategic salience of this region is such that any qualitatively important decline in American influence, especially if matched by a corresponding rise in Soviet political presence, is bound to have far-reaching and world-wide strategic consequences for the nature of the American-Soviet global equation.

Similarly, the manner in which the United States handles its new dilemmas in Central America, and in the longer run also the U.S.-Mexican relationship, is bound to affect the global balance, and therefore also the Soviet world role. As in the Middle East, it is again not so much a matter of what the Soviets may be doing as of how the United States conducts itself, either by commission or by omission. If American policy results in the "Americanization" of socio-political conflicts to such an extent that the Western hemisphere is increasingly turned against the United States—and the U.S.-Mexican problems become consequently so complicated that the United States loses the capacity for helping constructively in the resolution of Mexico's internal problems—the result will be a far-reaching decline in American global standing.

That, in turn, would reinforce the Soviet imperial consciousness and the expansionary impulse, while strengthening further the existing structure of Soviet power and the basic character of the system. Indeed, it is appropriate to recall in this connection that insofar as Russian historical experience is concerned, internal political change of truly significant character has tended to occur only in the wake of external defeats, whereas external successes have tended to reinforce centralism and ideological control. Moreover (as Arnold Horelick has shown in a recent Rand study) an improved Soviet domestic performance also tends to encourage a more assertive external behavior and the surfacing of greater external ambitions.

In contrast, external setbacks have induced profound reassessments of Russian internal policies and have occasionally produced even significant systemic changes. Thus, despite the internal weakness of the Czarist regime, its pervasive corruption and its mindless bureaucracy, the basic structure of its power endured for a long time—and collapsed finally only because of the massive military defeat inflicted upon it during the first three devastating years of World War I. Moreover, the occasional periods of internal reform that occurred in the first decade of the twentieth century, and during the 1860s, followed immediately upon external defeats suffered by Russia in the Russo-Japanese War and in the Crimean conflict, respectively. The great Russian historian V. O. Kluchevsky noted that "a Russian war carried to a successful issue has always helped to strengthen the previously compounded order"—but "progress in Russia's political life at home has always been gained at the price of Russia's political misfortune abroad."

By having become a global military power, the Soviet Union has *de facto* broken through the U.S. policy of geographic containment. At the same time, by expanding its exposure at a time when its own capacities are still profoundly one-dimensional, the Soviet Union is exposing itself to the possibility of overextension and even eventually to some major external misfortune, because of some protracted military-political misadventure. And in that respect Moscow's strategy of deliberate exploitation of global turbulence could turn out historically to have been a case of playing with fire.

The policy implications that follow from the foregoing analysis can be posited briefly as the following:

1. The military dimension of the East-West competition, notably of the U.S.-Soviet rivalry, is of critical importance negatively. Although the rivalry is not likely to be finally resolved by a clash of arms, the West must exercise every effort to make certain that the Soviet Union does not gain a military edge which would enable it to attempt political intimidation.

2. Arms-control arrangements should be assessed primarily in terms of their contribution to the maintenance of a stable East-West military balance. That is their central role. Arms control, moreover, should be pursued without historical illusions regarding the impact of any agreement on the character of the Soviet system and its relationship with the West, for the long-term political rivalry will not be ended by a comprehensive arms-control arrangement.

3. A major Soviet external misfortune is likely to have the most immediate impact on Eastern Europe. This region is manifestly restless and resentful of Soviet control. Any sign of Soviet weakness, any prolonged and debilitating Soviet foreign entanglement, will be exploited to break the weakest link in the Soviet imperial chain. Moreover, it is a region that is most susceptible to Western ideas and culturally attracted by Western Europe. It offers, therefore, a topical focus for Western policies designed to dilute the Soviet imperial impulse.

4. Western—and especially American—efforts to maintain and promote regional stability in such vital areas as Central America and the Middle East, are going to be decisive in determining whether Soviet global influence expands, to the detriment of international stability. American passivity in the Middle East and American over-engagement in Central America are the most immediate geopolitical dangers.

5. The positive task of shaping a wider international system that genuinely embraces the newly emancipated third world, and thus replaces the narrower European world order that collapsed in the course of World War II, will have to be pursued for quite some time to come without constructive Soviet involvement. The Soviet Union—too strong not to be a rival, yet feeling itself too weak to be a partner—cannot be counted upon to become a true participant in the constructive global process since its systemic interests are diametrically opposed to the preservation of the *status quo* in a world that Moscow can disrupt but not dominate.

6. Historical coexistence with the Soviet Union will remain dominated by the largely negative task of avoiding a nuclear catastrophe. It will be Western acts, of commission or omission, that will ultimately determine whether that historical coexistence—a coexistence that at best, for a long time to come, will be precariously peaceful—will eventually produce a more harmonious relationship or deteriorate into wider global anarchy.

CHAPTER TWENTY-THREE

———————— ■ ————————

The Crisis of Communism

IN THE CONTEXT OF THE NEW scientific-technological competition with the advanced West, the key issue that every ruling Communist party will have to address in the remaining years of the twentieth century is the problem of political participation. In examining this problem, I would first like to set forth the central impulses prompting the Communist governments to focus on the need to engage the citizenry in the political, economic, and social dimensions of national life. I would then like to examine how three Communist states—the Soviet Union, China, and Poland—have chosen to grapple with this dilemma and what problems have arisen from each approach. I will close with some observations about prospects for the resolution of the emerging crisis of communism.

*   *   *

The problem of participation is paradoxical in nature. By "participation" what is meant here is real participation: that is, participation in shaping the national and local decisions that are of consequential importance to the citizen. In its origins, the ideology and political movement of communism represented an attempt to create a basis for a fuller participation both in the social and political system of the early industrial age.

Yet, when its proponents have succeeded in seizing state power, communism has become an institutionalized system of highly regimented, disciplined, bureaucratized nonparticipation. It is, moreover, very difficult for Communist states to break out of this mold. None has been capable of transforming itself from a system in which an elite exerted top-down

This chapter appeared in *The Washington Quarterly*, vol. 10, no. 4 (autumn 1987). Copyright 1987 by the Center for Strategic and International Studies. Reprinted, with changes, by permission of the MIT Press.

control over society into one in which society participated in shaping its future from the bottom up, through indirection, choice, and freedom of information.

The original idea of communism was essentially utopian in nature. It called for the working class to govern itself. Leninism then superimposed the party as a political formula for elite control first over the workers' movement and then over the revolutionary government of the workers and peasants. Stalinism in turn institutionalized the supremacy of the party through the nomenklatura, thereby creating the hierarchical control mechanism that has become known as twentieth-century totalitarian communism. Yet, as successful as ruling Communist parties have been in controlling society, they have failed in mobilizing those same societies to achieve desired social objectives.

Therein lies the contemporary problem of participation under communism. Marxism-Leninism-Stalinism has proven itself capable of social mobilization for rapid industrialization, even though comparative data show that non-Communist countries have been able to achieve higher rates of growth and higher standards of living while incurring far lower social costs. Nonetheless, it is undeniable that rapid industrialization was achieved by Stalinist-type mobilization. The real failing of the Communist system, however, lies in its inability to transcend the phase of industrialization, to move from the industrial era into the postindustrial world.

We must recognize that this transformation will reshape the world as much as industrialization did. It involves three interrelated revolutions: a political revolution, a social revolution, and an economic revolution. Each revolution is independent of the others but at the same time feeds into the others. National success in the remaining years of this century and beyond will depend on the facility with which each nation harnesses these revolutionary forces.

The political revolution is animated by the idea of democracy. Human rights, self-government, and pluralism have become the universal aspirations of humanity. This was evident in Spain and Portugal, where one-party fascist regimes did not succeed in perpetuating themselves. It is also apparent in Latin America, where a proliferation of democratic government has taken place in the last ten years, and in the Far East, where the Filipino people ousted a dictator and where pressures have successfully risen for a more democratic order in South Korea. It is no exaggeration to assert that human rights and individual liberty have become the historical inevitability of our times.

The social revolution has been spawned by the appearance of new techniques of communication and for the processing of information. Advances in computer and communications technology have transformed the way people interact in modern society—and have on balance tended to break down the ability of a centralized state to control the flow of information through dogmatic censorship. These new technologies have also opened the way for vast increases in social productivity and will, over time, have the effect of increasing the gap between those societies that adapt to the new environment and those which do not.

The economic revolution involves the globalization of economic activity. Autarchy—even for the world's largest economies—is a fetter on efficiency. A country that seeks to develop solely within itself is likely to be a country that falls behind in development. The great national economic success stories of the last ten years—Japan, South Korea, Hong Kong, Singapore—all were based on capitalizing on the growth of world trade. Full exploitation of the potential of the world market will in the decades ahead be a precondition for continuing national prosperity—but that means sensitivity to the global market and hence flexibility and risk-taking in prompt and responsive economic decisionmaking.

We can expect that the countries that lead economically in the years ahead will be those whose political, social, and economic systems maximize individual and collective innovation. That requires that individuals be engaged—that they participate—in the system. Thus, for Communist countries, transcending the industrial phase requires a solution to the problem of participation.

Effective participation requires self-motivation. A system can motivate its members by ideas, by threats, or by incentives. Under Lenin, the idea of communism had a genuine appeal and impact. Under Stalin, the application of mass terror compelled obedience. Today, the idea of communism as a motivating force is dead, and no one even in ruling Communist parties wants to resurrect the mechanism of mass terror. Thus, incentives remain the only means to induce participation on the part of citizens in Communist countries—but Communist regimes have been singularly incapable of providing and structuring such incentives.

*   *   *

As they confront the crisis of communism, the Soviet Union, China, and Poland have a common point of departure: the heritage of Marxism-Leninism-Stalinism. In the political sphere, this involves the exclusive rule of the Communist party, with democratic centralism and a prohibition of horizontal communication imposing strict control over party members by the uppermost elite. In the economic sphere, it involves state control of all productive resources, with allocation based on central planning and with the price mechanism exerting minimal influence on economic decisions. In the social sphere, it involves a state-directed cultural and intellectual life and a strict prohibition on independent social organizations.

In the Soviet Union, Mikhail Gorbachev's three initiatives—openness, democratization, and economic restructuring—represent an effort to address the question of participation. In a recent address before the Soviet trade unions, he said, "The more democracy we have, the faster we will progress along the path of restructuring, socialist renovation, and the more order and discipline there will be. . . . So the question today is this: Either we have democratization or we have social inertness and conservatism. There is no third way here" (TASS, February 2, 1987). One must at least give Gorbachev credit for having put his finger on the critical problem.

Solutions, given the Soviet system, are more difficult to identify, however. On the political front, while Gorbachev has never questioned the importance of total party control, he has been grappling to find a way to make the Communist party more dynamic and to overcome the hide-bound party bureaucracy. He has used his campaign for glasnost to remove political adversaries, to create more participation at the lowest levels of the party, and to stimulate a higher degree of individual motivation. We should not, however, overestimate the significance of Gorbachev's glasnost. Michel Tatu has correctly noted that the campaign's concentration on the spheres of culture and information reveals its weakness and fragility. "It is not a sign of a leader's strength," he writes, "because if a leader were very strong he would do big things inside the apparatus" (*Soviet-Eastern Europe Report,* June 10, 1987, p. 3).

There is a joke circulating in Moscow that captures in an amusing way the essence of the glasnost campaign. A man visits his doctor and says, "Doctor, I have a problem, but I need two specialists: one for the ears, nose, and throat, and one for the eye." The specialists then arrive and inquire about the man's condition. He answers, "Gentlemen, I hope very much that you will be able to help me. It's a very worrying state I'm in: I don't see what I hear."

The fact is that reformist rhetoric is not the same thing as a concrete reform program. On the economic front, Gorbachev has so far announced reforms that nudge the country away from central planning, particularly in foreign trade, but that in no sense yet promote widespread market-based pricing or allocation of resources. Central planning will still prescribe national production quotas, but factory managers will have increased latitude in determining their production and in marketing their products. He has sought not to overturn the system but to rationalize it, with East Germany—not Hungary or China—as Gorbachev's model.

It is therefore too early to know how thorough a reform of the Soviet economy Gorbachev is seeking. Will collectivized agriculture be abandoned? We do not have the answer to the key question: How systemic—in the eyes of the Kremlin leadership—is the internal economic crisis?

Related to this is the question of how far-reaching a cultural revolution is the Soviet leadership prepared to promote both within the Soviet labor force and within Soviet management. After seventy years of the Soviet system, neither Soviet workers nor Soviet managers are predisposed toward self-motivation and risk-taking. The engrained habits of work emphasize conformity, laxness, bureaucratic security, and camouflaged privilege. The simple fact is that Soviet Russians are not Communist Prussians!

Beyond that, there is an enormous divide between economic decentralization from above and economic participation from below, between economic dispersal and political participation. Where to draw the line between the former and the latter is likely to be the major preoccupation of the Soviet leaders for years to come. This is the case not just because of the conservative nature of bureaucracy. The more important cause is the multinational character of the modern-day Great Russian Empire. The Soviet Union is the last surviving multinational empire in the world. The Great Russian people dominate a dozen major nations and scores of lesser nations. That national diversity ultimately represents the Achilles' heel of the system. A program of reforms for genuine participation— involving the dispersal of central power—could easily devolve into general national conflict between the Great Russians and the non-Russian nations of the Soviet Union.

Moreover, one must anticipate that Gorbachev's initial reforms may produce considerable confusion and almost inevitably some rise in consumer prices. A drop in the standard of living is thus likely—and that could trigger dangerous unrest. As Soviet citizens become more accustomed to even modestly enhanced participation, they will become emboldened in venting their dissatisfaction. One should not be surprised to see at that stage open manifestations of student unrest, of demonstrations by housewives, and even of strikes in the factories. The litmus test will be how the Soviet leadership then reacts to such unprecedented forms of participation from below.

In China, Deng Xiaoping's reforms have focused on economic decentralization. He has disbanded collectivized agriculture and introduced other reforms that, when completed, will remove 65 to 70 percent of production from state control by the year 2000. This will make profitability, not political pliability, the test of economic management. These reforms are not superficial—but consequential. They change the way the system works because they shift the locus and method of decisionmaking.

The central dilemma is whether economic reform will produce irresistible pressures for political reform. As evident in the recent student demonstrations for greater democracy, there is a link between the two. Fang Lizhi, who is the intellectual leader of the Shanghai student movement, addressed this question in a speech before his expulsion from the Communist party. He said, "Socialism is at a low ebb. There is no getting around the fact that no socialist state in the post–World War II era has been successful and neither has our own thirty-odd-year-long socialist experiment." He later added, "I feel that the first step toward democratization should be recognition of human rights" (*China Spring Digest,* March-April 1987, p. 15).

It was inevitable that the question of political reform would be posed, especially as the Communist party itself has formally diluted the importance of Marxist dogma. Deng Xiaoping's slogan calling on China to "seek truth from facts" cast doubt on the notion of ideological dogma itself. That made the rise of some kind of political challenges to the leading role of the party a matter of time. If truth lies in examining facts, anyone can deduce the truth—and competing interpretations of the facts will certainly arise. If no single truth exists and if others beside the party can divine this truth, no rationale exists for dictatorial rule by the party.

I discussed the issue of political reform with Hu Yaobang last year, several months before the student protests that led to his ouster. Hu told me, in the course of a five-hour-long conversation, that the reform program was far from finished and that future reforms would have to involve a restructuring of the Chinese political system. He said that initial discussions on this issue had taken place within the Politburo and that a party document would be finished on the subject in 1987. He explained that the fundamental nature of the party would not change and that the party would remain the leadership core of China. He added that the central party bureaucracy would be streamlined, that there would be considerable reform in the relationship between subordinates and superiors within the party, and that other political parties within China— the so-called democratic parties—would be given greater autonomy.

But the Chinese party leaders are clearly reluctant to take that giant step, leading from economic decentralization to political decentralization. In recent months, if anything, a reverse trend has manifested itself. A number of key Chinese political leaders have become alarmed that economic decentralization will spill over into the political realm, creating something that might be called a more liberalized political system. They have been quite explicit in their denunciations, and Hu Yaobang has fallen from power. Reflecting the ruling elite's anxiety, Hu Sheng, the chairman of the Academy of Social Sciences, said, "Some people have used the open policy and situation of letting 'one hundred schools contend' to preach bourgeois liberalism, refute socialism, advocate total Westernization and lash out at party leadership" (*The New York Times,* January 17, 1987, p. A4).

We can expect that the catalyst for China's political future will be the succession struggle after Deng passes from the scene. Given China's mass scale, one is entitled to expect a protracted conflict between the political imperatives of the Communist system and the economic requirements of the modernization program. My own expectation is that eventually the latter will prevail over the former, but only after quite a few zig-zags in domestic policy and after intense conflicts on the political level.

In Poland, communism has essentially broken down. Formally, the Communist party still rules the country. But in reality a combined military-police clique holds power in the name of the party, the Church is a significant force, and the leadership of Solidarity has become in effect an organized, if unofficial, political opposition.

What is significant here is that Polish society has in a very real sense self-emancipated itself. The Communist party has been unable to retain its monopoly on social organization and has had to accommodate itself to pressures from below to an unprecedented degree. When I traveled through Poland last month, I was genuinely impressed by the extent to which the opposition functions as a parallel social leadership. Its underground press publishes hundreds of newspapers, which are widely available and easily accessible. It even has managed to break the state's monopoly on the electronic media through the use of videocassette recorders. Whenever I arrived for meetings with opposition figures, it was always amid a battery of video cameras, not to speak of cassette tape recorders. While freedoms are not as great as they were at the peak of the Solidarity movement, we should not fail to note the significance of the fact that the opposition to the Communist regime feels so confident that it can hold "photo opportunities" for its own news media.

I was also impressed by the extent to which the confidence of the Polish Communist regime has been broken. As a result of state mismanagement of the economy, Poland is an economic calamity—and its Communist leaders know it. Even to begin the process of economic renewal, the state needs to engage the society—that is, to persuade the people to participate in the process. Since the imposition of martial law, however, Polish society has essentially adopted a strategy of passive resistance. To overcome this willful inertia, all the Polish Communist leaders with whom I met accepted the fact that they needed in some fashion to engage or co-opt the opposition leadership. But a political gridlock has developed over the question of how such accommodations might proceed. The government demands that the opposition operate in government organs, such as the official trade unions or the new advisory commission, but the opposition will not let itself be seduced into such subordinate status.

There seem to be basically three prospects for communism in Poland, with the precipitating catalyst for change being Poland's deepening economic crisis and the need for Western credits. The first is a continuation of the current political stalemate, with the growing risk of an eventual explosion from below. The second is a progressive return to repression, leading to a renewal of central control and administration. The third is a continuing transformation of the sociopolitical structure, leading eventually perhaps to formalized co-participation and even in the long-term to a system that (for geopolitical reasons) remains Communist in name only.

The bottom line is that genuine participation is incompatible with the rule of a Leninist-type party. In Poland, such a party no longer exercises a monopoly of power, but a new system of overt participation has not replaced it. The situation is one of an unstable stalemate. In the Soviet Union, political experimentation is confined to the lower political-social level, while the present economic reforms—to be truly successful—require a monumental change in the culture and working habits of both labor and management. In China, economic decentralization is in collision with continued political centralization, though China's commercial culture favors the progressive emancipation of the economic sector.

*   *   *

In conclusion, what is common to these three countries is that their Communist-type systems are encountering great difficulties in evolving beyond the phase of development associated with rapid industrialization. All so far have been unable to solve the problem of participation. At the core of the problem is the concept of an elitist party with a dogmatic conception of the truth. Such a ruling party is, very simply, incompatible with the notion of genuinely spontaneous social participation in the political, economic, and social spheres of a more modern, complex society. Until the nature of the party is changed or the party disappears, the issue of participation will continue to be a source of conflict both within the party and between the party and society.

Ultimately, the inability to resolve that conflict and to provide for genuine participation may prove to be the undoing of modern communism. There is considerable evidence justifying the belief that modern communism is becoming an increasingly sterile system in which the ruling party is viewed by society at large as the principal obstacle to social progress and to societal well-being. If one is correct in stating that the quest for genuine political participation is today's universal imperative, one is also justified to surmise that it augurs the approaching historical demise of the Communist system of social mobilization and political

TABLE 23.1

Participation in Communist Systems

	Marxism-Leninism-Stalinism	Soviet Union	China	Poland
Political Participation	Total party control. Centralized party discipline. Prohibition on horizontal communication. Nomenklatura.	Efforts to energize party bureaucracy. Minimal experimentation with low-level multicandidate elections.	Official dilution of Marxist dogma. Party recruitment of technical expertise. Experimentation with municipal electoral choice.	Military-party symbiosis. Church represents a political force. Solidarity leadership acts as organized but unofficial opposition which is excluded from policy participation.
Economic Participation	State ownership of productive resources. Collectivized agriculture. Centralized command economy. No role for price mechanism.	Proposed limited exposure to international prices and to price mechanism for production beyond state-fixed quota. Proposed elections for workplace managers.	Retrenchment in central planning. Decollectivization of agriculture. Widespread influence of price mechanism. Integration into capitalist world economy.	Private land ownership. Local trade unions, often run by former Solidarity members, influential in some industries. Stalemate between state and society over economic future.
Social Participation	Prohibition on independent social organizations. State-directed intellectual and cultural life. Communication tightly controlled.	More openness about problems within Soviet Union. More cultural and artistic freedom.	Nascent consumerism. More cultural and intellectual freedom, but suppression of "bourgeois liberalism."	Self-emancipated society. Party monopoly on independent social organization broken. Effectively free underground press. Independent cultural and intellectual life.
Key Issue	---	Scope and implementation of reform program.	Balance between economic and political reform.	Interaction between economic recovery, social austerity, and political participation.
Alternative Prospects	---	Slowdown of reforms. National unrest leading to reversal of reforms. Systemic reform.	Political retrenchment. Political decentralization. Collision between political and economic imperatives.	Continued stalemate risking political explosion. Progressive repression. Formalized co-participation.
Precipitating Catalyst	---	A politically activating and polarizing drop in the standard of living.	Succession struggle linked to programmatic debates.	Deepening economic crisis and realization of unavailability of Western aid.

Source: "The Crisis of Communism: The Paradox of Political Participation," Zbigniew Brzezinski, International Leadership Forum, Istanbul, Turkey, June 30, 1987 nonparticipation. Indeed, in many respects, the mood within large portions of the public in the Communist world is today reminiscent of the mood within capitalist states almost six decades ago, at the time of the Great Depression: There is a sense that a fatal flaw exists in the system itself. That flaw is called the Communist party.

CHAPTER TWENTY-FOUR

—————— ■ ——————

The Future of Yalta

YALTA IS UNFINISHED BUSINESS. It has a longer past and it may have a more ominous future than is generally recognized. Forty years after the fateful Crimean meeting of February 4–11, 1945, between the Allied Big Three of World War II, much of our current preoccupation with Yalta focuses on its myth rather than on its continuing historical significance.

The myth is that at Yalta the West accepted the division of Europe. The fact is that Eastern Europe had been conceded de facto to Joseph Stalin by Franklin D. Roosevelt and Winston Churchill as early as the Teheran Conference (in November-December 1943), and at Yalta the British and American leaders had some halfhearted second thoughts about that concession. They then made a last-ditch but ineffective effort to fashion some arrangements to assure at least a modicum of freedom for Eastern Europe, in keeping with Anglo-American hopes for democracy on the European continent as a whole. The Western statesmen failed, however, to face up to the ruthlessness of the emerging postwar Soviet might, and in the ensuing clash between Stalinist power and Western naivete, power prevailed.

Yalta's continuing significance lies in what it reveals about Russia's enduring ambitions toward Europe as a whole. Yalta was the last gasp of carefully calibrated Soviet diplomacy designed to obtain Anglo-American acquiescence to a preponderant Soviet role in all of Europe. At Yalta, in addition to timidly reopening the issue of Eastern Europe, the West also deflected, but again in a vague and timorous fashion, Soviet aspirations for a dominant position in the western extremity of the Eurasian land mass.

Reprinted, with changes, by permission of *Foreign Affairs*, winter 1984/85.

Yalta thus remains of great geopolitical significance because it symbolizes the unfinished struggle for the future of Europe. Forty years after Yalta that struggle still involves America and Russia, but by now it should be clear that the issue is unlikely to be resolved in a historically constructive manner until a more active role is assumed by the very object of the contest, Europe itself.

POLAND: THE KEY TO CONTROLLING EASTERN EUROPE

The setting for Yalta was prostrated Europe. That once globally dominant civilization had committed historical suicide in the course of two devastating wars fought within the span of a mere quarter-century. When the two leaders of the British and American democracies met with the Georgian tyrant of the Great Russian Empire to resolve the future of Europe, continental Europe was absent from the deliberations. In the meantime, much of Europe's future was being decided on the ground, by the great extra-European armies pushing from the east and the west into Germany, the heart of Europe.

Until Yalta, the key issue perplexing the wartime alliance was Poland, the key to control over Eastern Europe. Thereafter, the issue has increasingly become Germany, the key to control over Western Europe. Poland represented to Moscow the gate to the West, and thus the Kremlin in its wartime diplomacy adopted an attitude of utter intransigence on the question of Poland's future. Though in his memoirs Churchill later described the Polish issue as "the first of the great causes which led to the breakdown of the Grand Alliance," neither he nor his Atlantic partner, President Roosevelt, seemed to grasp the central strategic importance of the Polish issue; nor was either of them inclined to exploit Russia's initial weakness to obtain a satisfactory resolution of the Polish-Soviet dispute, initiated by the Soviet seizure of almost half of Poland in 1939 as a result of the Stalin-Ribbentrop agreement.

Stalin correctly saw in the territorial dispute the opportunity to transform Polish independence into dependence on Moscow. So did the Poles. Prior to the Teheran meeting, the Polish prime minister desperately warned Churchill (as recorded by Sir William Strang on September 9, 1943) that "what was at stake between Poland and Russia was not merely a question of frontiers but a question of general relations and indeed the question of the survival of Poland as an independent state. . . ."[1]

---

[1]This, and the other documents cited, are contained in the very useful collection edited by A. Polansky, *The Great Powers and the Polish Question*, London: L.S.E., 1976. See also V. Mastny, *Russia's Road to the Cold War*, New York: Columbia Press, 1979.

A month later, Foreign Minister Anthony Eden reported to the British War Cabinet that the Polish prime minister had told him on October 6, "The general attitude of Stalin towards Poland, towards Germany and the Free German movement and towards questions touching other occupied countries, as well as his record and his whole mentality, implied more extensive ambitions than ambitions only in the eastern provinces of Poland which were strategically important to Poland but in no sense vital to Russia." Finally on the eve of the Teheran meeting, Eden briefed the War Cabinet on November 22 that the Poles feared "that Russia's long-term aim is to set up a puppet government in Warsaw and turn Poland into a Soviet republic. . . ."

The British took a more benign view of Stalin's goals. Eden assured the Poles "that British experience suggested that Stalin was much less intransigent. . . ," and his internal memorandum on preparations for the forthcoming Teheran Conference makes it clear that the United Kingdom was prepared to satisfy Stalin's territorial goals in the hope that this would produce acceptable political arrangements. If anything, the Americans were even more inclined to gratify Stalin. In keeping with the foregoing, in Teheran in late November and early December 1943, both Churchill and Roosevelt agreed to changes in the Polish frontiers, without any further consultation with the Poles, and more generally conceded to Moscow a preponderant role in the Balkans.

To make matters worse, while pressing the Poles to make territorial concessions to Moscow in the hope of assuaging Russian desires, the British and Americans were unwilling to offer the Poles any assurances regarding compensation in the West. Adopting the position that changes in Germany's frontiers must await the end of the war, London and Washington made the Polish plight more desperate. As a result, most Poles simply refused any compromise on the grounds that a truncated Poland could not survive as an independent entity, while others, shocked and embittered, increasingly saw in Moscow the only sponsor of major Polish territorial acquisition of German territory as a compensation for what was to be absorbed by Russia. The price, however, was the inevitable emergence of Polish dependence on Russia, and through it Soviet domination over Eastern Europe.

By the time of Yalta, not only was Poland occupied by the Red Army, but a new government, sponsored by Stalin, had been installed in Warsaw. At Yalta, the West exacted Soviet promises that the Soviet-installed government would be enlarged and would hold free elections, following which the West would recognize it, but Western leaders agreed not to have any binding obligations regarding the elections inserted into the joint communiqué issued at the conclusion of the Yalta Conference. As a result, how free elections were to be organized remained an exclusive

Soviet prerogative, with the outcome thereby predetermined. (Indeed, the Western powers recognized the Warsaw government in mid-1945, even though—contrary to the Yalta agreement—no elections had been held.)

MOSCOW'S ENDURING GEOSTRATEGIC GOALS

By finally foreclosing the issue of Poland in Russia's favor, Yalta opened the battle for the future of Germany. Eastern Poland had been incorporated into the Soviet Union, but the West continued to oppose major Polish expansion at Germany's expense. The Russians at first hesitated in deciding how extensively they ought to support Polish claims. But at the Potsdam Conference in July 1945, following Germany's final collapse, Stalin apparently concluded that with his armies firmly implanted in the middle of Germany he could afford to satisfy Polish needs (thereby permanently cementing Polish dependence on Russia), while continuing to wage his struggle for a preeminent Soviet role in Western Europe.

For Stalin, that struggle was the vital substance of his war time alliance with the West. Late in 1943, on the eve of the Teheran Conference, Stalin, whose armies were then still fighting on Soviet soil, had succeeded in obtaining Western accord for a major Soviet role in both postwar Germany and Italy, and Western acquiescence to the scuttling of the Polish-Czechoslovak plans for a Central European confederation which might have presented an obstacle to Soviet domination over the region.

The Teheran Conference further nurtured Stalin's grandiose hopes that the British would be unable and the Americans unwilling to oppose his larger designs, which he revealed cautiously, while continuously probing the intentions and the will of his British and American interlocutors. Throughout, Stalin and his associates skillfully played on the anti-imperialist sentiments of the Americans to weaken the British role in any postwar arrangements and on the British rivalry with France to make certain that no center of effective power would emerge in postwar Western Europe. In the Soviet interpretation, Roosevelt's penchant for speaking of the world's "four policemen" could have had only one geopolitical meaning: America's central concern would be the Western Hemisphere, a weak China would be preoccupied with its own problems, and a bankrupt Britain would be enmeshed in its imperial dilemmas, leaving most of Eurasia to the care of the fourth policeman.

In testing Western reactions to his design, Stalin used as bait two somewhat varying schemes for Europe. Though one will never know to what extent these plans were alternative scenarios or competing concepts, both plans provided for a major Soviet role in all of Europe. The two options were succinctly summed up in a conversation on August 31,

1943, between British Foreign Minister Eden and the Soviet ambassador to London, Ivan Maisky, as reported by Eden:

> . . . Maisky continued that there were two ways of trying to organize Europe after the war. Either we could agree each to have a sphere of interest, the Russians in the East and ourselves and the Americans in the West. He did not himself think this was a good plan, but if it were adopted we should be at liberty to exclude the Russians from French Affairs, the Mediterranean and so forth, and the Russians would claim similar freedom in the East. If, on the other hand, we would both, and the United States also, agree that all Europe was one, as his Government would greatly prefer, then we must each admit the right of the other to an interest in all parts of Europe. If we were concerned with Czechoslovakia and Poland, and the United States with the Baltic states, then we must understand Russian concern in respect of France and the Mediterranean. . . .[2]

The latter variant was apparently advocated at least until Yalta by Maxim Litvinov, the former Soviet Commissar for Foreign Affairs and former ambassador to Washington. Postulated on the unstated assumption that America would disengage militarily from Europe but that at least a semblance of congeniality between the Soviet Union and its principal wartime allies would continue even after the war, and bound to appeal to the idealistic American dislike of spheres of influence, the plan envisaged not only a Soviet role in all of occupied Germany but in effect a thinly camouflaged arrangement for a Europe dominated indirectly by the Soviet Union, the only effective power in the region. British influence was to be confined to several narrow maritime enclaves, France was to play a negligible role, while continued Soviet-American accommodation would be tacitly premised on American noninvolvement in European affairs. There can be little doubt that the Soviets took seriously Roosevelt's repeated hints both at Teheran and even later at Yalta that the United States would not maintain a postwar military presence in Europe. Given their ideological cast, they must also have been reassured by Roosevelt's tendency to speak privately to Stalin in most negative terms both of the British and of the French, seeing in that confirmation of their theory of "inherent capitalist contradictions."

The alternative to this strategy of domination through Western acquiescence was associated with Litvinov's principal rival and successor at the helm for foreign affairs, Vyacheslav Molotov. It took more for granted that an American-Soviet collision would eventually occur, presumably after the expected U.S. disengagement from Europe and probably

---

[2]Polansky, op. cit.

in the context of sharpening intercapitalist conflict. Molotov's alternative strategy of exclusive control by fait accompli put more emphasis, therefore, on directly subordinating eastern Europe and as much of central Europe as possible, while vigorously asserting Soviet claims to a major role in the West and to a coequal veto-wielding status in relations with the United States. In more specific discussions regarding postwar arrangements for Germany, Stalin was careful to keep his options open. At times he seemed to be favoring a central German government, at other times he would opt for the fragmentation of Germany into several constituent states. In either case, he was always insistent that the Soviet Union have a major say in all of Germany, while making certain that no major West European power was reconstituted.

As the Soviet armies marched westward, Stalin's claims became more explicit both territorially and politically. In addition to retaining everything seized during the collaboration with Hitler, by late 1944 and early 1945 the Soviet Union made territorial demands on Norway (Bear Island and the Spitzbergen) and regarding the Far East (southern Sakhalin, the Kurile Islands, and a preponderant role in Manchuria and Outer Mongolia). Stalin also sought a share in controlling Tangier and a slice of the Italian colonies on the Mediterranean, in addition to proposals for joint action against Franco's Spain and increased political pressure on neutral Switzerland and Sweden. This was followed later by demands for territorial concessions by Turkey. Moreover, the Soviets consistently spoke of France as totally demoralized and worthless, underlining the proposition that Europe was a political vacuum.

Anglo-American surprise and protracted failure to come to grips with the scope of these Soviet ambitions is all the more remarkable when one considers the extent to which Stalin's aspirations mirrored traditional Russian goals. Indeed they so closely replicated Tsarist objectives in World War I that one may suspect that old Russian planning papers were disinterred for Stalin's and Molotov's use. Some 30 years earlier, in late 1914, the Russian Council of Ministers had also considered the related problems of Poland and of Russian postwar objectives. The majority report focused on the restoration of a Polish kingdom, but under Imperial Russian sway, as Russia's major postwar objective. However, the minority report prepared by the more reactionary members went beyond that priority and defined Russian war objectives much more ambitiously.

Russia's general aims were stated as involving the "strengthening of Russia herself, in an ethnic, economic and strategic way"; in addition to "the possible weakening of Germanism as the chief enemy of Slavdom and Russia at the present time"; and to "the possible liberation of other Slavic peoples from the authority of Germany and Austria-Hungary (insofar

as such liberation does not conflict with the direct interests of Russia)."
To accomplish the above, Russia was to attain the following specific goals
in order of importance:

1. Completion of the historic task of uniting all sections of the Russian
   people by reuniting eastern Galicia, northern Bukovina and Car-
   pathian Rus' with Russia.
2. Realization of the historic tasks of Russia in the Black Sea by the
   annexation of Tsar'grad (Constantinople) and the Turkish Straits.
3. Rectification of the borders of the Russian state at the expense of
   East Prussia and also in Asiatic Turkey.
4. The weakening of Germany internally in every possible way by
   means of her complete territorial reconstruction on a new basis,
   with a possible decrease in Prussian territory to the advantage of
   France, Belgium, Luxembourg, Denmark and the smaller German
   states as well, and, perhaps, the restoration of the Kingdom of
   Hanover, Hesse-Nassau, etc.
5. Unification and liberation of Poland within the widest possible
   boundaries, but, in any case, within limits which are ethnographic
   rather than historic (which would be contrary to the basic interest
   and entire history of Russia).
6. Liberation of the remaining Austrian Slavs.[3]

What is striking about these war aims, drafted by the more nationalistic
and reactionary members of the Council, is their identity with Soviet
post–World War II objectives defined by Stalin and Molotov. Every one
of the objectives became Stalin's: the incorporation of parts of Polish
Galicia never previously held by Russia and of Czechoslovak Sub-Carpathia
were identical with the first 1914 goal; the second objective was denied
to the Soviets, but they did press for it in their conversations with the
Western Allies (presumably recalling that in the spring of 1915 France
and Britain had conceded as much to Tsarist Russia); the third objective
was obtained in East Prussia (again a surprise to Westerners), and the
Soviets in 1945 pressed for territorial concessions from Turkey but
without success; the fourth was achieved in a different form in Germany;
the fifth pushed Poland further west than was thought possible in 1914
but with functionally the same result—the creation of a Poland highly
dependent on Russia for its territorial integrity.

---

[3]Gifford D. Malone, quoting *Russko-pol'skie otnosheniia v period mirovoi voiny* (Moscow,
1926), in *Russian Diplomacy and Eastern Europe, 1914-1917*, New York: King's Crown,
1963. pp. 20-21, 139-40.

One can thus classify Soviet wartime objectives as falling into three categories: first, recovery of the territorial status quo ante as of June 1941; second, securing politically acquiescent regimes in east-central Europe; third, gaining a preponderant voice regarding the political organization of the rest of Europe. The Soviets were totally unyielding and quite open about the first objective; they were prepared, however, to camouflage the second objective if it served to promote the attainment of the third goal. It is easy to forget how uncertain at the time was America's postwar role in Europe, while American unwillingness during wartime to focus concretely on postwar issues fortified the expectation that it would again turn inward. As Soviet forces moved westward, their pursuit of the second objective became more brazen, and it assumed brutal manifestations when it dawned upon the Soviets that there might not be an American acquiescence to the attainment of the third objective. That realization dawned on Stalin and his colleagues with increasing intensity after Yalta.

FROM COMPROMISE TO CONFLICT

Yalta can therefore be said to have initiated the postwar struggle for Europe. Yet it was hailed in the West as an unmitigated diplomatic triumph, foreshadowing a period of prolonged East-West accommodation. Forty years later this very same Yalta continues to evoke equally simplistic—though opposite—emotions. It is now the synonym for betrayal. At the time its decisions were said (according to a *New York Times* editorial of February 13, 1945) to "justify and surpass most of the hopes placed on this fateful meeting . . . they show the way to an early victory in Europe, to a secure peace and to a brighter world."

Sumner Wells might be accused of some partiality when he announced (in *The Washington Post* on February 28, 1945) that ". . . the Declaration of Yalta, whatever the future may bring forth, will always stand out as a gigantic step toward the ultimate establishment of a peaceful and orderly world." But even such an experienced observer as Walter Lippmann was not to be outdone. Writing in *The New York Herald Tribune* on February 15, 1945, Lippmann informed his readers that Churchill, Stalin, and Roosevelt "have checked and reversed the normal tendency of a victorious coalition to dissolve as the war, which called it into being, approaches its end. . . . The military alliance is proving itself to be no transitory thing, good only in the presence of a common enemy, but in truth the nucleus and core of a new international order."

Skeptical voices were few and far between. *The Wall Street Journal* warned on February 16, 1945, that the Yalta deal on central Europe "can only lead to increasingly unsatisfactory relations between the United

States and Russia"; while a perceptive Frenchman, André Visson, (writing in *The Washington Post* on February 18, 1945, in an article entitled "Big Powers and Small Nations") noted that the United States was finally becoming committed to the future of Europe and was showing signs of willingness even to contest the Soviet domination over Eastern Europe—unlike at Teheran, where it seemed uninterested in postwar arrangements and willing to settle for "the division of Europe into two zones of influence."

In fact, Yalta was the last effort by the wartime partners to construct the postwar world jointly. Unlike Teheran, where Churchill was still clearly Roosevelt's equal, at Yalta the lead was taken by the Americans, foreshadowing the bipolar world that was in fact emerging. The real collision at Yalta was between Roosevelt's well-meaning vagueness about arrangements for Europe's postwar future and Stalin's studied vagueness about the extent of Russia's desire to dominate that future. The former desperately wanted to believe in postwar cooperation while the latter deliberately exploited that faith to create facts on the ground while pressing for Western acceptance of Soviet claims in both the west and the far east of the Eurasian continent.

As a result, the Yalta declarations were manifestly escapist in character. The provisions regarding free elections in Poland were at best a transparent fig leaf for outright Soviet domination, while the rhetoric concerning future peace simply obscured the emerging and very basic differences between the major powers. However, that rhetoric did serve to further delude Western public opinion regarding Russia's true intentions, thereby making it more difficult for the Western democracies to cope effectively with the emerging East-West confrontation.

By failing to construct an agreed-upon world, while in effect sanctioning the concessions made earlier at Teheran, Yalta became subsequently the symbol of Europe's partition. The follow-on meeting at Potsdam was merely a contentious session to carve up the spoils. It was at Yalta that the Westerners belatedly had the first inklings that the concession of Eastern Europe to Soviet domination might be the beginning of the contest for central and Western Europe, while to Stalin Western reticence regarding satisfaction of the wider Soviet goals foreshadowed a more difficult political struggle than apparently anticipated earlier. Henceforth, the increasingly overt preoccupation of Soviet policy became one of driving the United States out of Eurasia.

THE CONTEST FOR EUROPE

That preoccupation has endured for the 40 subsequent years—and today it is still the central motif of Soviet foreign policy. Its concomitant is the determination to prevent the emergence of a genuine Europe motivated by shared political will. The last four decades, however, also reveal an important strategic lesson: what has come to be seen as the legacy of Yalta—namely, the partition of Europe—can only be undone either in Soviet favor through Litvinov's more subtle design of domination through acquiescence, or to Europe's historical advantage by the emergence of a truly European Europe capable of attracting Eastern Europe and of diluting Soviet control over the region. America does not have the power or the will to change basically the situation in Eastern Europe, while crude and heavy-handed Soviet efforts to intimidate West Europe merely consolidate the Atlantic connection.

Of the two principal sides, it has been the Soviet that has sought much more persistently than the American to achieve a geopolitical breakthrough, settling the fate of Eurasia. Yalta had stimulated Soviet anxieties that America might not in fact disengage totally from Europe; Potsdam reinforced them, while the subequent announcement of the Marshall Plan confirmed Moscow's worst fears: America, contrary to Stalin's hopes and expectations, was becoming implanted on the continent, de facto checking the expansion of Soviet power.

Subsequent history has been punctuated by more overt and direct Soviet efforts to challenge that reality head-on—above and beyond the relentless attempts to undermine it. The political campaign against the Marshall Plan, and Stalin's open decision to keep both Czechoslovakia and Poland out of it, were undertaken in the context of the strategic conclusion that not only would America remain engaged in European affairs but that a protracted political conflict was now inevitable. The subsequent Berlin crisis was thus an important test of will, designed to challenge America's suddenly improvised determination to play a major role in the truncated Germany.

It is important to be clear about it: neither Stalin's blockade of Berlin, nor Khrushchev's Berlin crisis of a decade later, was about Berlin itself. In both cases, the stake was the American security connection with Western Europe. This is why both Stalin and Khrushchev were willing to risk even a period of very high tension—dangerously high tension— with America, something which Berlin itself did not merit. Had the Soviets prevailed, Germany would have been panicked, and the vaunted American commitment to the defense of Europe would have been rendered impotent. The geopolitical effect of a Soviet success in Berlin would have been to establish Soviet paramountcy over Western Europe.

Though the two Berlin crises were the most overt indicators of the enduring Soviet determination to sever the Atlantic security connection, Soviet diplomacy throughout the postwar era has pursued also the cardinal objective of ensuring that a geopolitically vital Europe does not surface as a competitor or even as a neighbor. Soviet foreign policy—using all its diplomatic leverage as well as such overt and hidden tools as the West European Communist parties and the myriad of fellow travelers—has been active in opposing such schemes as the European Defense Community, and it has above all persistently tried to place obstacles in the way of the Common Market's evolution toward a political personality. Even if Western Europe cannot be severed from America, it must at least be kept divided and weak.

The commitment to the goal of expelling America from Europe is not just lingering in the Kremlin. It animates the current Soviet leadership, a leadership more Stalinist in substance than any since 1953. Attempting to exploit the West European "peace movements" and unease regarding the anti-Soviet rhetoric of the Reagan administration, the current Soviet leadership decided to elevate the INF (intermediate range nuclear forces) issue into a new test of will, again making the Atlantic security connection the ultimate stake. The Soviet decision to refuse to negotiate with the United States on arms-control issues unless the United States dismantles and removes its Pershing IIs and ground-launched cruise missiles is tantamount to an attempt to impose on America a public humiliation with wide-ranging strategic consequences. It is functionally equivalent to the earlier Berlin crises.

But the Soviet leadership has again overreached itself. Its heavy-handed tactics contributed to the defeat of the neutralist Social Democratic Party in Germany, to the discrediting of the unilateral disarmers in the Labour Party in Britain, and to the strong show of solidarity with America displayed by Europe on the issue. (Parenthetically, one may add that almost simultaneously the present Soviet leadership has stimulated in Japan the highest degree of anti-Sovietism since World War II.) It did so because it overestimated the depth of the neutralist sentiments and the extent of the West European, even the German, stake in the East-West détente. It may also have overestimated the impact on West European public opinion of the greatly increased Soviet strategic power, especially in comparison to the Berlin crises of the late 1940s and the late 1950s. The Soviet leaders may have calculated that the combination of a specifically West European interest in détente with the growing fear of Soviet military power (especially with massive deployment of the SS-20s targeted on Western Europe) might stampede the West Europeans—even if not the Americans—into a unilateral accommodation. They thus relied too much on simple political intimidation.

Nonetheless, in addition to noting Soviet persistence in seeking to achieve the subordination of Western Europe, it is important not to be overly reassured by the Soviet failure. For that failure is due more to the crudeness of the Soviet tactics than the resilience of Western Europe.

The fact is that Western Europe as such has not emerged politically. In that respect the Soviet Union can be said to have achieved at least a part of what it has been seeking since Yalta. In the meantime, the continued division of Europe breeds growing resentment not only of the direct Soviet domination over Eastern Europe but also of the American role in Europe, a situation which more skillful Soviet diplomacy could at some point more intelligently exploit.

The political reality is that America cannot undo Europe's partition, but the existence of that partition intensifies the American-Soviet rivalry which in turn perpetuates the partition. Though America has at times sought to loosen the bonds that both tie and subordinate Eastern Europe to Moscow, at the truly critical junctures America has chosen not to contest Soviet domination directly. American policy has aimed at carefully encouraging the peaceful evolution of a somewhat more pluralistic Eastern Europe, a process that is bound to take time and which can periodically be reversed by force, as through martial law in Poland in 1981. However, when the East German regime collapsed in 1953, when Hungary arose in 1956, when Czechoslovakia peacefully emancipated itself in 1968 only to be invaded by Soviet armed forces, the United States adopted a passive posture masked by anti-Soviet rhetoric. Whether more could have been done is debatable, but that not much was done is undeniable.

DIVIDED GERMANY: A PERMANENT CATALYST FOR CHANGE

American prudence is one reason why the Europeans sense that America cannot undo the division of Europe. The other reason is even more basic. America cannot undo the partition of Europe without in effect defeating Russia. And that the Russians must and will resist firmly— just as the direct expulsion of America from Western Europe would be resisted by America as an intolerable defeat. At the same time, the partition of Germany in the context of the partition of Europe makes both partitions a live issue. It ensures a continuing political struggle for the future of Germany and thus for the future of Europe. It locks America and Russia into a strategically central conflict, but with the stakes so high that neither can countenance a direct defeat. With divided Germany thus serving as the permanent catalyst for change, the issue of the future of Europe remains a live issue, despite the stalemate of the last 40 years.

The situation might have been altogether different if the division of Europe had not entailed simultaneously the division of Germany. If instead of the Elbe the geopolitical American-Soviet frontier had been fixed on the Rhine or on the Oder-Neisse line, the division of Europe into two spheres of influence would have been neater and politically easier to maintain. With the Rhine as the dividing line, the West European rump would have felt so threatened by the Soviet presence, backed by a Sovietized Germany, that henceforth its enduring preoccupation would have been to insure the closest possible ties with America, forgetting altogether about the fate of the Soviet-dominated central and Eastern Europe. If, on the other hand, Soviet sway had been extended only to the Oder-Neisse line, the Poles and the Czechs would have been so fearful that an American-backed Germany might resume its traditional *Drang nach Osten* that the partition of Europe would have been of very secondary concern.

As it happened, the existing stalemate is increasingly resented by all Europeans. The Germans—no longer dominated by feelings of war guilt, less mesmerized by the American ideal, distressed by the failure of Europe to become an alternative to divisive nationalisms—are naturally drawn to a growing preoccupation with the fate of their brethren living under an alien system. The notion that the destiny of a united Germany depends on a close relationship with Russia is not a new one in German political tradition. Frustration with the nation's division is giving it a new lease on life.

Moreover, for Germany especially but also for Western Europe as a whole, the East holds a special economic attraction. It has been the traditional market for West European industrial goods. As Western Europe discovers that in its fragmented condition it is becoming less competitive with the high-tech economies of America and Japan, the notion of a special economic relationship with the East becomes particularly appealing. The fear that America may be turning from the Atlantic to the Pacific has in this connection a self-fulfilling and a self-validating function: it justifies a wider economic, and potentially even a political, accommodation between an industrially obsolescent Western Europe and the even more backward Soviet bloc, a logical consumer for what Western Europe can produce.

More than most Europeans, the East Europeans, no longer expecting American liberation, long for a genuine Europe, which would free them from the Soviet yoke. That longing explains the extraordinary standing to this day in Eastern Europe of de Gaulle—simply because he raised the standard of "Europe to the Urals." It explains also the special appeal of the Pope, whose vision of Europe's spiritual unity has obvious political implications. But the East Europeans will settle for half a loaf if they cannot have the whole. Faced with the choice of exclusive Soviet domination, only contested by American policy, or of at least growing ties with even a politically weak Western Europe, the East Europeans clearly prefer the latter.

To register all of this is not to say that Europe will simply drift along into a separate accommodation with the Soviet Union, fulfilling long-standing Soviet ambitions. It is to note, however, the potential and growing West European susceptibility to a Soviet policy based more on Litvinov's prescriptions than on Stalinist practices. A Soviet policy designed to exploit more subtly the continued absence of a united Europe, the mounting American frustration with the low level of the European defense effort, and the inevitable appeal of escapist notions regarding disarmament, nuclear freezes, and the like could have a significant impact on both American and European public opinion. Indeed, under certain circumstances, one can even envisage a spontaneous American inclination to disengage from Europe, with conservatives advocating it out of irritation with European unwillingness to do more for the common defense, and with liberals propounding it because of their current tendency to deal with difficult security matters by evasion. The U.S. deficit will, in any case, drive Congress toward a more critical look at the cost of the U.S. NATO commitment.

In Europe itself, such a more subtle Litvinov-type Soviet policy would aim not at the dismantling of NATO as such but at depriving it of any political or military substance. Exploiting the duality of German feelings and the growing ties between Bonn and East Berlin, it would seek to transform Germany into a quasi-neutral member of NATO, thereby alarming and further fragmenting Western Europe. Instead of concentrating on trying to inflict on America a visible and direct political defeat in Europe, it would play on European unwillingness to associate itself with America in the wider global and ideological rivalry with Russia, in order to achieve European acquiescence to a subordinate relationship with Moscow.

It is not self-fulfilling pessimism to note that a Europe dependent militarily, fragmented politically, and anachronistic economically remains a Europe more vulnerable to such blandishments. In brief, a sustained Soviet peace offensive poses the greater danger that Moscow finally might succeed in splitting Europe from America and thus, taking advantage of Europe's continued historical fatigue, attain finally a Yaltanized Europe.

A STRATEGY OF HISTORICAL STEALTH

As President Mitterrand put it some two years ago, *"tout ce qui permettera de sortir de Yalta sera bon. . . ."* But how to escape from Yalta? Forty years later, there must be a better option for both Europe and America than either a partitioned and prostrated Europe that perpetuates the American-Soviet collision, or a disunited Europe divorced from America acquiescing piecemeal to Soviet domination over Eurasia.

And there is such a third option: the emergence of a politically more vital Europe less dependent militarily on the United States, encouraged in that direction by an America guided by a timely historic vision, and leading eventually to a fundamentally altered relationship with Eastern Europe and with Russia.

The third option requires a long-term strategy of the kind that the West simply has not devised in dealing with the enduring post–Yalta European dilemma. The point of departure for such a long-term strategy has to be joint recognition of the important conclusion which the experience of the last several decades teaches: the historic balance in Europe will be changed gradually in the West's favor only if Russia comes to be faced west of the Elbe rather less by America and rather more by Europe.

Thoughtful Europeans realize, moreover, that the future of Europe is intertwined with the future of Germany and of Poland. Without spanning, in some non-threatening fashion, the division of Germany, there will not be a genuine Europe; but continuing Russian domination of Poland makes Russian control over East Germany geopolitically possible. Thus the relationship between Russia on the one hand and Germany and Poland on the other must be peacefully transformed if a larger Europe is ever to emerge.

Both Americans and Europeans must also face up to the implications of the fact that the division of Europe is not only the unnatural consequence of the destruction of Europe in the course of two world wars; in the long run it is also an inherently unstable and potentially dangerous situation. It is likely to produce new explosions in Eastern Europe, and it could also generate a basic and destabilizing reorientation in Western Europe, especially since for many Europeans the existence of the two alliances across the dividing line in the middle of Europe is seen as an extension of superpower efforts to perpetuate the status quo.

Accordingly, concentration on the purely military dimension of the East-West problem, or trying to get the West Europeans to hew to the U.S. line in the Middle East or in Central America, is not going to preserve Western unity. America has to identify itself with a cause which has deeply felt emotional significance to most Europeans. Undoing the division of Europe, which is so essential to its spiritual and moral recovery, is a goal worthy of the Western democracies and one capable of galvanizing a shared sense of historic purpose.

But that objective, so essential to Europe's restoration, cannot be accomplished as an American victory over Russia. Nor will it be achieved by an explicit Russian acceptance, through a negotiated agreement, of Eastern Europe's emancipation from Russian vassalage. Moscow will not yield voluntarily. A wider Europe can only emerge as a consequence of a deliberately but subtly induced process of change, by historical stealth so to speak, which can neither be quickly detected nor easily resisted.

The West must shape that process and give it historical direction. As the point of departure for seeking the common goal, one can envisage a strategy combining five broad political, economic and military dimensions. Some involve relatively simple acts and can be summarized succinctly; some require more complicated process of change, are bound to be more controversial, and thus require a fuller justification.

First, on the symbolic plane, it would be appropriate for the heads of the democratic West as a whole, perhaps on February 4, 1985, to clarify jointly, through a solemn declaration, the West's attitude toward the historic legacy of Yalta. In publicly repudiating that bequest—the partition of Europe—the West should underline its commitment to a restored Europe, free of extra-European control. It should stress its belief that there now exists a genuine European political identity, the heir to Europe's civilization, which is entitled to unfettered expression. It should affirm the right of every European nation to choose its sociopolitical system in keeping with its history and tradition. It should explicitly reject and condemn Moscow's imposition on so many Europeans of a system that is culturally and politically so alien to them. Finally, by drawing attention to the positive experience of neutral Austria and Finland, it should pledge that a more authentic Europe would not entail the extension of the American sphere of influence to the European state frontiers of the Soviet Union.

Second, and in direct connection with the renunciation of Yalta's burden, the West should simultaneously reconfirm its commitment to the Helsinki Final Act. This is absolutely essential, for otherwise the repudiation of Yalta could give the Soviets the convenient argument that the territorial integrity of Poland and of Czechoslovakia is thereby again endangered. The Helsinki agreements confirmed the durability of the existing frontiers in central and Eastern Europe, and the eastern nations must be reassured on this score. At the same time, the Helsinki agreements legalized and institutionalized the notion that the West has a right to comment on the internal practices of East European governments and that respect of human rights is a general international obligation. Accordingly, the repudiation of Yalta's historic legacy should be accompanied by the reaffirmation of the West's commitment to peaceful East-West relations, to the maintenance of the existing territorial status quo, and to the indivisibility of the concepts of freedom and human rights.

Moreover, reaffirmation of the continued Western commitment to the Helskinki Final Act could help resolve the potentially fatal European ambivalence regarding Germany. The fact is that, while the Europeans resent their historic partition, they fear almost as much a reunited

Germany. Therefore, the renunciation of Yalta's legacy—the division of Europe—should be accompanied by an explicit pledge, through the reaffirmation of Helsinki's continued relevance, that the purpose of healing the East-West rift in Europe is not to dismantle any existing state but to give every European people the opportunity to participate fully in wider all-European cooperation. In that context, the division of Germany need not be undone through formal reunification but by the gradual emergence of a much less threatening loose confederation of the existing two states.

Third, much in keeping with the spirit of these symbolic acts, Western Europe should strive to create the maximum number of opportunities for Eastern European participation in various all-European bodies. There is today a proliferation of such institutions, both private and public. East Europeans should be encouraged quietly but systematically to increase their participation—even if initially only as observers—in such bodies as the European Parliament, as well as the myriad of more specialized technical agencies. The fostering in Eastern Europe of the European spirit, and of greater East European recognition that there is more to Europe today than meets the eye, is clearly in the interests of all Europe. But a new burst of energy in this regard is much needed.

It would also be appropriate for the major West European nations, as well as for America, to sponsor during the Yalta year of 1985—on either a private or public basis—a series of seminars and conferences on the future of post-Yalta Europe. A special effort should be made to invite East Europeans to participate, on whatever basis is possible, in deliberations designed to forge during that year a wider consensus on how best to undo peacefully Yalta's legacy.

In addition, Western Europe should reactivate efforts previously initiated but lately dormant designed to encourage closer contacts and eventually even some form of collaboration between the Common Market and Eastern Europe. In different ways, both East Germany and Yugoslavia today have practical relationships with that important Western European entity. Precisely because the present Soviet leadership has stepped up its efforts to integrate Eastern Europe into COMECON and thus to bind it to the Soviet economy, additional initiative on the part of the Common Market is now badly needed. Even if the East Europeans, under Soviet pressure, were to rebuff such Western efforts at closer contacts, exchange of information and some cooperative projects, the Western initiative would still have a positive effect. The recent East German willingness to risk Soviet displeasure at growing inter-German ties reflects the widespread desire as well as economic need of Eastern Europe for closer links with the rest of Europe. The continued economic stagnation of the Soviet-type economies makes the timing for greater Western activism in this regard particularly propitious.

Fourth, and in no way in conflict with the preceding, Europe should intensify its aid to those East Europeans who are struggling actively for the political emancipation of Eastern Europe. That struggle is the necessary concomitant and at least partially also the cause of evolutionary change in Eastern Europe. Only too often do West European well-wishers of a more independent Eastern Europe look askance at those in the East who undertake more direct forms of struggle. While cultivation of East European officials enjoys a certain fashionable prestige in Western circles, tangible assistance to those resisting totalitarianism is viewed only too frequently as somehow "in the spirit of the cold war."

Yet a division of labor between America and Europe in which the former is seen as alone in supporting dissident "subversion" while the later engages exclusively in official courtship would be self-defeating. West Europeans should undertake to provide support for some of the activities that America has quite generously, for Europe's sake as well as for its own, sustained for more than three decades. The French recently have done so for the Polish Solidarity movement, and so have some other Europeans. Radio Paris has been gaining more East European listeners. But much more needs to be done. Germany, for example, after Chancellor Helmut Schmidt in effect endorsed Wojciech Jaruzelski's martial law in Poland, confined itself to truly humanitarian private philanthropy; it has not been as active as it could be in sustaining various forms of East European political activity designed to induce the existing regimes to transform themselves.

In subtle but sustained fashion West Europeans could aid the East Europeans in such efforts, because in the age of transistors and mass communications totalitarian control can be pierced, with positive political effect. Western Europe should, after all, be a direct partner in the struggle for Europe's future, and a well-funded Franco-British-German-Italian consortium (a Foundation for a post-Yalta Europe) to aid East European efforts to emancipate peacefully the eastern portion of Europe would be an appropriate and long overdue contribution.

Fifth, the time has come for a more fundamental rethinking of the relationship between Western security and political change in Europe as a whole. The West can make the needed adjustment, and America— since it plays the central military role—should take the lead to that end. America is needed in Europe to deter Russia not only from military aggression but from political intimidation. That is obvious and it justifies NATO and the American military presence on the continent. But an American military presence that reduces the incentive for the Europeans to unite politically, yet simultaneously increases the incentive for the

Soviets to stay put militarily in central and Eastern Europe, is a military presence not guided by a subtle political-historical calculus. A more sensitive calibration of the political-military equation is needed in order to safeguard Western Europe while promoting change in the East-West relationship.

If Europe is to emerge politically, it must assume a more direct role in its own defense. A Europe that plays a larger defense role will require a lesser, or at least a redefined, American military presence. A Europe that can defend itself more on its own is a Europe that is also politically more vital, while less challenging to the Soviet Union from a purely military point of view, than a Europe with large American military presence in its very center. Such a Europe would then be better able to satisfy the East European yearning for closer association without such association being tantamount to an American defeat of Russia.

But Europe must be prodded to move in that direction. Left as it is, Europe's cultural hedonism and political complacence will ensure that not much is done. Even the modest 1978 NATO commitment to a three percent per annum increase in defense expenditures was not honored by most European states. America should, therefore, initiate a longer-term process to alter the nature of its military presence in Europe gradually, while making it clear to the Europeans that the change is not an act of anger or a threat (a la the Mansfield resolution) but rather the product of a deliberate strategy designed to promote Europe's unity and its historic restoration.

Ultimately, the United States in NATO should be responsible primarily for offsetting Soviet strategic power, thus deterring both a Soviet attack or nuclear blackmail. But on the ground, the defense of Europe over the next decade should become an even more predominantly European responsibility. The needed process of replacing gradually but not totally (and certainly not in Berlin) the U.S. ground combat forces could perhaps be accelerated if, through the Mutual and Balanced Force Reductions talks or otherwise, the Soviet Union were willing to reciprocate by comparable withdrawals of its own ground forces. But, in any case, it should be accompanied by appropriate European efforts to assume greater responsibility for the defense of Europe not only on a purely national basis but through enhanced European defense coordination.

The United States should particularly encourage efforts at increased Franco-German military cooperation and eventual integration. France has a historic awareness of a European identity while Germany chafes under Europe's partition. A Franco-German army would have the manpower, the resources, and the fighting potential to pick up the slack created by a gradual decrease in the American combat presence on the ground. The eventual fusion of these two national forces into a joint combat force would represent a giant step toward a politically more vital Europe, yet a Europe which would be less conflictual with the Soviet Union than a Europe hosting a large U.S. army and less threatening to Eastern Europe than a Europe with a powerful separate German army. A gradually reduced U.S. ground presence would in turn create pressure from even the existing East European regimes for a commensurate Soviet redeployment, thereby gradually creating a more flexible political situation.

To move Europe in this direction, the United States will have to take the first steps, even perhaps unilaterally through a ten-year program of annual cuts in the level of the U.S. ground forces in Europe. But these steps should be taken in the context of an articulated strategy that has a constructive political as well as military rationale. Its political purpose should be openly proclaimed: to create the setting for Europe's restoration and, through it, also for a more stable East-West relationship. It would also have to be made clear that some American combat forces would remain in Europe, as they do in Korea, thereby ensuring immediate American engagement in the event of hostilities. Moreover, continued American strategic protection of Europe should not remain confined only to the possible employment of nuclear weaponry. It should over time, with technological advances, be enhanced to include also some strategic defense. As strategic defense for America becomes more viable, it should be a major American goal to extend some of its protection to Europe as well.

A division of labor in NATO along the foregoing lines would make it much easier to consider by Yalta's fiftieth anniversary also those East-West security and political arrangements which at the moment seem premature, unrealistic, or excessively threatening to America or to Russia. These could include demilitarized or nuclear-free zones or extension of the Austrian-type neutrality to other areas, including later even to a loosely confederated Germany. It would encourage a process of change permitting the latent or frustrated West and East European impulses for the resolution of Europe gradually to surface. Eventually, it would permit Europe to emerge, and to play a major role on the Eurasian continent, along with the Soviet Union, India and China, while helping to ensure through its links with America that no single power dominates that geopolitically vital continent.

YALTA: EUROPE'S PAST OR EUROPE'S FUTURE?

The fiftieth anniversary of Yalta is only ten years away. It should be our shared goal to fashion by then political-military arrangements which, instead of perpetuating the division of Europe—and perhaps even prompting West Europe's political decay, create the preconditions for peacefully undoing Yalta. A Western Europe essentially self-reliant in regional defense, while covered by the U.S. system of nuclear deterrence and also eventually by U.S. strategic defense, would be a Western Europe more capable of pursuing a positive policy toward the East without fear of domination by Moscow. In the final analysis, only Europeans can restore Europe; it cannot be done for them by others.

To be sure, Moscow will resist the aspirations of the Europeans. No empire dissolves itself voluntarily—at least not until it becomes evident that accommodation to gradual dissolution is preferable to the rising costs of preserving the imperial system. So it will be also with the Soviet empire. Moscow will violently protest any Western disavowal of Yalta's legacy and will accuse the West of worsening East-West relations; that is only to be expected. But such public disavowal is the necessary point of departure for more focused efforts by all the Europeans gradually to undo their continent's division. Once that historic commitment has been made, these efforts, as recommended here, need not be either aggressive or initially even very explicit. As time passes, with the organic growth of a larger Europe gathering momentum, it will become more and more difficult for the Kremlin to resist a process that over time may acquire the hallmarks of historical inevitability. At some point, then, even the Soviets may find it useful to codify some new neutrality arrangements in central Europe and to reduce and eventually to remove their occupation forces.

One should not underestimate in this connection Moscow's adaptability. Despite his ruthlessness, even Stalin accommodated himself to the reality of an independent Catholic Church in Poland; Khrushchev to a Polish peasantry free from collectivization and to a separate Romanian foreign policy; Brezhnev to "gulash communism" in Hungary and to army rule in Poland. Why then should not the next generation of Soviet leaders be pressed also to come to terms with the fact that even the interests of the Soviet people would be better served by a less frustrated and oppressed east-central Europe, partaking more directly of the benefits of all-European cooperation?

As divided Europe enters the fifth decade after Yalta, it is important to reiterate that undoing Yalta cannot involve a precise blueprint or a single dramatic initiative. The shape of the future cannot be reduced to a neat plan, with specific phases and detailed agreements. Rather, it requires an explicit commitment and a sense of strategic direction for a process of change that is bound to have also its own dynamic. In any case, for America the emergence of a more vital Europe would be a positive outcome, for ultimately a pluralistic world is in America's true interest. Moreover, such a development would avert the major danger that if Yalta's legacy is not deliberately—though peacefully—undone in the East, it will eventually become the reality in the West. In other words, Yalta must be consigned to Europe's past if it is not to become Europe's future.

CHAPTER TWENTY-FIVE

———————— ■ ————————

The U.S.-Soviet Relationship: Paradoxes and Prospects

THE PAST YEAR HAS WITNESSED a rising tide of Western analyses of developments in the Soviet Union under the leadership of Mikhail S. Gorbachev. Indeed, as the coverage of British Prime Minister Margaret Thatcher's recent visit to Moscow demonstrated, the new Soviet General Secretary is becoming something of a "media star" in the West.

That Gorbachev and his policies have evoked a great deal of interest and sympathetic reaction in the West clearly is not surprising. We have become accustomed to the image of a Soviet system that is rigid, stalemated, frozen in mediocrity, and stifling in its weight on Soviet society. Hence, a new Soviet leader who is seen to introduce some spark into that system is bound to emerge as a novel oddity. And if he does so with some degree of civility, it is understandable that he should evoke sympathetic responses from the West.

Some of these reactions have gone further than would seem warranted. Recently Denis Healey, the former British Defense Minister and now Foreign Secretary in the Labour Party's shadow cabinet, when asked to identify his favorite current foreign personages, named Gorbachev. This may be going a bit too far.

Still, one can understand why Gorbachev has attracted so much favorable attention. Our relationship with the Soviet Union has been fraught with chronic anxiety about the future. Those anxieties have been nourished in the past by a succession of wooden-faced Soviet leaders who seemed to personify the dull totalitarian conformity and ideological fetters of the Soviet system, and the sinisterness of its global ambitions. Hence, any new leader who projects a more urbane, more dynamic, more

This chapter appeared in *Strategic Review* (spring 1987). Reprinted by permission.

"Western" image is bound to spur hope of better things to come in the relationship.

SIGNS OF ATMOSPHERIC CHANGE

Beyond the sheer personality factor, however, we are obligated to recognize that something, indeed, is brewing in the Soviet Union that is real. It would be mistaken to dismiss developments in the Soviet Union in the last several years as strictly superficial or irrelevant.

Anyone who regularly reads the Soviet press must be struck by a certain change in atmosphere, a certain shift of emphasis—indeed, a certain degree of openness in the discussion of issues which hitherto were taboo. The Soviet press accounts, for example, of the riots in Kazakhstan were remarkably detailed and frank—particularly in their acknowledgement that the disorders in Alma-Ata, even if they may have been initially stirred by displaced and disaffected elements in the local leadership, represented a genuinely nationalist reaction against the Great Russian overlordship exercised from Moscow—and that this nationalist reaction was far-reaching, commanding a great deal of popular support.

Another telling example was a recent televised interview of the Soviet minister in charge of the police, in which people telephoned questions from throughout the Soviet Union. Most of the callers identified themselves and raised questions about the behavior and the conduct of the police, their manners, their frequent lack of education, and even their primitive behavior. In one particular instance, a caller asked the minister "whether it is true, as has been rumored, that it was militiamen who participated in a bank robbery in which some people were killed." The minister acknowledged that this, indeed, much to his shame, was the case. A woman telephoned and complained about corruption in her factory. The minister asked for her name, noting that she failed to give it. She replied on the air: "I will not give you my name, because if I do so, I am likely to be punished for telephoning. Hence I prefer to remain anonymous." The minister said: "That's fine. Let me at least know the details so we can help with it." Again, this is a sign of a new atmosphere in the Soviet Union.

Still another example is provided by a series of articles in *Izvestia* dealing with economic reforms in Communist China. Surprisingly the articles contained a fairly balanced treatment of the reforms, including a very frank discussion of the decentralization of the Chinese economy and the introduction of the profit motive, of the changes this has wrought in the Chinese countryside and of the innovative experiments being conducted in Chinese cities. To be sure, the articles contained some criticisms. By and large, however, the criticisms seemed reasonable; nor were they excessively ideological in nature. The Soviet reader could infer from the overall thrust of the articles a certain legitimacy of the Chinese reforms.

All such indicators add up to the fact that something is happening in the Soviet Union. Therefore, it would be a mistake if we were to view the phenomenon as simply a superficial exercise designed to deceive the West. Some effort at change is clearly underway. Yet, the question remains: how far will the process go, and how far-reaching will its consequences be?

THE NATURE OF GORBACHEV'S LEADERSHIP POWERS

Here I do entertain two very basic reservations. One pertains to Gorbachev's personal power. In my judgment, Gorbachev is a totally new type of Soviet leader, in that he is the first one in the entire history of the Soviet Union who has not seized power himself, but instead was selected by his predecessors. Stalin was not Lenin's choice. Nikita Khrushchev was not Stalin's choice. Brezhnev's seizure of power was rather a surprise to Khrushchev. Andropov was not Brezhnev's choice. But Gorbachev was the choice of his predecessors, who functioned essentially in a bureaucratic setting in selecting him, the youngest member of the Politburo, to be the next General-Secretary. In that sense his power is far less personal and more an expression of a certain institutional consensus.

Gorbachev has not come to that power with a dedicated group of personal supporters who had risen through the party hierarchy, as they did with Stalin or Khrushchev. Rather, Gorbachev has emerged as the spokesman of a generation of leaders, more or less in his own age bracket, who share his sense of frustration over the failure of the Soviet Union to move forward and his aspirations to do something about it, but who do not see themselves as personally beholden or devoted to him as an individual. This means that his power is not quite that of a dictator, and closer to that of a strong chief executive who depends for the maintenance of his position and power on the success of his policies.

A dictator typically, if his policies fail, can blame his associates for the failure: this, in many respects, is the true test of a dictator. He can execute the alleged malcreants (or scapegoats), as did Stalin, or he can send them into exile, as did Khrushchev. But I do not believe that Gorbachev yet wields that degree of personal power. If his policies succeed, he will continue in his position of quasi-chief executive; if they fail, he could well be displaced. This means that he must be much more cautious than his predecessors in pursuing his policies, but at the same time also much more determined to make them succeed. And it is an open question whether his reforms can successfully penetrate a system that is so notoriously resistant to change—and to do so in the face of a *nomenklatura* that so jealously guards its privileges and levers of control over the system.

THE TEST OF CONSEQUENTIAL REFORMS

Indeed, thus far there is no evidence of a single reform adopted by Gorbachev of the type that could be characterized as consequential— that is to say, a reform that bodes significant consequences in and of itself for the way the Soviet system works and/or is likely to breed a dynamic with widening impact. Gorbachev's innovations have been fairly limited, involving some tampering with the margins of the system. Perhaps the true measure of "innovation" in the Gorbachev approach thus far is a public relations campaign intended to generate more zeal, more enthusiasm and more dedication in the Soviet system. But the reforms adduced by him thus far neither are consequential in their implications, nor are they irrevocable.

As an example of "consequential" reform, the economic measures adopted by the Chinese leadership in Beijing are deserving of that term. They promise to result in a new relationship between the system and the citizen—and, more than that, to create pressures for changes in the political system, such as already have been evidenced in the street demonstrations of Chinese university students. A consequential reform in the Soviet Union would be, for example, a secret-ballot election in which voters could choose among several candidates for a big position. If this were to be adopted in the Soviet Union, it would begin to change the nature of the exercise of power at the top. But that has not happened. Incidentally, a proposal to that effect, which Gorbachev did articulate at one stage of the last meeting of the CPSU Central Committee, was omitted from the committee's final resolution.

Hence, a review of Gorbachev's performance in the domestic arena thus far shows interesting dimensions, as well as some positive and encouraging aspects. But the report card thus far also reflects on a leader who wields power in a novel and much more tenuous fashion than his predecessors, and who has at this stage made only a very limited attempt to deal with the margins and the atmospherics of the system, but not its essential substance.

THE CHIMERA OF WESTERN
"HELP" TO GORBACHEV

What then, are the emergent implications of Gorbachev's internal policies for our relationship with the Soviet Union? Here the point needs to be posited at the outset that, whatever may be one's judgment about the nature and scope of Gorbachev's reforms, they should not be interpreted as affecting the substance of the American-Soviet relationship. Indeed, the notion that domestic reforms in the Soviet Union should somehow be "rewarded" by the United States in the form of foreign policy concessions is both illogical and fraught with danger. After all, domestic reforms in the Soviet Union are, in the final analysis, revocable by the regime. By contrast, once rendered, concessions by the United States with respect to vital issues related to its national security and global stability—for example, in arms control agreements—are not so easily recallable or redressable. Beyond that, we must bear in mind that Soviet domestic reforms are designed to improve the Soviet system, its efficiency, its long-range staying power and thereby also its weight in world affairs.

Therefore, it is difficult to justify changes in U.S. policy toward the Soviet Union on the basis of the argument that Gorbachev's domestic policy should be rewarded, that he should be encouraged—indeed, as some have argued after visits to Moscow, that he should be assisted by the West. Rather, issues in our relationship with the Soviet Union must in all prudence be dealt with on their merits, in terms of their own substance, irrespective of whether the given leadership in the Soviet Union is presumed to be progressive or conservative, reformist or aggressive.

The second point that needs to be made about the external implications of Gorbachev's internal policies relates to their "public relations" context noted earlier. It is rather interesting to observe that Gorbachev has surrounded himself with people who are essentially communicators and mass-media managers. He is relying on public relations campaigns to consolidate his own position, to change the atmospherics of the Soviet system and to stimulate some of the changes he deems desirable.

The public relations aspect has been even more marked in the foreign policy realm; in fact, thus far this element has been dominant in Gorbachev's external endeavors. Hardly a month passes without a major proposal by Gorbachev in foreign policy, or at least a major address couched in sweeping, conciliatory terms that appeal to the sentiments of world public opinion. This is the case with respect to the Far East with the "new spirit" launched in Gorbachev's Vladivostok address; it is the case in regard to Western Europe and particularly in the context of strategic issues.

A great many of Gorbachev's foreign policy endeavors, therefore, are not substantive, but rather are designed to take advantage of the new perception of the Soviet leadership in order to exact changes in Western policies, particularly from the Soviet Union's principal rival, the United States.

Certainly, the massive conclave on "world peace" staged in Moscow last February, which was attended by some 900 leading personages from the West, fits the public relations mode. Lenin once spoke of a category of people whom he called "useful idiots"—members of the bourgeoisie who could be drawn into unwitting support of the Bolshevik cause. It is not clear whether Lenin would apply that label today to the participants in that Moscow forum. Still, even if many of those Western participants were individually sophisticated, discerning and critical of what they observed, their presence was blatantly used in a public relations exercise, the obvious purpose of which was not to spur equitable East-West movement toward a possible arms agreement, but rather to put maximum pressure on the rival power, the United States, to render unilateral concessions in the ongoing negotiations.

ASYMMETRY IN THE U.S.-SOVIET INITIATIVE EQUATION

Against that general background, let me now turn to some of the major issues in the U.S.-Soviet relationship and their short-term prospects. Again, a general observation is in order: What we are witnessing in the Soviet Union today is some measure of a systemic crisis in which a new leadership is groping to define its policies in the face of bureaucratic rigidity and amid considerable uncertainty as to what needs to be done. But it is, according to all indications, a vigorous leadership that has displayed manipulative skill in the use of public relations at home and propaganda abroad to promote its objectives.

The Gorbachev regime confronts in the United States, its principal rival, a situation which, while not quite a "systemic crisis," does warrant the term "leadership crisis." In other words, in the Soviet Union there is an activist leadership in a setting of a systemic crisis; while in the United States, a reasonably stable and dynamic system is afflicted by a leadership crisis that inhibits it from taking the initiative and perhaps even from effectively formulating policy on complicated issues.

This contrast suggests that in the short run the possibilities of any real movement in the American-Soviet negotiating process will be more dependent on decisions in Moscow than on decisions in Washington. It is unlikely that the U.S. Administration, in its present condition, can in fact fashion proposals toward resolving some of the issues which perplex the American-Soviet relationship. But if the Soviet leadership should choose to do so, there are in fact some possibilities for some limited East-West agreements in the relatively near future.

THE INF ISSUE

The Gorbachev regime already has demonstrated this asymmetry in the capacity for initiative-taking with its latest proposal on INF—the issue of intermediate-range nuclear weapons in Europe. This Soviet gambit, which has been advertised as a major concession to the United States, was eminently predictable in the wake of the Reykjavik summit meeting last October. In the INF issue, the Soviet Union has managed in effect to hang the United States on the petard of its own negotiating position.

It will be recalled that in 1982 the Reagan Administration proposed to the Soviet Union a "zero-zero" solution with respect to INF: the removal of all Soviet SS-20 missiles in return for the non-deployment and/or removal of all comparable American INF systems then scheduled for stationing in Western Europe. Whatever its potential in the nego-tiations, the "zero-zero" proposal was regarded at the time as a needed political move to overcome the resistance in Western Europe to the pending deployment of 572 U.S. Pershing-2 ballistic missiles and ground-launched cruise missiles (GLCMs), as mandated by the NATO agreement of December 1979.

The Soviets with indignation rejected the "zero-zero" proposal, and the American INF deployments began in early 1984. In the face of this *fait accompli* the Soviets obviously began to entertain some second thoughts—until at Reykjavik they accepted the basic American proposal with some slight modifications. Both parties agreed to a formula in which there would be a "zero" solution for Europe, including the European part of the USSR, but with 100 SS-20s remaining in Soviet Asia and 100 intermediate-range delivery systems being redeployed from Europe to the United States. Yet, this formula—which both sides accepted— did not become an agreement when the Soviet Union chose, abruptly and in conflict with its previous position, to link the INF question to the larger issue of the U.S. Strategic Defense Initiative.

In their latest proposal, the Soviets have revived the Reykjavik INF formula, but no longer insist on the linkage to SDI. That concession clearly reflects a reading in Moscow of post-Reykjavik trends in Western Europe—in particular, a great deal of anxiety there about the possibility of the "decoupling" of the American-European strategic relationship that is implicit in the INF issue. It will be recalled that the original rationale behind the NATO decision to deploy INF in Europe was to maximize the interconnection between the security of the United States and that of its European allies in the setting of nuclear deterrence. Especially after the political costs that were entailed in implementing the INF deployment decision over a vociferous opposition in Western Europe, the fear has grown that a removal of those weapons would impact all the more sharply on the "coupling" relationship.

Moreover, most Europeans are aware of the fact that the Soviet Union does not require the grant of special permission to redeploy its SS-20s from Soviet Asia to the Western Military Districts of the USSR, but that in a crisis the United States would in fact require the agreement of the relevant European countries to redeploy any intermediate-range missiles from the United States to Europe. Hence, there is a rather significant political asymmetry in this arrangement, not to speak of the logistical reality that Soviet Asia happens to be closer to the European parts of the USSR than Western Europe is to the United States.

Finally, there is the complicating factor of shorter-range nuclear forces. In the past several years, the Soviets have deployed in growing numbers modernized SS-21, SS-22 and SS-23 missiles. While these weapons command shorter ranges than the SS-20, when forward-deployed they can reach most of the targets in NATO countries now covered by SS-20s. Western analysts believe not only that such short-range systems can function with greater mobility and accuracy than SS-20s, but that they are also "triple-capable"—that is, can be armed with conventional and chemical as well as nuclear warheads, thus adding a substantial new dimension to the imbalance in conventional forces that already favors the Warsaw Pact in Europe.

In deference to European apprehensions, the United States apparently is endeavoring to introduce these concerns into the INF bargaining at Geneva, with emphasis on the short-range missiles issue. Yet, it is patently both difficult and awkward to retreat from a formula solemnly agreed to by the President at Reykjavik, even though that agreement may have been hastily and imprudently rendered. The Soviets already are taking full propaganda advantage of the American predicament, accusing the United States of bad faith and deliberate obstructionism, while playing on the divided opinion in Western Europe on these issues.

The United States thus faces a very difficult dilemma on INF. The logic of its previous negotiating position, augmented by political pressures both within the United States and the Alliance, are pushing the U.S. Administration toward early consummation of an INF agreement. Yet, unless the Soviets completely accede to a renegotiated accord that allays the U.S. and Allied concerns that have been described, any agreement is likely to impact adversely—in the short or longer run—on the interests and cohesion of the Atlantic Alliance. The Soviets thus hold the upper bargaining hand and can hope to profit from either outcome—the failure of an INF agreement or its conclusion.

NEGOTIATIONS PROSPECTS IN STRATEGIC ARMS

A second short-run prospect in U.S.-Soviet relations—if on a lower order of likelihood than INF—concerns an at least limited agreement on strategic offensive forces. That is more problematical, but it is useful to bear in mind that at Reykjavik there was also preliminary agreement on at least a partial strategic formula: namely, that the strategic offensive arsenals of both sides would be reduced to approximately 6,000 warheads, 1,600 launchers, and on the Soviet side to 154 SS-18 missiles, which would mean a reduction of 50 per cent in the Soviet heavy ICBMs that have been a principal concern of U.S. strategic planners.

Again the Soviets at Reykjavik linked such an agreement to the Strategic Defense Initiative, and they have used this since in their campaign to mobilize opposition to SDI. Yet, the possibility cannot be excluded that here too the Soviets might be willing at some point to accept a formula whereby a strategic agreement confined to the above-mentioned categories would be viewed as an interim arrangement pending a more comprehensive pact on strategic weapons, with the SDI issue "shelved" in some fashion.

The Soviets might be tempted to move in that direction if they concluded that its political effect would be greatly to strengthen those forces within the United States which are against any further strategic modernization, both in U.S. offensive capabilities and with regard to SDI. They could calculate that such a political effect is worth the price of some flexibility on SDI in relation to a limited strategic agreement, so long as they still reserve for themselves the fall-back option of rigidity on the issue of SDI linkage with respect to a more comprehensive agreement on strategic arms reductions.

THE OUTLOOK ON AFGHANISTAN

The third short-term prospect in the U.S.-Soviet relationship pertains to Afghanistan. Here the principal issue centers on the duration of any Soviet timetable of withdrawal. The East-West differences over Afghanistan have narrowed somewhat, but they remain substantial. The Soviets have made some gains in creating the impression that they would like to withdraw—whereas so far, at least in my estimate, they have not in fact reached that conclusion. Instead, they are striving to obtain two objectives at the same time. The first is greater flexibility in the pursuit of what can be described as a "fight-talk-fight" strategy vis-à-vis the West—a strategy that has the effect of focusing greater attention on negotiations rather than on the continuing bloodshed in Afghanistan, thus lowering the political costs of the engagement for Moscow.

The second Soviet objective is to promote division among the powers that are critical to the sustaining of the resistance in Afghanistan: the United States, Communist China and Pakistan, with other powers playing lesser roles. If the Soviets can use the negotiating lever to weaken the will and the determination particularly of the Pakistanis, they could gain commensurately greater freedom of action in imposing their objectives in Afghanistan.

In a sense the Soviets are today in regard to Afghanistan roughly where the United States stood in 1970–1971 in regard to the Vietnam issue. By that time, a general consensus had taken root in the country-at-large, but particularly among U.S. policymakers, that we could not stay the course indefinitely in Vietnam—that we had to get out. Yet, we still desired a withdrawal that would leave behind a government in Saigon acceptable to us. We had not yet crossed the Rubicon of realization that a U.S. withdrawal would mean the collapse of any American-sponsored government. That Rubicon was crossed in 1973–1974. The Soviets have not yet reached a similar realization with respect to Afghanistan. For that reason, it will be some time before we can look for a genuine change in the Soviet approach to Afghanistan.

LONGER-RANGE TRENDS
IN THE STRATEGIC ARENA

That brings me to some longer-range concerns in the U.S.-Soviet relationship. The major such concern relates to the military-strategic arena. This arena remains as the crucial one in the relationship between the superpowers. In contrast with the other realms of U.S.-Soviet global competition—political, ideological and economic—it is in the military-strategic arena that the position of the United States shows signs of dangerous deterioration relative to that of its adversary.

There was a time when economically and ideologically the Soviet Union seemed to be on the historical upward curve—on what its leaders characterized as the "wave of the future." Khrushchev fervently believed that the Soviet Union would surpass the United States in economic performance. The fallacy of that vision is attested to by Gorbachev's desperate efforts today to make the Soviet economy function, let alone to enable it to compete with the U.S. economy.

There was also a time, only a decade ago, when various revolutionary movements in the world openly professed and aspired to the ideological model of the Soviet Union. Today, there is not a single such movement, even when it is self-avowedly "Marxist-Leninist," that would dare to assert that if it came to power it would try to replicate the Soviet historical experience. The reason is obvious: The overriding image of the Soviet Union in the world is that of a sterile, bureaucratically stifled, economically malfunctioning and otherwise thoroughly unattractive system.

Yet, militarily the Soviet Union is a powerful rival. Hence, a key question for the future centers on U.S. management of its side of the strategic equation. The question assumes greater salience in the context of the U.S. leadership crisis alluded to earlier.

The fact of the matter is that the current Administration has mishandled badly the needed modernization of U.S. strategic forces. That is particularly true of the MX intercontinental missile. The Reagan Administration inherited an MX deployment program, congressionally approved and mandated, on a scale of 200 launchers with 10 warheads each, which meant 2,000 time-urgent and accurate warheads deployed in a survivable mode. Through a series of rather inept decisions this whole program has been emasculated to the point where today, six years later, the United States has only ten MXs, and will be fortunate if it ends up with 50 missiles, all of them deployed in a highly vulnerable mode.

Beyond that, there has been very little change on the U.S. side of the strategic equation—which means that the Soviets have moved forward and we have remained essentially stationary.

The Strategic Defense Initiative represented a creative and imaginative initiative, one with strong potential relevance for security conditions in the remainder of this century and beyond. Yet, SDI has also been handled politically in a manner which poses the ominous prospect that the initiative will be killed by the next Democratic President or quietly abandoned by the next Republican President.

Today we are engaged in an essentially legalistic debate over the meaning of the ABM Treaty of 1972—a debate which permits the opposition to SDI to be mobilized on the grounds that sacrosanct treaties are being deliberately stretched on behalf of the so-called Star Wars program. It seems that the political tactics being used by the Administration and its own internal decisionmaking regarding SDI are counterproductive to the goal of progressively moving forward with SDI, using it as leverage to exact concessions from the Soviets on their own offensive strategic forces, and deploying some elements of a ballistic missile defense as a means to stabilize the overall strategic situation. Yet, when one looks to the likely strategic requirements of the next two decades, some strategic defenses clearly would help to stabilize the strategic equation, especially if balanced with some degree of self-restraint in the deployment of strategic offensive systems.

PORTENTS IN CENTRAL AMERICA
AND THE MIDDLE EAST

I am also concerned that over the course of the next several years the geopolitical security of the United States will progressively deteriorate in an area close to us: Central America. Indeed, we may be on the brink of a protracted "Bay of Pigs," in which an American-sponsored military undertaking is gradually defeated, with the United States either unwilling or unable to support those whom it has dispatched on an essentially military mission on behalf of goals which in significant measure reflect our own national interest.

It is not an edifying spectacle. It was not edifying to see the 3,000 Cubans dispatched to the Bay of Pigs in 1961, and then abandoned when they were being defeated. It will be an even less edifying prospect if 20,000–30,000 Nicaraguans, fighting against the Sandinista regime and directly supported by the United States through a legislative mandate, are then abandoned to their own fate in the face of superior military forces. That is bound to have a devastating impact on our interests in Central America. Should the consequences of this begin to merge with growing political instability in Mexico, we could, in the course of the next decade, confront a truly significant security problem immediately to the south of our territorial borders.

Finally, one can only speculate about the evolving geopolitical situation in the Persian Gulf and Middle East. Certainly U.S. policies over the past several years have not been conducive to higher American standing, greater American influence, in the area or greater regional stability. Yet, this region is of crucial importance to our overall global position—if only because our principal allies in Western Europe and in the Far East depend on access to the oil reserves for their economic survival. If the region were to fall under Soviet influence or into anarchy, our alliances would be in jeopardy. Yet, both prospects have been heightened in part by the policies we have pursued and by the kind of passivity we have adopted in recent times.

A PARADOX OF VULNERABILITIES
AND OPPORTUNITIES

All of the trends I have described could not only affect the stability of the American-Soviet relationship as a whole, but also provide the Soviet Union with openings which heretofore it did not enjoy. Not only would this be dangerous to our national interests, but it would mark a double tragedy in terms of missed opportunities for the United States. The Soviet Union is probably more vulnerable than ever before to purposeful Western policies designed to promote change within the Soviet empire and within the Soviet Union itself. Its vulnerabilities are glaringly evident. Its ideology has lost appeal. There is growing restlessness and frustration with the system in the Soviet orbit especially, but also within the Soviet Union as well.

Hence, in the broad historical sense one ought to be able to say that the Soviet Union is losing ground and that the West is prevailing. Yet, a judgment of this kind is, alas, contradicted by some of the specific tendencies which I have noted, over which we should exert greater control.